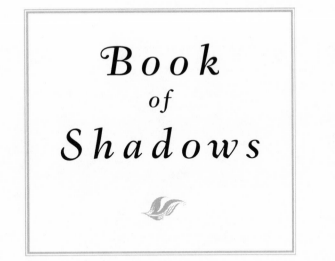

Book
of
Shadows

Book

of

Shadows

A MODERN WOMAN'S
JOURNEY INTO THE WISDOM
OF WITCHCRAFT AND THE
MAGIC OF THE GODDESS

Phyllis Curott

Wiccan High Priestess

BROADWAY BOOKS
New York

BROADWAY

Broadway Books titles may be purchased for business or promotional use or for special sales. For information, please write to: Special Markets Department, Bantam Doubleday Dell Publishing Group, Inc., 1540 Broadway, New York, NY 10036.

BROADWAY BOOKS and its logo, a letter B bisected on the diagonal, are trademarks of Broadway Books, a division of Bantam Doubleday Dell Publishing Group, Inc.

Library of Congress Cataloging-in-Publication Data

Curott, Phyllis.
Book of shadows : a modern woman's journey into the wisdom of witchcraft and the magic of the goddess / Phyllis Curott. — 1st ed.
p.   cm.
ISBN 0-7679-0054-5 (hardcover)
1. Witchcraft. 2. Goddess religion. 3. Curott, Phyllis.
I. Title.
BF1571.C87   1998
133.4′3—dc21   98-18231
CIP

FIRST EDITION

Special thanks to Zsuzsanna Budapest for granting permission to reprint excerpts from We All Come from the Goddess.

DESIGNED BY DEBORAH KERNER

98 99 00 01 02 10 9 8 7 6 5 4 3 2 1

For my parents,
and for all those who have
suffered and resisted Witch-hunts

Acknowledgments

This book was written with the encouragement and aid of many wonderful people to whom I extend my deepest thanks.

From the outset, my agent and friend Joanna Pulcini has been a gift of the Goddess, nourishing this effort with love, graciousness, devotion, and enthusiasm. With all the instincts of a natural Priestess, she has been the midwife to my literary magic. Also at the Linda Chester Literary Agency, I could not ask for a stronger iron grip in a more elegant velvet glove than that of Linda Chester; Gary Jaffe was endlessly helpful and delightful; and Meredith Phelan, Judith Ehrlich, and Laurie Fox all lent valuable critical input.

My editor, Lauren Marino, encouraged me to reach for the stars, and supported me as I risked it. She has been this book's stalwart knight on the field of publishing jousts where she carries the scarf of the Goddess, and I am grateful for her courage, vision, and confidence. I am grateful to Janet Goldstein and Betsy Thorpe for acquiring the book. The hard work of others at Broadway has also brought this work to a global public: Bill Shinker, John Sterling, Trigg Robinson, Nancy Clare Morgan, Robert Allen, Kathy Spinelli, Sharon Swados, Ann Campbell, Roberto de Vicq de Cumptich and many more from copy editors to sales reps. Thank you all. And thanks as well to all the foreign publishers who are helping to return the Goddess to her world.

Nancy Peske's editorial input helped me hone a galaxy of light into a guiding constellation, and she did so with warmth, skill, humor, and intelligence. Lara Webb brought her excellent sense of story to my efforts and helped me hold to the course I'd charted.

I am grateful for the efforts of an extraordinary group of people who have helped to bring this book, and its message, to the public: Arielle Ford, Lynn Goldberg, Grace McQuade, Lynn Ludlam, and Mitchell Feldman.

Patricia Kennealy Morrison blessed me with her wisdom, her wit, and most importantly, her loving friendship. She is an inspiration.

The members of my circle, who are both my students and my friends, have blessed me with love and leant themselves to many arduous and important tasks: Mary Alagna, Charles Boyce, Jeff Courtney, Gene Dratva, Tracy Grandstaff, Marilee Hartley, Anna Hill, Debby Horton, Judy Landon, Linda Maglionico, Lorenza Menegoni, Anne McCord, Mikaele Pearson, Cory Rochester, Bruce Smith, Tana Freya and my familiar, Webster. In our extended family, help in many forms also came from Rodger Parsons, Lisa Cady, Sally-Jo O'Brien, and Caitlin Creed.

My deepest thanks to the two priestesses with whom I studied and who initiated me: Lady Rhea and Lady Miw Sekmet, a/k/a Carol Bulzone. The content of this book necessarily reflects my perspective, in my words, but they are present in these pages, and I hope they find that the book expresses my abiding respect and appreciation. The women of the first circle of the Mother Grove of the Minoan Sisterhood will also find themselves in the story I have told. I have altered and disguised them, but I hope that when they recognize aspects of themselves, they will find I did them justice as the extraordinary women I knew them to be. I hope they also know how deeply I honor our time together and the sisterhood we engendered.

Thanks also to the following who have nourished, challenged, and inspired me: Alan Barnes, Herman Benson, Rev. Darrell Berger, Edith

Deutsch, Philip and Phyllis Deutsch, Max Evans, David Friedman, Jane Froman, Ampere Giguere, Matthew and Leigh Grant, Marjorie and Philip Gross, Susan Hellerer, Hans Holzer, Henry Jaglom, Betty Jensen, Paula Keogh, Leonore Krieger, Ruth Lehr, Deborah Anne Light, Howard Lorber, Patrick Miller, Barbara Nevins-Taylor and Nick Taylor, Phil and Beth Press, Basil Pollitt, Dr. Eleanor Rae, Professor Duncan Smith, and Barbara Zahm. And special thanks to Giorgio Armani, Linda Gant, Judith Smitten, David Webb, and Stanley Silberstein.

I am grateful for the brave and often public efforts of many remarkable women and men of the Wiccan and Goddess traditions. Their willingness to work for and speak out on behalf of our growing community has laid a foundation of public acceptance and interest. I have met and worked with many of them over the years. Others I know only by reputation. It is impossible to list them all here, and there are many who remain private, but whose efforts have been equally invaluable to the growth of this important spiritual movement. My heartfelt thanks goes out to all of them, with special thanks to Margot Adler, Z. Budapest, Andras, Deirdre and Annya Corbin Arthen and the Earthspirit Community, Janet and Stewart Farrar, Selene Fox, Macha Nightmare, and Brightshadow. And I especially mention the following notable individuals who have bravely let their convictions and recognition of the Goddess be publicly known: Tori Amos, Deepak Chopra, Olympia Dukakis, Erica Jong, and Cybill Shepherd.

I cannot thank my parents enough for teaching me to believe in the goodness of the human heart. Though they cannot read it, I know that they know this book is dedicated to their courage and love.

And finally, without my husband, Bruce Fields, without his endless expressions of love and support, this book would never have been written. He let me go, he held me close, and he never doubted I could do it.

Contents

Preface

Thousands of years ago, the Sumerians created a legendary collection of invocations to the Goddess, ordaining their magical corpus of poetry and songs a "Book of Shadows." Over time, *Book of Shadows* has come to refer to a Witch's journal, a record of spiritual wisdom, a diary of spells, songs, chants, rituals, and invocations. This is my *Book of Shadows,* the story of my first encounter with the ancient ways of the Goddess. It is the true story of a modern woman's spiritual journey into a realm long forgotten by Western culture. It is a chronicle of discovery, challenge, and transformation.

Over the past two decades, as a High Priestess and a teacher of the Old Religion, I have found when I mention the word *Witch,* it often brings to people's minds images of hurly-burly hags casting spells, licentious young women consorting with the devil, and wizards commanding supernatural demons to appear. On the lighter side, they might think of glamorous Veronica Lake in *I Married a Witch,* sexy Kim Novak in *Bell, Book and Candle,* or the adorable TV Witches in *Bewitched* and *Sabrina* lending some desperately needed excitement, as well as some unexpected morality, to the American suburbs. Or perhaps they will remember, with a child's delight, *The Wizard of Oz* and Glinda, the Good Witch of the North, who tells young Dorothy the power to find her happiness, and her way home, has been with her all along. This last image comes closest to capturing the real and unknown truth about Witchcraft.

Like most people, there was a time when I thought Witches existed only in the realm of make-believe. Whether they were real, and whether they actually had magical powers, were not questions I even considered as a philosophy student at Brown University, and certainly not later as a young practicing Manhattan attorney. After all, why would a well-educated, professional woman be interested Witches, let alone willingly become one?

Then, twenty years ago, a series of mysterious coincidences led me to a world where I discovered the answers not only to these questions, but to questions buried at the center of my soul—questions, it turns out, millions of people also want answered, for the answers are the hope for humanity's future as we enter a new millennium. How are we to find our lost souls? How can we rediscover the sacred from which we have been separated for thousands of years? How can we live free of fear and filled with divine love and compassion? How can we find and fulfill our magical destinies? How can we restore and protect this Eden, which is our fragile planet?

The answers were not found in the domain of make-believe, but in the place one might least expect to find them—in the hidden world of real Witches. But contrary to the clichés in fairy tales and Hollywood films, Witchcraft is not a subculture of satanic rites enacted by wacky spinsters or mad demonologists. It is an ancient, elegant spirituality that revives the magic of being alive—the kind of magic we have always longed for, but sadly assumed only came true in storybooks.

Wicca, as Witchcraft is most often referred to by contemporary practitioners, is the renaissance of a pre-Hebraic, pre-Christian, and pre-Islamic Goddess spirituality. The word *Witch* actually comes from the old Anglo-Saxon word *wicce,* meaning "wise one," a seer, a priestess, or shaman who is able to work with unseen, divine forces. Witches were the singers of sacred songs, the midwives and healers, guides and teachers of the Goddess's spiritual wisdom. Like Native Americans, Taoists, Australian Aborigines, the Yoruban tribes in Africa, Eskimos, Hawaiians, Lapps, and other indigenous peoples, the people of old Europe and the Fertile Crescent lived close to the earth and respected their relationship with nature as sacred, for they experienced their world as the embodiment of the divine.

The shamanic practices of the Old Religion enabled women and men to attune their psyches and their daily lives to the cycles of nature and the mystical wisdom found in the earth's profound rhythms. A spirituality of divine empowerment, the holy magic practiced by Witches, shamans, priestesses, and mystics celebrated an enlightened connection to the earth.

Their sacred truths have been passed down by magical orders and within families, who carefully preserved the religion of the great Goddess. Those who practiced the old ways—in southern Italy, in the small towns of the British Isles, and, several centuries later, in rural parts of West Virginia and New England—were forced to do so secretly, having been driven underground nearly five hundred years ago, when accusations of Satanism first arose. From these accusations came the "Witchcraze," the Church's crusade to suppress the Old Religion of the Goddess and establish religious hegemony in Europe. Hundreds of thousands were killed in an unholy campaign, most of whom were women, who suffered great losses in economic and social power. But this was not the only wound to Western culture. The ancient knowledge of the village wise woman, and man, was nearly lost, as the sacred rites that maintained the connection between people, the earth, and the divine were rent asunder.

Hundreds of years after the Witchcraze, the archetype of the horrific hag continues to hold tremendous power as a repository for modern culture's fear of women, sexuality, and individual freedom. The repulsive crone has become our guardian at the gate, challenging our readiness to enter a world of ecstasy and enchantment. Those with courage, curiosity, compassion, and a taste for adventure may confront her, and when they do, behind the mask of the wicked Witch, they will find the beatific face of the Great Goddess.

As a young woman at the start of my career, I began studying with priestesses of the Goddess. They introduced me to the timeless arts of spiritual transformation, imparting tools and techniques that anyone can use to experience the divine within themselves and in the world around them. I entered a realm of magic that was as ancient as the history of humanity, and as modern as the theories of quantum physics. And their ways enabled me to see the world as vibrantly, divinely alive, rich with wisdom and beauty.

Since I first began practicing the secret arts of the sacred earth, Goddess spirituality has emerged from the shadows of misunderstanding as the fastest growing spiritual practice in the United States. I have addressed the public, the media, the legal system, Church congregations, the Parliament of the World's Religions, and United Nations conferences. I have taught the wisdom of the Great Goddess. I have found a beacon of truth, a torch that I offer for your journey into the future, into realms of wonder, magic, and divinity.

We are entering a new era, an age of the Divine Feminine, when the illumined power of women and men will bring new life to a dying world. It is a time of critical change that depends upon our spiritual awakening, a collective epiphany, a summoning of the sacred into our lives. Now is the time for the Goddess's return, for the return of our lost souls. For the return of life to a world laid waste by spiritual and environmental crises. Through the re-empowerment of the feminine principle, our world can become a holy vessel of connectedness, grace, and joy for all. With Her return, we will rediscover the Paradise which dwells within and which encircles us on this sacred, beloved planet.

The story that follows is true. In an effort to safe-
guard the privacy of individuals whose lives have
touched mine, all of the names and many identi-
fying details of the people mentioned in this book
have been changed. In some cases, composite characters have been created and some events altered
for the purpose of further disguising the identity of
individuals.

CHAPTER I

The Dark Side of the Moon

If a man could pass through Paradise in a dream,
and have a flower presented to him as a pledge
that his soul had really been there,
and if he found that flower in his hand when he awoke
—Ay! and what then?

—SAMUEL TAYLOR COLERIDGE, *Anima Poetae*

In dreams begins responsibility.

—WILLIAM BUTLER YEATS, *Responsibilities*

Moonlight filters in through the city skylight. The air is fragrant with the scent of flowers and the smoke of burning incense. Candles flicker and glow, bathing our bodies in golden light. Holding hands, we begin a quiet chant: "Isis, Astarte, Diana, Hecate, Demeter, Kali, Inanna. . . ." Singing the names of ancient goddesses, our voices blend and rise, our bodies sway and dance, faster and faster we circle.

The room around us blurs, the earth slips away beneath our feet and we are spinning together, weaving a wild and timeless web of energy. Suddenly the circle stops. Our arms fly upward, the power we have raised shoots from our fingertips into the night sky above. A shout explodes from our lips, then disappears into the thinnest whisper of breath.

I inhale slowly, feeling the energy rushing through me. I have never felt so alive. I look around the circle of women who stand with me—their *eyes full of fire, skin flushed and glowing, their hair dancing about their radiant faces. "Thou art Goddess," the woman next to me says. "Thou art Goddess," I reply and turn to send the blessing around our circle.*

Our magic is done.

I awoke that Monday morning to the perfume of roses filling my room, a silver mantle of moonlight draped across my bed. I reached for the pen and notebook on my nightstand. The images were already disappearing as the words appeared on the page. I sat, head in hands, grasping for wisps of my evaporating dream. *Isis!* There it was again—the name had been floating in and out of my sleeping and waking consciousness for weeks, weaving a spell of strange anticipation. I knew only that Isis was an ancient Egyptian goddess, but her name reverberated inside of me, as if it were a magic word that could unlock the doors of paradise.

Outside, a siren shattered the sleepy morning. I threw off the covers and went to my window. Across the street, an ambulance and a police car pulled to the curb, their red lights flashing. A small crowd gathered on the sidewalk below, drawn by the magnetism of calamity, or the fear that it could be someone they knew. Though it was early, New York never fully slept and I could see those who'd been up all night, or who had reason to rise before dawn—Mr. Rocco on the way to his bakery around the corner on Bleecker Street; Mr. Tomanello coming home from the late shift; and the old women, in their black dresses, clustered like crows portending a final journey.

A feeling of sadness pressed in upon me as I pictured a man, perhaps in his late sixties, or just prematurely aged by a hard life of too many disappointments, a weekend's worth of grizzle still on his chin, an old T-shirt stretched across his belly. His wife stood in their bedroom doorway wearing a robe covered with vivid roses. She shook with grief as two young men in white uniforms settled a clear plastic mask over her husband's face. A name flashed in my mind: Paul Berzini. As a student, I lived on the periphery of this community, but two weeks ago, my neighbor Renata had told me that Berzini's wife was afraid he was going to lose his job as an insurance salesman. He'd worked thirty years for the company, and was too old to be hired by another. The recession of the seventies was still taking its toll.

Somehow I knew what I had imagined was real. Staring at the old apartment building, a wave of fear overwhelmed me. It was too much pain and I pushed it away, raising my eyes westward, toward a river I could not see. Scanning a black asphalt landscape, I looked for the few rooftop gardens that grew red tomatoes, yellow sunflowers, and hope, until the sense of panic faded. A vivid blur of blue landed on my fire escape—the blue jay that visited every morning, screeching exuberantly for crusts of bread.

I checked the clock and realized I had only twenty minutes to get to class. I rushed through my shower, threw on my clothes, and raced down the stairs, almost crashing into Renata on the front stoop.

"Don't run like that, you'll live longer," Mrs. Tomanello chided me. She was a tough old bird, dressed in her perennial widow's garb. Her husband had been a stonemason, and she lived in my building, in the same apartment her husband had grown up in.

"So, Mikey's one of the cops, he told Tony it's Pauli Berzini—a heart attack. Poor Maria, what's she gonna do? Two sons dead in the war and now this?" Renata crossed herself, a gesture quickly copied by the small gathering of women who turned, as I did, to see the figure of a man, strapped to a gurney, being lifted into the ambulance.

"Blessed Mother," Mrs. Cardozi murmured, and the little prayer, like the invocatory gesture, rippled through the group.

"They'll be O.K.," I tried to reassure Renata. She nodded sadly and, knowing there was nothing to be done, I left, running down the block toward New York University Law School. Knowing my vision of what had happened to Mr. Berzini was real, I felt myself caught between the pleasure that came with my strange new talent, and repulsion for what it had shown me.

The visions had started a few months back—coming in psychic flashes, premonitions, and even precognitive dreams. It was 1978, my final year in law school, and while most of my fellow students were narrowing their sights on which corporate or tax law firm they wanted to work for, my world was expanding in ways I could not comprehend.

My sixth sense had begun with small things—like knowing that the phone was going to ring before it did. And then knowing who was on the other end of the line. I knew the answers to a professor's questions without having read the assigned case law or text, and I often sensed what people were going to say before they spoke. And though it was temporary, I had developed a photographic memory that allowed me to scan pages with tremendous speed, later calling them to mind as if they were lying right in front of me.

I rushed beneath an arched gateway and through a courtyard into the large brick building that housed the law school. Standing before a bank of elevators in the lobby, instinctively knowing which set of doors would open before me, I entered the elevator feeling as if the "normal" world had once again shifted, showing me a side of reality ordinarily hidden from view. This ability to see the dark side of the moon was thrilling, even when it was disturbing. It was the provocative opposite of the rules and regulations, the laws and codes that had, until recently, held my complete attention.

Perhaps it could be traced to the old Sicilian lady who lived and died in my building, the one Mrs. Cardozi called a *strega,* whose powerful and mysterious presence seemed to linger long after her soul left her body. Perhaps it was triggered by the little bundle of blue corn and strange herbs given to me by a young man who taught on a Hopi reservation. He had called it a medicine bundle, and told me it was given to him by an elderly woman, with instructions to give it to the butterfly girl who came to her in dreams seeking justice. There were times when I thought it came from my practice of yoga, or from a contact high from the sweet-smelling marijuana smoke that curled out from beneath my roommates' doors when their boyfriends came to call.

It may have all started because deep within me, hidden somewhere beneath my well-trained, analytical mind, an instinct was guiding me to break out of the chrysalis of my rational self. And perhaps it was all in the timing, for I later learned that others underwent similar epiphanic experiences at that remarkable moment in time, when Jupiter and Saturn were about to conjoin—an astrological occurrence that happens once every twenty years, bringing a new spiritual vision.

Memory selects events with significance, discerning a pattern that is invisible in the moment. I now know that my shift in consciousness came from a magical combination of all of these things, stirred together in the cauldron of a young woman on the threshold of life. What was unique was not the latent gift, for I now know it resides within all of us, but my ability, my willingness, my desire to pay attention to the signs and summonings that drew it forth. But that year, all I knew was that amazing things were happening, and the universe seemed alive and aware of my existence. It seemed to be sending me messages, as if to guide me in a direction I'd never considered. The question was: where?

Once in class, I pushed my musing aside and concentrated on mastering the intricacies of pension and welfare plans, for I had some plans of my own. I had accepted a position as legal director for a rank and file union reform group fighting against organized crime in their union. In a few months, after I passed the bar, I'd be heading to work in the group's main office in Washington, D.C.

But the name *Isis* continued to echo through my mind, haunting me as I walked down the busy streets of Manhattan. She was a mysterious figure that beckoned to me, summoning me to steal an hour here or there, during the day, between or after classes, to search for her name, her face, a clue to her meaning. I soon found myself among the ruins and artifacts in the high marble halls of the Egyptian collection at the Metropolitan Museum of Art.

I stood for hours in a gallery of beautiful frescoes that climbed to the ceiling. The colors were breathtaking—sea green and lapis lazuli blue, honey gold, and carnelian red. Women with wide jeweled collars and long black hair, dressed in sarongs of pleated white linen, stared at me with their large almond eyes across the abyss of time. I could hear the hypnotic shaking of their rattles, the sistrums in their hands, the *ting* of golden finger cymbals, the provocative, soul-summoning *thock* of drums made of hammered silver, ceramic fired mud of the fertile Nile, or carved from the trunk of the fragrant myrrh tree in the shape of the full moon or a woman's body, and covered with antelope skin.

I envisioned these graceful women in their ancient serpentine dances of sex, death, and rebirth, the mysteries of the moon, of desire and the womb so powerful in its summoning forth. I longed to dance with them in the presence of grand ibis, the birds with black beaks that curve like scimitars spearing fish in the emerald waters of the Nile. I saw men with crescent horned oxen plowing brown fields, and everywhere, lotus flowers in colors of a desert rainbow. It felt vibrantly alive, the energy as vivid as the colors that dazzled me, and I was inexpressibly happy. The beauty there made it difficult to return to the canons of law, which seemed as dead and dusty as I had once thought the world painted on the museum's walls.

Long before I dreamed the name Isis, I had longed for the colors of the Nile. When I first moved into my West Village apartment over a year before, I had painted my bedroom the very same coral I found on these walls. I hung posters on my wall with portraits of Egyptian priestesses and queens, papyrus fronds billowing in unseen breezes, and lotus buds looking like spherical dreams waiting to be opened. I slept on terracotta–colored sheets marked with ancient Egyptian hieroglyphs. These silent symbols of venerable magic, these incantations of reincarnation and ecstasy, which I could not read with my waking mind, summoned the part of me that walked in dreams each night.

In those dreams I found truths and precognitions I could not have logically foretold—the sudden death of a beloved aunt, the return of a long-lost friend, my father's recovery from a coma. There was also a terrifying nightmare about an accident that appeared in the headlines the next morning. And several times I had the same mysterious dream in which I felt more awake than asleep: Each time it began, I was alone in a great hall. Music like rippling water filled the room, and a woman sat before me. Her face was pensive and serene; a book lay open in her lap. A shining light crowned her head and a necklace with a six-pointed star hung at her throat. The power that radiated from her crown and her throat became so bright I was momentarily blinded. I blinked and she was gone. Who was she? I wondered. Could she be Isis?

I searched my memory for answers, but it seemed they came to me only in the dark cave of sleep, when the portal opens into a mysterious realm of power. In our dreams, we willingly pass through to the other side, journey to far-off places, encounter demons and lovers, fly like birds, and swim like dolphins. We learn a language of symbols, and spirits speak to us, guiding our waking days, though we may not remember when the sun rises why we suddenly know the truth or choose an unexpected path. We are rewarded with signs and talismans that transform our waking world with the magic of dreams come true. And one day, we awaken at the precise moment when the moon sets and the sun rises and we realize that new life begins with a dream.

I turned twenty-five during my last term of law school, and among my birthday gifts I received a biography of the actor James Dean, who was also born on February 8. I longed to sit in the park and read, but it was a bitter cold day and so I took it with me to the Metropolitan Museum. I sat in the cafe, reading, when a quote from *The Egyptian Book of the Dead* rose startlingly from the page: "Give to me my mouth that I may speak with it. May I follow my heart at its season of fire and night, they come forth the souls upon earth. . . ."

I felt as if I'd opened a time capsule and found a note from Isis with my name on it. And the added coincidence of finding those words at the museum thrilled me. From the collection's statues and artifacts, I knew that Isis was a mother who suckled her son as she sat upon a throne, she carried emblems of divine power, wore a crown of vulture's wings and a serpent's head, was glorious and beautiful. But I longed for more.

The next day, during a break between classes, I ran to the undergraduate library and quickly prowled between the bookcases until I found my quarry—*The Egyptian Book of the Dead,* translated by E. A. Wallis Budge. The leather binding of the ancient edition cracked open, and the afternoon quickly fell away. I missed my classes, caught in the spell of the enchanting prose. Carefully turning the yellowed pages, I read of how Isis—goddess, wife, sister, and Witch—journeyed to the Underworld and by her magic restored life to her beloved husband, the lost and sundered god Osiris.

My law books remained closed that night as I read Isis's lamentation for the death of Osiris. I traveled with her into the nether realms to heal his wounded form, journeyed through the rich Nile valley and through the desert gathering the thirteen pieces of Osiris's body that had been torn asunder by his envious and angry brother, Set. I watched as she knelt above his lifeless body, heard her voice singing riddles of rebirth, saw her hair spill forth to shield them from view as she worked her magic. I marveled at ancient mysteries and the magical powers of love that could summon back life from the realms of death. But still I wondered what these lost miracles had to do with me.

In the past, everything about my life had been thoughtful and sensible. My parents were intellectuals who had left the superstitious constraints of religion behind them long ago. As a young girl, I remember asking my mother whether we believed in God. She replied that we believed in the goodness of the human heart and, when I grew up, I could find out for myself whether God existed. I was satisfied with her answer and lived my life as I had been raised—by the Golden Rule and the basic conviction that human beings were responsible for their own destinies. Life was what we made of it and it was up to all of us, together—not some distant God—to create the promised land here on earth for everyone.

But though my parents' moral beliefs were founded in reason, they were still two of the most spiritual people I had ever known. I'd learned from example as they practiced their beliefs. My father, who'd gone to sea at the age of twelve, was a union organizer; my mother was a diplomat who, despite her wealthy upbringing, was part of the early fight for racial equality. I'd been raised with Woody Guthrie and the Metropolitan Opera, John Steinbeck and William Shakespeare, in a family that defied the boundaries of class, religion, and race. As my parents had, I defined myself by my intellectual capacities and convictions. I studied philosophy at Brown University and attended one of the top law schools in the country.

My idealism, and my career choice, seemed resolutely sensible: Democratic unions meant a democratic society, and an agenda of social justice was the only rational course for a great nation. My recent psychic experiences, however, were not "sensible." They were extrasensory, and the world I lived in had no explanation for them. And so I kept my secrets to myself.

I was unaware that I was experiencing a shamanic break—a break with the socially defined reality opening to the greater reality of a sacred, living universe. Some Native Americans, and Witches, would describe it as "a calling." Aldous Huxley referred to these experiences as an opening of "the doors of perception." In other cultures, other epochs, I would have been swiftly sent off to study with the village shaman, or to attend the college of priestesses. Or I might have been burned at the stake. But this was New York City in the 1970s. I'd been too young for the psychedelic sixties, I'd never read Carlos Castaneda, and Esalen was a world away in California. I had no frame of reference for understanding or cultivating what was happening to me. Yet because my psychic flashes were objectively borne out by events, I turned to science for sensible and rational explanations.

Between classes I returned to the undergraduate library. In books on physics, the original "natural science" devoted to the study of matter and energy, I read that physicists had discovered a new level of reality. Underlying the three-dimensional, physical world described by Newton's Laws, they found an "invisible" realm, a quantum level of subatomic particles and energy. It is a realm that underlies, pervades, and forms the world we "see" and live in each day.

At the quantum level, everything is interconnected energy, even matter. Quantum reality is another level of existence, another dimension. Here the energy field is the underlying order, a hidden or shadow reality of our daily lives. We see solid material objects as separated from one another—a rock, a table, a human being—but on the quantum level, they are all actually bundles of vibrating, interacting energy. And though we perceive them to exist separately, these energies—the rocks and tables and ourselves—are interconnected. As

Einstein said, "Our separation from each other is an optical illusion of consciousness."

Even more extraordinarily, I learned that quantum physics experiments have shown that we can influence objects, even people, and events in ways I never imagined. Science opened the doors of my perception to an astonishing reality: The role of the human mind in this realm goes far beyond that of an analytical tool. Experiments have actually proven that we can influence the movement of subatomic particles. In other words, the experimenter can directly affect the outcome of the experiment, through thought and will alone. Our simple observations and our expectations of subatomic particles will alter their course. The magic of yesterday is today's science.

I sat at my desk with a pile of physics books to the right, law books to the left, and *The Egyptian Book of the Dead* in the center. Though it was three o'clock in the morning, I was unable to sleep, awestruck at the implications. With unrealized powers, we create our reality in virtually magical ways. But what of the longings of the heart, and the fears that lurked in the shadows? What realities would they create?

With growing excitement I learned that my experiences reflected an entirely different set of rules about reality. These rules defied the expectations with which we were all raised, and by which we lived. And more important, physics provided a hook for me to hang up my skeptic's hat. Like a child whose storybook had suddenly come alive before her, I had stumbled into a universe of astonishing possibility. Still, science couldn't help me explain the quality of my experiences—why the world was now intoxicatingly alive, full of wonder and miracles, strange events and shimmering beauty. Most exhilarating of all was the unshakable feeling of a presence observing, accompanying, and even guiding me. I began to sense I was in touch with an *élan vital,* an intelligent and creative universe.

There were times when I felt the universe come to me like a mother's encompassing embrace, and other moments when it seemed to be the enchanting magnetism of a lover's presence. But why these events were happening to me, what they meant, and what role I played in them as the "experimenter," remained a mystery.

After my graduation, I studied intensely for the bar exam, marveling at the usefulness of my enhanced memory. When the exams were over, I packed and left for Washington, D.C. But, once there, I missed

New York and soon realized I dearly missed the magic I had left behind, for the premonitions, dreams, and insights had stopped. Pushing aside my disappointment at having the door to this other world closed, I hoped it was only a matter of time before it would open again. In the meantime, I threw myself into my work with complete devotion. Like so many young idealists who head to our capital, I was determined to help make a difference for those who lived in the shadow of the American dream.

With a religious zeal, I lobbied Congress, counseled drivers with problems in their locals, and testified before congressional committees on the appalling absence of truck and bus safety and the devastating damage to the health of drivers. I consulted with lawyers about litigation to clean up the union, dealt with the press, worked on grant proposals and legislation for workers' health and safety, and traveled the country on organizing drives, urging union members to battle for change. Unfortunately, less than a year after I'd begun, the Washington office was closed and my job was sacrificed in a merger of reform organizations, victim to budget cuts, differing priorities, and most of all, politics, of which sexual politics was certainly a part.

A shadow had fallen on my idealistic expectations, and though disappointed, I was also relieved to return to New York City. I now knew life without magic was no longer enough for me. So I settled into a tiny studio apartment, and waited for the magic to begin. I went back to the foundation I'd worked for in law school. I filed briefs to democratize corrupt unions, wrote articles, organized plaintiffs from around the country for lawsuits. And I waited.

Months passed without sign or stirring of enchantment. Maybe the magic needed jump starting, I thought, so I began to hang out at rock and roll clubs like CBGB's and Max's Kansas City, rubbing elbows with the Lower East Side's black-clad punks and rockers. It was a culture of rebels who knew that music could be a magic carpet to a world of passionate intensity. And there was always the hope that my romantic dreams might materialize in human form, wearing old blue jeans and a beat-up leather jacket, with a light in his eyes and a heart full of poetry. It was an instinctual choice to roam among this crowd, and though I couldn't prove it yet, I was certain that passion, music, and magic were inextricably interwoven.

I soon found myself managing a band. After finishing up work, I would head for the Music Building, an old warehouse on Eighth Avenue, alive with the sounds of all kinds of bands rehearsing: heavy metal, rhythm and blues, punk, new wave, and rockabilly. It was a scene, vital and alive, full of raucous jubilation and the rapture of amazing harmony. I accompanied my band to gigs or hung out with musicians until dawn. Many nights I crashed on a mattress on the floor of the rehearsal studio, and made love with my new boyfriend, a volatile and handsome left-handed drummer. In the morning, I donned my business attire and raced off to fight corruption in trade unions. But though the music was magical, and the work was gratifying, there was still no magic within me.

And then the music brought Sophia to me. She arrived in the Music Building like a messenger sent to set me back on course. We hit it off right away, hanging out on the third floor where the band she managed rented a space. Equipment was jammed all along the walls and there were piles of clothes scattered around the floor, soda bottles, the usual mess made by lost boys. Sophia and I were a couple of Wendys, but we drew the line at cleaning up after them. Sharp as a tack, Sophia was funny and hip. But there was one odd thing about Sophia: She called herself a Witch, a white Witch.

My parents had taught me not to judge by labels, for beneath stereotypes there was often a very different reality. I decided to ignore this one, to dismiss it as an idiosyncrasy. And then one afternoon while we were waiting for the roadies to load her band's gear for a gig downtown, my curiosity overwhelmed me and I finally asked her: "So exactly what is this Witch thing?"

Sophia dropped into the sagging couch at the front of her studio and a cloud of dust lifted into the air.

"First of all," she said, "before I can tell you what it is, I have to explain what it isn't. It has nothing to do with Satanism. That was a completely false accusation made by the Church in an effort to suppress the Old Religion. They called it Satanism and that justified their use of torture and violence to do away with the competition."

I nodded. I was all too familiar with the practice, and consequences, of witch-hunts. "Go on."

"The word Witch comes from an old Anglo-Saxon word *wicce.*" She pronounced this word just as she said the word Witch, adding a soft *a* to the end of it. "It meant a wise one, a seer, a shaman. And, it may also reflect an old Nordic word, *vitke,* which meant a singer of sacred songs. The Old Religion is a lot like Native American spirituality—it's the indigenous earth religion of Europe. There's a Goddess as well as a God, and everything that exists in nature is experienced as sacred, as part of the Goddess, and the God. There are also remnants of the Mystery Schools of ancient Greece and Egypt in Wiccan cosmology."

"Mystery Schools?" I asked, my attention caught by her mention of goddesses and Egypt. I thought of Isis, my dreamkeeper.

"Yes, they were the dominant religious traditions for several thousand years throughout Greece and the rest of the Fertile Crescent. The Mystery Schools centered on the worship of the Great Goddess. Their primary mythos was the story of the Goddess's descent into the Underworld and her divine gifts of restoring life to the world."

It was Isis's story. A thrill shot through me with the hope that my magic was returning.

"Anyway, the way we practice now has remnants of ceremonial traditions that sought to preserve those mysteries, and the folk practices which are very shamanic."

"Shamanic? You means like shamanism, European shamanism?"

Sophia nodded.

I knew from my college anthropology classes that shamanism was an ancient religious practice that enabled the shaman, or "medicine man, or woman" to enter a state of ecstatic consciousness. He, or she, would then receive the aid and guidance of spirit helpers, who often came to the shaman in the form of an animal. My excitement grew as we discussed how, in this state of ecstatic consciousness, the shaman could diagnose and heal illness, commune with the divine, and receive information about practical matters such as where to hunt, plant, or live. I had read that shamanism was practiced throughout the world by indigenous peoples, such as Native Americans, Aborigines, Africans, the Inuit (Eskimos), Lapps, Siberians, Hawaiians, Tahitians, Japanese, and others. But I'd never realized Europeans had also practiced shamanism.

"Do you belong to a . . . coven?" I hesitated saying it, anxious at how quickly dark and frightening images came to my mind.

Sophia shook her head. "No, I prefer to work alone. But I know some other Witches, if you'd like to meet them. They're mostly hidden, for obvious reasons, but there are certain . . . portals."

I smiled. "No thanks. One Witch in my life is more than enough for me."

"You'd be surprised," she said mysteriously, and got up to let the roadies in.

I let the subject drop, feeling too awkward to ask more questions in front of others, unable to understand how a bright person like Sophia could be involved in anything so . . . offbeat. I could accept her explanation that it had nothing to do with Satanism, but what about casting spells on people, and riding on broomsticks, and magical potions, and . . . still, I respected her and enjoyed her company. Who knew, maybe there was more to Witchcraft than met the eye. And certainly, when I thought of Witchcraft I thought of magic—perhaps knowing Sophia would lure the magic back into my life.

A month later, I woke up with a stiff neck to the sound of unfamiliar voices and the smell of strong coffee. Where am I? I wondered, groggy with sleep. And then it came back to me with a rush of sadness: Last night I'd finally broken up with my boyfriend and Sophia had let me crash on her couch. She was standing over me with a cup of steaming java.

"Good morning. I've got an idea. Have you ever had your cards read?"

I shook my head. It was too early for this stuff. It was too early to be conscious. It was Saturday, and I just wanted to sleep.

"Well, I want you to meet Maia. I called her and she says she can read you this morning."

Too tired to protest, I murmured my assent, then left the room to take a quick shower. I want to go home, I thought as I dressed. Actually, though, I didn't want to be alone. We were headed out the door when I remembered my silver and jade ring. Sophia had taken it from me last night to "charge" on her altar and, while it sounded a little weird, I humored her. I had watched as she slipped it onto a long willow branch tied with feathers and bells that jingled softly as she handled it. She placed the wand, with my ring, on a small table beside her bed. It was low to the floor, covered with a pink silk scarf. Spiraling nautilus shells and roses, gemstones, crystals, and a statue of a female figure were also carefully arranged on the table. As I drifted off to sleep on the couch the night before, I could have sworn I heard the sound of women's voices singing, and laughing.

"Here it is." Sophia raced back and handed my ring to me. I slipped it on the third finger of my right hand. I shook my hand, my eyes opening wide in disbelief—my finger was tingling with electricity.

"Come on. We don't want to be late," Sophia said, smiling at my astonishment. She lived in the Village, not far from my old apartment.

We quickly walked up Sixth Avenue, turning off onto a block in the upper teens.

We stopped in front of the last place on earth I would expect to find myself—on an incidental side street, in front of a dusty storefront window, and beneath a long green banner with large, gold, Gothic lettering: MAGICAL CAULDRON. I peered into the dusty window and saw a small black cauldron, a statue of an Egyptian goddess, and bookcovers with strange markings. There were decks of Tarot cards, an odd assortment of silver jewelry, green stone scarabs, and a large crystal ball. A broom with a rough-hewn handle and long yellow straw leaned against the glass. And in the middle of all this was an apparition, a face that appeared and disappeared as swiftly as the clouds racing across the sky. I blinked, and there it was staring back at me—my own startled face reflected in the plate glass. Joke's on me, I thought. Then I looked down and found myself standing in the middle of a large symbol that looked like a medieval number four surrounded by indecipherable characters all marked in green chalk on the sidewalk. I heard the sound of bells and saw Sophia disappearing through the old front door. What the hell, I thought, think of it as an adventure.

I walked into a perfumed cloud of smoke that hung in the air like drifting cobwebs. I surveyed my surroundings uneasily. It was unlike any bookstore I'd ever seen. Instead of being brightly lit, the shop was dark, illuminated only by a few dim bulbs hanging from the tin ceiling high above. Along my left, running down the center of the store, was a long, crowded bookcase. To my right, a brick wall was lined with large glass jars of strange herbs, twisted roots, dried flowers, and powders the color of the desert at sunset. I hurried to catch up with Sophia and found her at the back of the shop, sniffing the contents of an exotic little bottle with a red jeweled top.

"Mmmm, a new oil. Smell." She waved it under my nose and images of tigers and elephants, crowded open air marketplaces, and billowing curtains of pink and saffron silk blew past my mind's eye. I smelled the spices coriander and cardamom, then ginger, cinnamon, and flowers I did not know.

"It makes me think of India."

"Very good—it's a Lakshmi oil. Lakshmi is an Indian goddess of fertility and love."

Dark brown and cobalt blue apothecary bottles filled the narrow shelves along the back wall of the shop. "Oil Office" noted a little calligraphied sign. Several leather-bound books with yellowed pages sat open on a wooden table, next to funnels of various sizes and scores of tiny clear glass bottles.

"I wonder where Maia is?" Sophia asked, and smiled at me reassuringly.

"Maybe she's invisible," I quipped. The bookstore was just a little too peculiar for me. "Listen, I'm perfectly happy to come back another—"

The wall in front of me started to shake and the colorful robes hanging from a wooden pole began to dance as if ghosts had jumped into them for a midnight romp. The wall wrenched open and before me stood a small, olive-skinned woman with thick raven hair and a lovely round face.

"I keep telling Herman we've got to get this damned door fixed."

Hugging Sophia while laughing warmly, she turned to me.

"I'm Maia. So, Sophia told me you need to have your cards read? Sit down." Waving me to a seat at a small table, she carefully began to unwrap something from a purple silk bundle.

It was a deck of Tarot cards. They were larger than playing cards, with an elegant blue and white mosaic pattern on the side facing me. She began shuffling them nimbly and I glimpsed flashes of color as they flew from one hand to the other.

"Have you ever had your cards read?" she asked, her voice rich and full, with the earthy tinge of a Bensonhurst accent.

I shook my head.

"Ah," she murmured, a little smile appearing, and nothing more was said.

My gaze shifted to her face—she was the image of a Sicilian madonna. Though her movements were quick and energetic, her composure was tranquil. She looked up, her deep black eyes meeting mine. "What's your question?" she asked.

My mind flashing on carnival gypsies, I ran through a sensible list of possibilities—Will my grant be renewed so I could stay at the foundation? Will I find true love? Should I continue managing my band?—as if this were a mere sideshow game, but I had been yearning for more of the magic that had invaded my life. And in spite of my skepticism, I found myself speaking from the heart.

I asked: "Where does the path lie?"

Without hesitation she replied, "It lies within."

"But how do I get there?" This was no minor question, for the one thing I knew with certainty about myself was that my life had always been thoughtfully directed toward the outside world—to get good grades, work hard, fight for social justice, try to make the world a better place. The idea of an inner life was only just beginning to take shape in my mind. But events had awakened my heart to its unsuspected capacity to know this hidden realm of being and I hungered for a portal back to the magic that had enchanted my life.

She replied by shuffling the deck of Tarot cards and smiling.

"Cut the deck into three piles, then put them back together, any way you want, into one pile."

I could feel by their well-worn edges that the cards had been used in many readings. Thinking of all the fortunes they must have foretold, I wondered about mine as I lifted and rearranged the piles. Maia picked them up, held them between her hands, closed her eyes, and sat for an infinite moment.

She opened her eyes and, very slowly, turning over one card at a time, spread sixteen cards in an intricate pattern on the table before me. Though they were upside down as I viewed them, I could see brightly painted images of people, animals, cups, staves, swords, and shining disks. I watched and wondered if it was possible that the unconscious powers of the mind—my mind—could instruct the placement of these cards. Would this ancient set of symbols fall into patterns that revealed more truth about me to a complete stranger than I knew about myself? Would the laws of quantum mechanics work as my expectations influenced the movement of energy, and particles, and cards?

The answer went beyond my conscious anticipation. But it wasn't Maia's prophecy of a new job where I would make a great deal of money, or her insights into my restless heart, that persuaded my skeptical soul that this woman had a talent for the truth. As she interpreted the cards' meaning for me, Maia spoke of things I had told no one, small things that astonished me—like my missing carnelian ring, which I usually wore on my left hand, taken from me by Antonio, a man I'd met at a party, to ensure that I would see him again. Maia could have known about my work as a lawyer, my family background, dozens of things from Sophia. But no one knew about Antonio and no one knew about the ring. I couldn't help but wonder whether it wasn't just a lucky guess, despite the precise details with which Maia described both my ring and Antonio. But then she paused, as if startled, and said, "There's a spirit that leads you . . . the woman with the star."

A chill ran up my spine. How could she know? I'd never told a soul about my dream.

"You've met her, haven't you? In your dreams."

I nodded, knowing some force of mystery and intelligence was at play in the field of my unspoken consciousness.

"You've been wise to follow where she leads you."

I stared at the brilliant array of cards that illuminated and bemused me. Closest to me, at the top of a line of four cards, was the picture of a woman. She was seated beneath a large tree, and a shield that bore the symbol of Venus rested by her side. She was pregnant and sat, smiling beatifically, working at a spinning wheel. A basket filled with fruits and grains also rested beside her and in the background was a vast and fertile landscape. Beneath it was the Roman numeral III. I later learned this is the Empress card, the card of the Goddess. As I stared at the image, suddenly, somehow I knew: Things didn't just happen randomly, but were the extraordinary effects of a force of destiny, or desire, so profound that it could animate a lifeless universe.

Events were spinning like silken threads from a cocoon of longing, and unseen hands were weaving them into an enchanted tapestry. Sitting in front of me was a woman at ease with the spinning of the wheel and the mysterious movements of the shuttle that flew through the loom of life. Here was someone who understood there was meaning in the pattern. Perhaps she even knew the weaver.

In the space of less than an hour, my perception of the world, like the cards spread before me, had again been turned upside down. Topsy-turvy, I thought, and in the instant I thought it, Maia had me pull two final cards from the deck. She handed me the first one—it was a man hanging upside down from a tree. Beneath the man were the words "The Hanged Man."

"This is the god Odin."

I felt my heart race, for I already knew of the Scandinavian god Odin. My father passed on tales from his Norwegian ancestors, and Odin was a principal divinity of the Norse pantheon. I remembered my father's bedtime stories of Odin, his wife, the goddess Freya, and Thor, Loki, and the other Scandinavian divinities. Odin had suffered for nine days, hanging upside down from the Yggdrasil tree, helpless and alone, until a raven plucked an eye from his head. He lost the ability to see "normally." In exchange for his sacrifice, Odin was given the runes, the first letters of a sacred alphabet, which enabled him to see within, to see into the past, and into the future. Without the runes, there would be no language, no poetry, no stories of love and valor. And there would be no prophecy, for each letter bears a magical meaning. To win the power of wisdom and the gift of inner sight, Odin had to be willing to sacrifice the way in which he had always seen the world.

"In some readings, it is a card that can mean selfishness, but in others it means sacrificing for wisdom." Maia pulled the card from my tight fingers. Our eyes met as she asked me, "Can you make this sacrifice?"

I knew that I had to be absolutely truthful. "I don't know," I replied.

Maia grinned. "Honest—that's good. You just might find the answer to your question." She handed me the second card. "Do you know what this card means?"

I looked at the tiny painting in my hand. It was gorgeous—a mysterious woman, dressed in a white gown embroidered with dark red pomegranates, sitting between two poplar trees, one white, the other black. Behind her was a shining moon, and in her hands she held a scroll. Across the bottom of the card were the words "High Priestess" and the Roman numeral II. I thought of the mysterious woman in my dreams. "The mysteries of life?" I asked.

Maia nodded. She seemed satisfied, as if my reply had answered more than the question she had asked me.

"And she who seeks them," she added. I felt her study my reaction and sensed in her approval a heightened curiosity. As quickly as Maia had handed the card to me, she now took it back, pushing it into the deck, then giving the cards a quick shuffle. She wrapped them carefully in the silk cloth and put them aside.

"I've just started a women's group. It meets once a week," she said matter-of-factly. "Why don't you come? Who knows, you might find the answers you're looking for."

"Thank you," I said. "The reading was amazing. And thank you for the invitation, but I may have to work."

I felt dazed as Sophia and I emerged from the quiet cave of the dark shop into the frenetic blare of the street.

"So what do you think?" Sophia was dancing around on the sidewalk like a schoolgirl after her first kiss behind the bleachers. "Is she amazing or what?"

"Are you going to this thing tomorrow?" I asked, avoiding her inquiring look. Back in the usual world, as we struggled just to cross the street without getting run over by terrorist taxis, Maia's spell was rapidly breaking.

"I'm really not into group stuff, I prefer working alone, but if it'll make you more comfortable, I'll go with you. You know, just to get you started. There aren't many opportunities to work with someone like Maia. I wouldn't say no 'til you've at least checked it out."

I hesitated. In the stark light of day, I was starting to feel uncomfortable with the idea of going to a meeting of strangers—and Witches at that. "Mmm, I guess I have to think about it."

We hugged good-bye and I headed off to the office to restore my sense of normalcy. At the tiny nonprofit organization I worked for, we had to make the most out of every penny, so the office was small, cramped, old, and donated. I put the reading out of my mind as I settled behind my battered desk. Work kept me busy, and I lost track of time. Finally, I switched off my desk light and leaned backward as far as I could in my chair. Stretching my aching neck and shoulders, I watched the brilliant blue Manhattan dusk fill my office with stillness. I closed one eye and squinted at the upside-down world out my window. Upside-down and one-eyed like the Hanged Man. How could I approach the world like that and survive? It sounded more like a prescription for cracking your head open than finding your way. I doubted I'd return to that strange little shop.

On any other night I would have headed to my rehearsal studio at the Music Building. But that night I felt as though the world had slipped out from beneath my feet, and somehow, I needed to get in touch with magic again.

The path lies within.

"CBGB's," I told the cab driver.

The club down in the middle of the Bowery was crowded and loud, but the pressure of people and noise wasn't enough to push Maia's words out of my head. Looking around the room, I saw a legion of young men dressed for a part they didn't know how to play. I had given up looking for my incarnated rebel, my other half, my unknown love, my god-come-to-earth in a pair of old jeans and a fast car. I was tired and bored with looking on the outside. Somehow I knew what I needed had to be found within myself. I finished my drink, said good-bye to my pals, and headed home.

I showered off the smell of smoke and climbed into bed. I thought I was awake when the dream came again. She was seated beside me, and larger than life, with a blinding light emanating from a star at her throat. Then, suddenly, I was awake and the magic was gone yet again.

A year had passed since my return to New York, and the universe was forcing me to surrender another set of expectations. It was clear I had to find a new job with a salary I could live on, since there wasn't enough money to renew my grant. Calls, interviews, lunches, and coffee with partners at various progressive labor law firms and unions had left me with statements of respect, accompanied by polite apologies of nothing available except shared office space.

But I didn't give up. I wore my banker's gray suit, the pink silk blouse with the bow tie, and a string of pearls my mother gave me. I pulled my hair back into a neat chignon. I carried letters of recommendation from congressmen and civil liberties lawyers who'd made history. I waited in reception areas larger than my apartment, sat on slippery leather chairs, gave firm handshakes, and made steady eye contact. The futility of my efforts escaped me until finally a lawyer who had worked in the labor movement for years clued me in. I was looking for someone to help me fight on behalf of the rank and file, against the mob, against corrupt leadership. No large firm wanted to take on that battle. I was feeling lost and without direction, but events were conspiring to teach me an important lesson: You cannot have the great adventure of finding your way until you've gone astray.

I headed home, with tears of frustration shattering a dam of control I'd kept in place for weeks. I wept, and just as I was climbing into a tub of steaming water to soak away my sadness, the phone rang. I wrapped myself in a towel and raced down the hall to answer it.

"Did I dream that I took you to see Maia? Or were you there too?" Sophia asked.

"Yes—it was a dream and yes, I was there too."

"So, what's the deal? You've had plenty of time to think it over—are you going to her women's group or what?"

"Well, I've been a little busy with unimportant matters like survival, you know."

"Well, it's your decision. Maybe you've been hunting for the wrong thing. I mean, you can survive, or you can thrive—it all depends on which path you choose. Call me when you make up your mind. If you can't trust yourself to decide, maybe you should trust fate. Some opportunities come along once in a lifetime—*carpe diem,* darlin'.'"

Make a decision. That sounded good—as though I had control, as though I could choose, instead of waiting to be chosen. Or maybe Sophia was right, and fate had already chosen me. I had been, after all, learning to do nothing if not follow signs over the last couple of years. Was the decision to try this circle, as Sophia called the women's group, so difficult to accept because it had been placed directly in front of me? Or because it was such a damned strange choice to make? After all, they were Witches. I pulled out my diary from the drawer of my nightstand, opening it to record my thoughts. When I looked down, I found myself reading from an entry written years before: "Moonlight filters in through the city skylight. . . . I look around the circle of women who stand with me. . . ."

A shiver passed through me. I scrambled into my comfort clothes—jeans, T-shirt, and leather jacket—and headed for my Egyptian oasis at the Metropolitan Museum of Art, remembering how it had nurtured me through that last strange year of law school. I relived my fascination with the images of Isis and the ancient invocations of Horus, the mysterious little amulets, and the grand Temple of Dendur. And then I took a detour, leaving the Egyptian collection behind and wandering into the American Wing, which I learned had a new garden extension. I pushed open the large glass door, entering a beautiful glass-enclosed greenery.

Set within a niche, formed by the outer stone walls of the museum, the garden's gracious proportions were grand, cleverly combining the neoclassical architecture of the original building with a modern encasement. A glass wall, running along the northern side, was several stories tall and allowed soft light to fill the space. Through the glass I could see the rolling green of Central Park. Along the walls were Arcadian Tiffany panels, a statue of a bacchante feeding grapes to an infant, and an enormous fireplace held aloft by caryatids. The pieces were as majestic in scale as the garden itself. Four squares of English ivy divided the space, tall papyrus fronds grew from a rectangular reflecting pool, and in the center of it all was a golden statue of Diana, goddess of the hunt, naked, standing like a ballerina on one pointed foot, her bow pulled taut.

I walked slowly, allowing the beauty of the sanctuary to fill and soothe me, strolling from one great marble statue to another, not thinking about my decision, just enjoying the silence and magnitude. And then I saw her—crown upon her head, six-pointed star at her throat, seated with a book in her hand—a luminescent white marble statue of the woman in my dream.

I felt as if I would choke on my own breath, my heart missed beats and a terrific pressure squeezed my temples. The room became blindingly bright and a wave of dizziness hit me as I sank into a chair beside my miracle.

I was almost afraid to look at her, astonished to see my dream come to life. I looked instead at the discreet little plaque by her beautiful bare toes: "The Libyan Sibyl."

My eyes followed the graceful folds of sculpted stone draped across her lap. In her left hand she held a sheaf of papers; her chin rested in the cup of her right hand. As in the dream, she was bare breasted. Her hair fell in plaits around her bare shoulders. A six-pointed star hung from a necklace that encircled her ivory neck, and a simple triangular crown rested upon her brow. Her face was strong, intelligent, with an aquiline nose and full lips. I studied every nuance of her face, as she stared into the realm where dreams come true.

The afternoon passed while I sat in the presence of an inexplicable revelation. At closing time, I left the great conservatory, descending the great stone steps of the Museum. I walked up Fifth Avenue and headed into the park, adoring the brilliant blue twilight and dewy green grass. I was so energized by the encounter that I practically ran all the way back to 86th Street and Riverside.

"Sibyl, sibyl, sibyl," I sang, rushing into my little room. I pulled my favorite dictionary, the 1933 edition of the *Shorter Oxford English Dictionary,* from the shelf and found her name: "Sibyl . . . 1. One of various women of antiquity who were reputed to possess powers of prophecy and divination . . . 2. A prophetess; a fortune teller, *witch.*"

I decided to accept Maia's invitation.

The Hidden Children of the Goddess

An accusation of Witchcraft casts a long shadow.
—ANNE LLEWELLYN BARSTOW, *Witchcraze*

Nothing could have prepared me for what I encountered when I stepped into the room behind the hidden door. I had never thought that Witches were real, and, despite lovely, blonde Sophia with her stylish haircut and impeccably hip wardrobe, when I did think of them at all, I couldn't help but recall images from a lifetime of fairy tales and Shakespeare, movies and television. There were the hurly-burly hags who predicted Macbeth's fate, poisoned Snow White's apple, and coveted Dorothy's red shoes—ugly old crones with warts on their noses, wearing black hats, riding broomsticks, brewing potions in their cauldrons, and casting evil spells in the company of black cats.

I surveyed the room—not a pointy hat in sight. I stood surrounded by dozens of women of all ages, shapes, sizes, and colors, all utterly normal. Looking around, I thought of the positive images of Witches I'd also grown up with, like Glinda, the Good Witch of the North, sexy Kim

Novak in *Bell, Book and Candle,* beautiful Veronica Lake in *I Married a Witch,* and Elizabeth Montgomery, star of *Bewitched,* one of TV's most popular shows. Chatting amiably, and standing about in small groups or sitting in old red velvet theater seats that encircled the room, they were dressed in jeans, elegant pantsuits, and dresses. Some looked like artists, others like professionals, and some like friends of my mother, or my grandmother.

Walking into the midst of their animated conversations felt like walking into a cloud of sparkling electricity. As I moved through the room, I passed bits of exotic dialogue:

"It's the best piece I've ever choreographed, I just need to find a dancer for the role of Demeter." A young woman in paint-splattered overalls was conversing with a two other women in their early thirties. She nodded and smiled at me, and kept talking as I passed them.

"I haven't told him yet. . . . I mean what am I going to say—Darling, there's something I haven't told you: I'm a Witch!" A stunning woman, tall and slim with high cheekbones and a twenties-style bob, was talking animatedly to her companion, a short plump woman with green eyes, red hair, and skin like the petal of a flesh pink rose.

I slowly picked my way through the groups, hoping Sophia was here as she had promised she would be. Four brightly colored banners— yellow, red, blue, and green—ornamented with various geometric shapes and mysterious symbols, hung on each of the four walls. Beneath the yellow banner at one end of the room was a raised area, a small stage, with an ornately carved podium. Below each banner stood a tall wrought-iron candlestick holding a thick white candle. Several faded Persian rugs covered the floor and the distant ceiling was crowned with a smoked glass skylight. Tucked into the room's corners were old wooden chests and bookcases. Music played softly in the background, Eastern tones mixing with Celtic melodies. A chorus of women's voices was accompanied by pipes and drums, finger cymbals, and stringed instruments, and I imagined myself standing on a high cliff in the north country, a wild sea below. . . .

Just then I spotted Sophia waving from across the room, standing with two women who were looking my way. As I approached them, I felt as if they'd been talking about me.

"I'm so glad you decided to come." Sophia hugged me. "This is Nonna." I reached out to shake her hand and found myself bundled into an enthusiastic hug.

It's been so long, so long, I heard with my inner ear. *She's just as I remember her. Does she recognize me?* Were these her thoughts, or mine? I knew I'd never met her before, yet she seemed comfortably familiar.

"Nonna's a very respected crone, that's a title of honor for an elder. She's been practicing since before you and I were born," Sophia continued her introduction.

"Well, what a gracious way to call me ancient." Nonna threw back her head, and as she laughed the scent of rosemary filled the room. Everything about her was generous—her laughter, her figure, the features of her face, her thick black hair.

"And this is—" Sophia began to introduce me, only to be interrupted by Nonna.

"No need. I know exactly who this is. *La fia.*" I wondered what she meant as she tucked my arm around hers. Beneath my awkwardness, I enjoyed this feeling of familiarity. Nonna introduced me to the other woman standing with us. "This is Bellona. She's also a High Priestess and she's Maia's partner."

Tomboyish Bellona was lean, wiry, and muscular. Her reddish brown, tightly curled hair crowned a face with sharp cheekbones and large green eyes. She looked just like a cat. In contrast to Nonna's cryptic words, Bellona was immediately straightforward, and her directness was equally reassuring. As she shook my hand firmly, I sensed the mettle of a warrior.

"Glad you could make it. You'll have to excuse me, Maia needs me to set up the altar. Sophia, would you give me a hand?" And I found myself alone with Nonna.

"Sophia tells me you're a lawyer," Nonna turned to me. "You fight criminals?" Her attention felt like sitting in the sun on a chilly winter afternoon.

"Well, I used to. I worked for several foundations, fighting organized crime inside trade unions. Trying to get the unions back for their members."

"Sounds dangerous."

"For the union members it is. But it's hard to make a living with that kind of practice, so I need to find something else." Speaking about it in the past tense, made me feel a little lost. Who was I without the work that gave my life its meaning?

"You will," she reassured me and untucked my hand from her arm.

"What a lovely ring. The stone is carnelian, yes?" I nodded. I had taken Maia's advice about getting my stolen ring back from Antonio and was happy to have it back on my finger. "Carnelians are good for enhancing psychic gifts." She turned my palm upward and I thought she was going to read it, but she simply held it between her thumb and forefinger, closing her eyes. I felt very self-conscious, and then strangely relaxed.

"Don't be discouraged. Something is coming, totally unexpected. Lots of money. It will seem like a dream come true . . . but. . . ." She opened her eyes.

"But what?"

"But things are not always as they seem. Learn to follow your heart and you will come to know that it is not the destination, but the journey that matters. You'll learn much about yourself, and about where your true path lies. Eh, you love adventure, don't you?" Nonna was smiling again.

I was surprised by the way she seemed to read my thoughts, but quickly dismissed her poetic predictions with practical concerns. "Yes, I suppose I do, but I also like to eat and jobs are not about adventure, at least not anymore. Now they're about paying bills."

"I know what you mean about liking to eat," Nonna laughed, putting her hands on her hips. I loved the way she laughed, full and throaty. "But life is wasted if it's not lived as an adventure. And after all, you're here, aren't you? So, you must have questions, a smart lawyer like you."

I had a million questions, and none. "Why do Witches wear black? I mean do they?" I felt like an idiot. But what was I going to say: Do you really kill cats, eat babies, worship Satan? Somehow I already knew instinctively, those questions and the stereotypes they belied were truly idiotic.

Nonna's eyebrows went up and her roaring laughter suddenly filled the room. Everyone turned to look at us, and I wanted to disappear.

"From the look of your face—sometimes they wear red!" Nonna chuckled at her joke.

"But I'm not a Witch," I protested.

"Well, you think not, eh? But I happen to know there's a little Witch in every woman today."

As I looked around at all the smiling faces, my awkwardness vanished and finally, I too was smiling.

"Actually my dear, your question is as good as any. I wear black because it's slimming. And it is New York after all—everyone wears black." We laughed again, enjoying her jokes together. She was full of humor, and though regal in her carriage, she was genuine and accessible, like a wise grandmother, not at all intimidating, nor transcendentally aloof—the way one often thinks of a religious leader. "The fact is, Witches don't wear black any more than anyone else does. It's the Catholic Church that uniforms its clergy in black. The idea that Witches wear only black is just one of many distortions about Witches. So what's troubling you?" She amazed me with her apparent ability to read my mind.

"Well, it's just . . ." I hesitated, feeling suddenly self-conscious, as if by asking I would insult her. "To be honest, I've been a little uncomfortable. It's just that I've always thought that Witchcraft was Satanism."

Nonna patted my arm. "No wonder you looked like your shoes were too tight. Come, I want to show you how these distortions got started."

I followed her from the crowded room back out to the bookstore, where women were still arriving for today's gathering. Nonna perused a bookshelf with a little sign that said "History."

"To understand what the Craft is really all about you must confront the negative stereotypes, the perverted images."

"Well, Sophia did tell me that Wicca has nothing to do with Satanism, but . . . ," I began politely.

"It's a mistake most people make. You need to understand how that misunderstanding arose historically. Here it is." She pulled a large black book from the shelf and handed it to me.

"*Malleus Maleficarum,*" I pronounced slowly.

"*The Hammer of Witches.* Between its covers you will find the most vicious lies ever told about Witches. And women. When this book was written, they were considered one and the same, and both were declared evil. This codified the misogyny of the Catholic Church. It was written by two Dominican inquisitors in 1486. The preface is a papal bull. . . ." As she spoke the book opened in my hands to the exact page upon which the Pope's endorsement began.

" '*Summis Desiderantes,* issued by Pope Innocent VIII in 1484,' " I read aloud.

"That Vatican edict, which has never been rescinded, branded Witches as worshipers of Satan," Nonna explained. "But it was not true then, or now. It authorized the use of torture to secure confessions and spurred a terrible anti-Witch hysteria throughout Europe. With that ecclesiastical order in it, it was a bestseller, outselling everything except the Bible. It became a guide for Witch-hunters, and they used it to commit some of the most heinous acts of cruelty and violence that the human mind has ever conceived. And it was all generated by the Church's fear of women and repression of sexuality," Nonna sighed. "Go on. Turn to any page and read."

I began: " 'Witchcraft comes from carnal lust, which is in women insatiable . . . When a woman thinks alone, she thinks evil. . . . Women are intellectually like children. . . .' " Women are liars, it said, wicked-minded and in need of constant male supervision. They are responsible for impotence in men, for seducing them and destroying their souls. It accused Witches of making pacts with the devil and engaging in sex with him, sacrificing babies and eating children, flying through the air, and making a priest's penis vanish. It ended with praise to God, "who had so far preserved the male sex from so great a crime."

My hands were shaking as I slammed the vile thing closed. A small group of women had gathered as I was reading.

"It's hateful," said Maia, her presence a bundle of warmth that blazed with anger. "Hidden behind their lies is the truth—their history of hideous violence against women. If you read on you'll find all the grisly details on how to try, torture, and execute an accused Witch."

"It was the women's holocaust. Everyone knows about the Inquisition, but people don't realize the extent of this persecution," Nonna added, "not only against the various so-called Christian heretics and Jews, but against the Old Religion of Europe, and against women. For several hundred years a terrible Witchcraze swept over Europe. At least a hundred thousand people, mostly women, were executed on the basis of 'confessions' that were obtained through the most vicious and sexually perverted forms of torture.

"The grotesque distortion that we still contend with today, that Goddess worship is Satanism, was perpetrated by the Church to destroy the Old Religion. There is no Satan in the Old Religion. He belongs entirely to the patriarchal religions; he is their figure of evil." Nonna continued, "Really, the Church's assertion that Witchcraft is Satanism, or demonology, is a projection of their own fears and phobias. And they used this accusation to justify their violence. Those whom the Church could not convert, they finally tried to destroy with the Witch-hunts. And they were brutal."

Nonna pulled another book from the shelf and handed it to me. I opened it and was confronted by scores of grotesque torture devices: Iron Maidens that enveloped victims, piercing their bodies with metal spears; racks that pulled limbs from bodies; beds of nails; a "witch's chair," a metal seat that was heated by fire from beneath; the "scold's bridle," an iron cage that drove spikes through the victim's tongue, and worse. I held it, sickened and horrified, unable to look and yet unable to look away.

"Most of the tests to determine if someone was a Witch were *very* sexually perverse. Women were always stripped naked for these so-called tests, and the Witch-hunters were always men. A common test was pricking—they jabbed needles and hot pokers into their victims' naked bodies," Maia said grimly.

We winced collectively.

"The persecutors justified their madness by claiming Witches were supposed to have a mark somewhere on their bodies, made by the devil, that was insensitive to pain," Maia continued. "People were encouraged, and paid, to inform against each other, and professional Witch-hunters were paid a fee for each conviction. It was an era of terror, particularly for women, and it went on for hundreds of years."

"There was also a water test," an elderly woman with long gray hair quietly added. "A woman was tied up, then thrown into a body of water. If she sank, she was innocent, but if she managed to stay afloat, she was found guilty. Either way, the woman was dead. Many, many of the women who were murdered were elderly and widowed, like I am, like Aldegonde in France who was seventy years old. She turned herself in to clear her name and was strangled and burned."

"Chiara Signorini was an Italian peasant and healer, who was imprisoned for life," Maia said angrily, her Sicilian temper flaring as she seized the book and slammed it shut. "Most women were tortured into confessing and then put to death. They were raped, sodomized, and there were other forms of sexual torture. All of this, and worse, in the name of their male God. They embodied the very things they claimed to be fighting."

"But these practices were the furthest things from the teachings of Christ," Nonna shook her head sadly. "Most people don't know this terrible history, but there are extensive records. The victims of terror, most of them women, had names and faces and families. I'm haunted by the terrible story of Walpurga Hausmanin. She was a midwife who lived in Dillingen, Germany, whose breasts and arms were torn with heated irons; they cut off her right hand; and then she was burned at the stake, all under the jurisdiction of the bishop of Augsburg, who received all of her property. These women are only a handful from the hundreds of thousands murdered all across Europe and Russia. But we remember their names, and so we remember them all." Nonna's quiet voice had remarkable power. Giving Maia a reassuring hug, Nonna returned the book to the shelf.

We fell silent, taking in the enormity of the horror. We had all grown up with the term "Witch-hunts," but I had never realized how gruesome, nor how pervasive they had been. Nor that women had been their principal victims.

"Come," said Nonna gently, to all of us who had gathered, "let's get started and you can see for yourselves what Witchcraft is really all about." She held the door to the temple open and I no longer had doubts about following her through the portal. Nonna walked to the center of the room, stopping before a small table covered in a cloth of coral silk and rang a small bell. It echoed through the room, mixing with the laughter, and I experienced déjà vu. Then I remembered—I'd heard bells ringing and women laughing as I had fallen asleep on Sophia's couch weeks before. The room fell silent and the women gathered into a large circle. A shiver of excitement passed through me as I joined them, standing by Sophia. On the table was an intoxicating bouquet of rubrum lilies, a basket filled with oranges, a large silver bowl, and a simple statue of the goddess Isis. I was comforted by the beauty that so vividly contrasted with the hideous images I'd just seen and grateful to feel Sophia squeeze my hand. Her presence helped me feel more connected to this unfamiliar experience.

"Welcome to our circle." Nonna was radiantly poised as she slowly turned to meet the eyes of each woman. Maia and Bellona stood beside her and I was struck by how unique each was, and yet how well they complemented each other—Nonna reminded me of my grandmother, Maia seemed so motherly, and Bellona was like a warrior maiden. "We gather today to remember the ancient ways of the sacred Mother Earth. We gather to give thanks for her blessings, for without them we would perish. She is mother of all. It is she who nourishes and sustains us. She is the soul of nature who gives life to all things. We come to honor the Great Goddess from whom all blessings flow." Nonna lifted the bowl from the table. Raising it high above her head, she spoke her final words of prayer: "We gather to give thanks and to remember the ancient ways, for we are the hidden children of the Goddess."

Carefully she drank from the beautiful bowl, then she passed it to Bellona, who raised it to her lips. Slowly, it was passed around the circle. Some women drank in silence, many spoke.

"I send a prayer for my mother, who is ill."

"I send a prayer for the Mother Earth, who is ill. Let us help her heal."

"I ask the Great Goddess to help me become pregnant. Bless me with your gifts of fertility, share with me your greatest gift, the power to bring forth life."

"You also need to send a little prayer to the God for that one," Maia added and many of the women laughed. I was surprised at their relaxed humor in the midst of solemnity. Rather than detracting from the spirit of what was occurring, it seemed to add to the intimacy and openness. As I looked at their smiling faces, I felt more at ease.

Their poetry and sensitivity were moving, and I was impressed with the honesty and relevance of the remarks I was hearing, but the closer the bowl came, the more I started to worry—what was in it? Sophia handed it to me and I felt my heart racing. I looked down into the purple liquid and before me floated images of bats and eyes of newts and blood and . . . did I see something moving?

Don't be ridiculous, I thought to myself. Either drink it, or leave. I looked up at Sophia, who was smiling at me.

"I give thanks for friendship, and for trust." I lifted the bowl to my lips and found myself drinking some of the most delicious grape juice I had ever tasted. Another stereotype dissolved as I drank from the Goddess's bowl.

It took a long time to travel full circle back to Nonna, as each of the dozens of women drank and gave thanks, and yet I was neither bored nor impatient, my attention held by each woman's heartfelt eloquence. She placed the bowl on the table and slowly surveyed our shining faces. "Look at the sisters who surround you. We are many in number and each day that passes there are more of us. Some of us are too young to bear children, some of us are too old, and many of us are mothers. We are white, black, Hispanic, Native American, Asian."

As Nonna spoke I looked slowly around the circle. We were as varied as she was describing.

"We are straight, and we are gay. We are married, we are single, we are widowed. We are students and we are teachers. We are wise women and we are Witches. And though they are not with us today, there are also men, our brothers, husbands, sons, and lovers, who walk this path with us. We are the hidden children of the Goddess. Our circle is now open, but never broken. Thank you all for coming. Please stay and get to know each other."

The women turned to each other, hugging and laughing. It had been simple and moving, and as I glanced at my watch I was surprised to see the service had taken much longer than I had thought. Nonna and I hugged; as I felt her warmth enfold me, the words she offered were as strange and provocative as this adventure now beckoning.

"I've been waiting for you for a long time . . . we've all been waiting for you. It's good you're finally here."

"What do you mean?" I asked pulling back from her, but Sophia was spinning me into another embrace, and Nonna disappeared into a room of women with bright eyes and joyful voices.

"So, what do you think? Interesting huh?" Sophia was already throwing on her jacket.

"You were right—it certainly wasn't what I expected. It was lovely, actually. Are you leaving already?"

"Yeah, I hate to ritualize and run, but I've got to go. I've got a meeting with my band, but you should stick around, get to know people."

I returned to the temple to find a large group of women had already settled in around Nonna. She smiled at me and patted the empty chair beside her as she continued speaking. "There is a hidden history that few people know, a history that holds many interwoven truths—about women, about the earth, and about how Western civilization lost its soul. The Old Religion is very old. It predates the three patriarchal Western religions—Judaism, Christianity, and Islam—by thousands of years. It is an ancient earth-based spirituality, a religion that experiences the divine as both feminine and masculine. For our ancestors, the Goddess was as important, often more important, than the God. The Old Religion is the shamanism of ancient Europe and the Middle East. It is very similar to Taoism, and Native American and other aboriginal spiritual practices."

"Then why do people always think of Witchcraft as Satanism?" asked a young raven-haired woman, her voice revealing Southern roots. "I mean, to be perfectly honest, I was very reluctant to come because of that association."

I was relieved to hear I was not the only one who'd been struggling with this stereotype.

"Of course you were afraid. Everyone is raised with these terrible images of devil worshipers," Nonna said. "Or people think that it's just silly or kooky. They don't know the real history of their own culture. The Church demonized women to hide its own evil deeds. The Witch-hunts went on for hundreds of years and did tremendous damage to the status of women—laws were passed forbidding them to inherit, to own property, to receive an education, to divorce, to have an abortion. We're still fighting the restrictions and the negative stereotypes about women's power today that arose during the Witchcraze. This is why the truth is so important, to free us from the bondage of lies and terror."

"So how did Goddess worship survive?" I asked.

"Those who worshiped the Great Goddess had to go into hiding, or they would be killed. And traditions were passed down secretly, within families or magical orders," explained Nonna.

"Is that why you called us the hidden children of the Goddess?" I asked.

"Exactly. You see, when the Crusades failed, the Church and the nobility that had supported these wars found themselves in serious financial and political trouble. And they were confronted by upheavals and challenges to their authority throughout Europe. The so-called heresies of the twelve and thirteen hundreds, and the rebellions of serfs and peasants that stretched into the fourteen hundreds and beyond, threatened their power. And a tremendous amount of the wealth and power had devolved into the hands of women during the Crusades, because they were left to run everything from vast estates to small trades while the men were off at war."

"Another reason the persecutions took place was because of the development of the medical profession," Maia said, joining us. "Only men were allowed to be educated, and only men could be doctors. They usurped the role of the village herbalists and midwives, most of whom were women, and made it illegal for them to practice. They wiped out their competition by force."

"Unbelievable," exclaimed a young woman in a purple T-shirt and long brown hair. A small silver double-headed ax, which I learned was called a labrys, a symbol of the Goddess, hung from a delicate chain around her neck.

"I know it seems unbelievable," Bellona said, standing with her arm around Maia's waist. "But it's true. It was a period of tremendous repression, and the misogyny of the culture had deep theological roots."

"I heard that over nine million people were killed," said the woman with the labrys.

"It's difficult to determine the precise number because the record keeping was not exact, but the number was most likely between one and two hundred thousand. But proportionally, relative to the overall population of Europe at the time, those hundreds of thousands would be equivalent to about nine million people today," Bellona answered. "All because of their fear, and hatred, and ignorance."

Maia shook her head. "And greed. The Church was actually responsible for the Plague—they were the ones that killed all the cats."

"Killed all the cats!" I exclaimed. "What for?"

"For being Witches' familiars. And with the cats away, the rats sure played." Bellona had scooped up Abramelin, a beautiful orange tabby with enormous green eyes who purred happily in her arms. "They also burned all the drums. Any kind of music, other than ecclesiastical, was forbidden."

"Between eighty and ninety-five percent of the people killed in Witch-hunts were women," Nonna added. "Sometimes as much as ninety-five percent. Entire villages were wiped out, even children. A terrible murderous madness swept over Europe. But it wasn't just the Church and the doctors. The nobility seized and consolidated their land holdings and forced the peasantry off of the land and into the growing cities, and government officials used the persecutions to enforce their control."

I remembered studying about the land enclosure acts in England, how they had created terrible poverty and suffering for those forced off the land, and phenomenal wealth for the aristocracy. I remembered the songs of Woody Guthrie, the stories my father had told me of the struggles he'd lived through to build a union and of how the poor in this country had been forced off their land during the years of the Great Depression, and how they too had been used as forced laborers. I thought of the migrant workers who toiled on the great corporate farms of today and how I now fought on behalf of unionists in the same age-old battle for justice.

Maybe this wasn't such a strange place for me after all.

"It was a prolonged period of ferocious persecution. The churches and their political allies seized the property of their victims and became very wealthy. And they were able to consolidate their power and control. Of course, the different forms of Christianity then turned on each other. Theirs is a very bloody history. And the lie that Witches are Satanists persists. But not here—here, the truth lives." Nonna smiled, and the sun returned to the dark world we had just encountered.

"I hope you'll come back next week," Maia said as I was gathering my things to go.

"Thank you for inviting me. I will," I answered as she was enveloped by a group of women anxious to talk to her.

I stood at the entrance to the temple, listening to the laughter inside. I had traveled a great distance that afternoon—from fear to friendship, ignorance to understanding. And I knew that without this first inner change there could be no magic.

I sensed someone behind me and turned around to see Nonna, her hand outstretched. "Take this. It will help you find a job." She placed a small bundle of green cloth in my hand. I closed my fingers around it and felt its mysterious contents through the cloth—something small and hard, like a stone with an indentation in its center, surrounded by something soft and crumbly. Its fragrance was rich and sweet, the way the earth smells after a spring rain.

"Carry it next to your skin, sleep with it beneath your pillow, do not let it out of your possession. The job will come by the time the moon is full. Then open the pouch and scatter its contents upon the earth. And give thanks."

"Thank you," I whispered, feeling strangely awed by the feeling of power burning in my palm. A sudden rush of confidence hit me: I would find a job, and soon. I knew it. Call it magic, or luck, or persistence—it didn't matter to me. My fingers curled around the little amulet. I wanted to believe in magic—who wouldn't? Whether it existed or not, it couldn't do any harm, I told myself. I carefully placed the bundle in my pocket, then walked out into the moonlit night.

12:12, I thought to myself as the taxi pulled up in front of the Russian Tea Room. I checked my watch. I was right on the dot. I was developing little games, exercises to flex psychic muscles—one was to guess what time it was, then check my watch. Another was to think of a song, then turn on the radio, hoping to catch it, which I almost always did.

Synchronicity. Jung had coined the term, but I'd only recently begun to understand its meaning: A coincidence that's more than a coincidence because it is filled with meaning. Synchronicities seem to arise at the quantum level. They are clues the universe provides, and they can direct us to the meaning of our lives. They are magic. And considering my nervousness about the meeting that was about to take place, magic was exactly what I needed.

A red-coated doorman opened the door, and I entered the restaurant. It was the ultimate point of convergence for indulgence and the entertainment business. I was here to meet John Hadus, one of New York's best known entertainment lawyers. And an ex-lover. He had said it was business, and said no more. I assumed it had to do with a record deal we'd both worked on. Since managing my band, I'd picked up several musical clients whose business was keeping me financially afloat, and it was through this business that we'd met. Business lunches became business dinners. Arriving in a long black limousine, he'd swept me off to a world of opulent pleasures—four star restaurants, benefit balls, downtown gallery openings. I was dazzled by him, his self-confidence and success, his polished seductiveness and determined courtship. He was a man used to getting what he wanted, and for a time, I had wanted him. Or thought I did.

It wasn't the quarrels—for passion can explain rage. It was the dark subtleties of character revealed in a single moment, like the night he gripped my wrist as we left a dinner party. Sensing a perilous side to Hadus, I closed the door on our relationship. Months passed and, in pursuit of a record contract for a new client, our paths crossed again. We established a cautious equilibrium of courtesy and distance, and I was relieved as he assumed a posture of formal indifference. No, I thought, Hadus wouldn't risk his pride trying to rekindle our affair. He probably just wanted a piece of my clients' promising future. Though the record industry was in a post-disco slump, their single was climbing the charts. Their career was taking off, and so was mine.

I followed the maître d' through the Christmas-colored dining room, past Woody Allen at his usual table, Warren Beatty with his most recent trophy, Tom Wolfe in white, and countless lawyers, to Hadus's table. He rose to greet me, clasping my hand and pulling me toward him. I was momentarily thrown off balance as he planted a kiss on my cheek. I silently scolded myself for not expecting his move. Hadus was in his late forties, tall and trim, with thinning black hair, and sharp black eyes. As always, his suit, his tie, his shoes, his regularly manicured and buffed nails, were all impeccably elegant.

"I'm so glad you could make it," he smiled ingratiatingly.

"So, what business prompts this elegant lunch?"

"Well, I understand congratulations are in order—your song is on the charts and we should celebrate."

"Thank you, but it really wasn't necessary," I turned to the waiter. "I'll have the beluga, a quarter ounce, and a glass of Cristal, and the salmon. Thank you." I handed back the menu, unopened.

"I'll have the broiled chicken, ask the chef to remove the fat. And another Stoli, on the rocks."

"So what else is up?" I asked, uncomfortably recognizing the mixture of annoyance and fascination that had once beguiled me.

Hadus lifted his Stoli. "Always to the point. I like that. You're going to do very well in this business. And if you'd like to do well with me, I'd be happy to make a toast to my new associate. If she'll have me."

A waiter brushed the back of my chair and my purse slipped to floor. Out tumbled Nonna's little amulet. *Was it possible?* I scooped it up quickly.

"What happened to the old associate? Did he get a better offer?"

"There is no better offer. There is no better music firm in New York. Everybody knows that. His wife got a job in Chicago and, being a truly liberated male, he's giving up his job to go with her. Asshole. But his loss is my gain, if you'll say yes. You can keep your clients. We'll work something out."

He made me a very attractive offer. A dream come true, actually. Since the recession in the music business, jobs had become rare. It was a precious prize and it had fallen right into my lap. It was also very dangerous territory.

"I'm flattered. And I'm certainly interested. Who wouldn't be, but there are scores of attorneys out there, with a lot more experience than I have in this field, so . . . please be straight with me." I felt awkward bringing up our personal past, but I knew I couldn't work for him if that was his real agenda. Looking around the room at all the success stories, I suddenly wanted this job very badly. "I'll know within ten minutes of starting, and I won't stay if you've got a hidden agenda. We need to be absolutely clear—this is strictly business."

Hadus smiled. I'd told him what he wanted to hear—I was interested. "Strictly business. One hundred percent. No hidden anything." He leered at me and I raised my eyebrows. "Come on—just a little joke for old times' sake." He smiled sweetly.

Too sweetly, I worried as I sipped my champagne.

"I know how we work together—the Turner deal went down very well. You're sharp, you don't impress easily, and you certainly are easy on the eyes. You've got my word—no hidden agendas." He laughed, and with a tinge of condescension, offered his winning argument. "And once you meet my new girlfriend, you'll see you have nothing to worry about."

Over lunch, which he barely ate, we talked terms, clients, and my desire to continue pro bono labor work. By the time we'd finished coffee, and the dozen assorted stars, rockers, movers, and shakers had stopped by the table to pay their respects, Hadus's artfully staged pitch had worked. We shook hands and I felt like he'd handed me the keys to the kingdom.

"I'll see you on Monday." He reached into his jacket pocket and pulled out an elegant silver card case. "Here are a few of my cards, use them until yours are printed."

I felt the raised lettering on the silky stock between my fingertips. It felt important, like a talisman of power. I placed them carefully in my purse, next to Nonna's bumpy little green pouch.

In the time it took to wash down a spoonful of caviar with a goblet of champagne, my career anxiety had vanished. It was as if someone had read my mind and waved a magic wand. It had to be magic—in an instant I'd gone from struggling to survive to working for one of the top firms in the entertainment business. I was blinded by the light as I stepped out onto Fifty-seventh Street and didn't see the man I slammed right into.

"I'm so sorry."

"Not to worry, lovely lady. Can you help me out?"

I dropped a five-dollar bill into the cup of the homeless man, and feeling I'd spread some of my good fortune around, I floated to Bendel's with dreams of sugar plums, and I. Miller shoes, dancing in my head. I was halfway to shopper's heaven when I remembered Nonna's instructions about releasing the amulet once it had worked its charm. *Was this kind of magic possible?* I wondered.

I took a hard left on Fifth Avenue up to Central Park. The ground was frozen and patches of ice made the going slippery and slow. The trees were barren of leaves, the landscape lifeless and gray. Carefully, I climbed out onto a rocky ledge over the pond. I opened the little green bundle and flung its contents to the winds. Powdery dust disappeared into the sky and a small, shiny nugget flew off into the water. Softly, so none of the lovers, or mothers with baby carriages, or old men on the benches would hear me, I said, "I don't know who it is I'm supposed to be thanking, but whoever you are, thanks."

I couldn't wait for Sunday's gathering to tell Nonna about my new job. In my elation, I'd forgotten her words of warning about my future. Though the skeptic in me doubted, it was exciting to grab on to the idea of magic as some Santa Claus–like ability to bring about good luck. Part of me dismissed the effect of Nonna's amulet, but part of me was fascinated by the possibility that she had somehow harnessed a benevolent power. The full moon sat skewered on the top of a skyscraper as I climbed out of the subway and headed for the Witches' circle. In the past I'd rarely paid attention to the moon—sometimes I noticed when it reappeared as a dramatic sliver of silver, or when it rose above the city skyline particularly large and golden. But tonight I realized it was full, and I remembered the timing of Nonna's prediction.

"I've got the most amazing news!" I grabbed Sophia, who had agreed to attend a few more circles with me, and pulled her aside. "I'm starting work at Rosen, Meiser, Dutton and Hadus tomorrow. I may have to leave early tonight—I've got so much to do."

"Very impressive." Sophia worked for a record label. She knew.

There were noticeably fewer women this week. Sophia told me they had not been invited back and I could see a winnowing was occurring.

While Sophia helped Maia and Bellona set up, I drifted to the small table in the center of the room. It was covered with a soft, green velvet cloth and a collection of female figurines, some of which I recognized from my reading. A lovely woman, with skin as brown and glowing as the rich earth in spring, came and stood beside me. She looked as if she were in her late thirties, and I heard in her gentle voice a subtle, lilting West Indian accent as she pointed to a small statue of a large woman with a round belly and breasts.

"That's the Venus of Willendorf. She was found in Germany and comes from the late Paleolithic period. Figures like her have been found all over the world. A full-figured lady, like me. It's nice to see feminine beauty and power that I can identify with. Not that I wouldn't mind losing a few pounds. But it's been such a struggle." She sighed and then brightened as swiftly as she had saddened. "Now that one's more like you." She carefully handed me a long, thin figure. "She's from the Cycladic Islands. In the Mediterranean. Very old. And that wonderful creature with the head of a lion is Sekmet, the Egyptian goddess of destruction and rebirth. She's the sister of Maat, the goddess of truth, and she helps Maat by eating liars."

"I can think of some offerings for her."

"So can I," she agreed and our laughter dispelled my shyness.

"I'm Jeanette. Maia and I have a mutual friend, a *manbo*. She thought I'd enjoy working with a group of women."

"A *manbo*?"

"A Vodou priestess. Very wise woman. Very generous. How did you get here?"

"My friend Sophia introduced me to Maia and she invited me. Who's that?" I asked, pointing at a beautifully carved statue of an Asian woman. Her swirling robes gave her a feeling of gracefulness and movement and she held an orb in her hands.

"That's Kuan Yin, an ancient Chinese goddess of compassion."

"Now this Goddess I think I recognize," I had picked up a heavy brass statue, clearly from India. She had full breasts, almond eyes, round hips, and gorgeous jewelry. "Looks like Shakti, beloved of the god Shiva. She's also called Parvati, the creative force of the universe, the power of desire manifest in the world's beauty."

Jeanette looked surprised.

"I used to do a lot of yoga," I explained. I was excited to spot a small green figure of the goddess Isis among the statues. "Who's that?" I asked, pointing to another striking figure.

"This is the Japanese goddess of the sun, Amaterasu. The emperors are said to have descended from her. And here's a Celtic goddess— Brigid, which is where the name *Britain* comes from; she's the muse of poets. The one carved of ebony is the Yoruban goddess Yemanja, the ocean mother, giver of wealth. She's African in origin, but she's worshiped throughout Brazil and the islands, in New Orleans, and in the Santeria and Vodou traditions where they call her Yemaya. So tell me, how long have you worshiped the Goddess?" she asked.

"I don't worship the Goddess," I replied honestly. "I can't really say I have a religious interest. It's the history I find fascinating, from a feminist perspective. I mean, I don't even believe in God, so it's kind of a major stretch to imagine a Goddess."

"Ah," she exhaled in a lovely sliding tone, like a silvery Caribbean breeze. "Well you see, you don't really believe in the Goddess so much as you experience Her." She smiled at me, and I looked down at the dozens of sculptures. It was an irrefutable collection of a long-forgotten history from all over the world.

"And how do you experience the Goddess?" I asked.

My answer was about to come from Maia, who welcomed us, standing at the center of the circle with Bellona and Nonna. "Please form a circle and take each other's hands."

She began to move around the circle, stopping four times and speaking about birds and lions, dolphins and bears, air and fire, water and earth. It sounded like poetic gibberish to me, and I didn't understand what she was talking about. Each time she stopped, the women turned with her to face the same direction. Some of them raised their hands, and others waved their arms in the air, making peculiar gestures.

I felt foolish and the skeptic within me began to rise up in rebellion. I wondered, looking around at them, what an intelligent, soon to be highly successful, lawyer like me, who had just had lunch at the Russian Tea Room, was doing here. I had moved from discussions of history, with which I was quite at home, to ritual, which pushed all my buttons about religious superstition.

Maia returned to the center of the circle and spoke: "Isis, Astarte, Diana, Hecate, Demeter, Kali, Inanna. Goddess of a thousand names."

With the utterance of the name Isis, an unfamiliar wave of emotion moved within me, quelling my uneasiness and lifting my mask of intellectual distance. The rushing river of mysterious names caught me up and carried me far from the shores of my conditioned resistance to an island of magical women. I felt a strange sense of déjà vu, as if I had dreamt of this moment.

"Great Goddess who is one and from whom come the many. Maiden, Mother, and Crone. Lovely Moon that monthly changes in her mysterious journey. Mother Earth without whom we would not be," Maia continued.

Perhaps it was the language of poetry reaching me in ways that logic and prescriptions, edicts and commandments never could. Perhaps it was the effect of weeks of delving into the Goddess's ancient realms and recitations, or the impact of subtle revelations, but I heard a language of feeling that turned me inward upon myself, a realm of unfamiliar but thrilling mystery.

Maia asked us to be seated. She lit a green candle, sat down, and closed her eyes. She was completely composed and seemingly unaware of the many eyes upon her. At some inner signal, she raised the silver bowl, which shimmered with reflected candlelight. "Great Mother, may the truth be reborn with your children and may the earth once again be revered as your sacred form." And, in an entirely imperfect yet lovely voice, she began to sing:

"We all come from the Goddess
And to her we shall return
Like a drop of rain
Flowing to the ocean."

Some of the women already knew the haunting melody and they joined in, swiftly adding harmonies. Tentatively, unused to the sound of my voice and self-conscious about whether I could remember the words or carry the tune, I began to sing. As the song filled the room, my confidence rose and I began to enjoy myself. I was carried, raised and uplifted, in a chorus of women's voices.

The bowl was passed and when it came to me, I found myself speaking words that came from a place other than my conscious intention.

"To finding the Goddess who lives in each of us."

When the bowl had returned to the altar, Maia had us stand, as she walked around the circle, stopping in each of the four directions. "Thanks to the spirits of air, the spirits of fire, the spirits of water, the spirits of earth. Thanks to the Great Goddess from whom all blessings flow, and thanks to her daughters for returning to the ancient ways of the Mother."

The circle fractured into a score of chattering, laughing women. I stood as if nailed to the spot, unable, or unwilling, to let go of the joy that filled me.

And then Nonna was beside me, encircling me in a warm hug, whispering words of welcome and reassurance. "The world is full of beauty, but the greatest beauty of all is the light that shines from you heart. Don't be afraid to let people see it."

A floodgate of emotion suddenly opened, releasing feelings I'd lived with since before I'd been born, feelings locked behind a dam of mistaken purpose built by schooling and social upbringing and eons of history. I cried. Not for very long, but long enough for me to realize a river of longing, like the Nile when Sirius rises, was about to flood the desert of my life. And I sensed how fertile the soil, how fragrant the trees of myrrh, and how delicious the fig trees growing within that sacred delta would become as this ancient star now rose on my horizon.

These Witches, these women were members of an ancient college of priestesses and keepers of the Old Ways. Sophia called them shamans, visionaries with knowledge of the spirit world, carrying on the ways of the sacred earth and the Great Goddess. Since the beginning of human history, priestesses had played the vital, though long hidden role of spiritual guide. They were wise women, they were Witches, and they were to be my teachers of the ancient wisdom of the Goddess.

As I headed home, walking down the moonlit street, I felt oddly thrilled at the secret I carried within me, yet I remained uncertain about this strange netherworld I was entering. Descending into the subway, I did not realize that everything was upside down. I was not far enough along on my path to see that my blissful miracle of professional ascent actually marked my abduction into an Underworld realm of enticing, but ultimately barren, terrain. Nor did I know that my confrontation with our culture's age-old images of darkness was the beginning of my journey toward true illumination.

But I had not yet lost my eye and gained my sight.

CHAPTER 3

A Coven
of Witches

Flow backward to your sources, sacred rivers,
And let the world's great order be reversed.
Story shall now turn my condition to a fair one,
Women shall now be paid their due.
No more shall evil-sounding fame be theirs.

EURIPIDES, *Medea*

It only makes sense to me that God is a woman.

PRIVATE LETTER OF JIM MORRISON
TO WIFE PATRICIA KENNEALY MORRISON,
FEBRUARY, 1971

It's not a dream—I've really arrived, I thought, stepping into the offices of Rosen, Meiser, Dutton and Hadus. The rush of exhilaration was as strong now, eight weeks after joining the firm, as it had been the very first day. The minute I pushed open the heavy mahogany door I knew I was in a world unto itself—weather and season, worry and uncertainty, all disappeared in this carefully constructed domain of accomplishment. The palette of this world—black, white, and shades of gray—shone from all the polished and mirrored surfaces with a brightly reflective sheen.

Magically granted entree to this world of privilege, I was under its spell. Walking past gold records glittering like talismanic disks, I was assured, like the artists who entered here, that though the outside world might be filled with vermin, poverty, and plague, within these halls of power there was nothing but radiant prosperity. Masters of an Olympian universe dwelled here and, if you had the talent, or the connections, and certainly the cash, they might lend you aid in your quest for riches and fame.

The music of an infamous British band that was represented by Hadus played on the premium sound system. The thought of meeting them, one of my rock and roll fantasies, flashed through my mind. From my small but elegant office each day I could see stars and megastars and icons walking into the partners' offices for conferences, contract signings, meetings, and the even more mind-blowing "In the neighborhood, thought I'd drop by and say hi" visits. It was intoxicating, and I couldn't wait to be included in the inner sanctum.

"Good morning," the receptionist Madeline greeted me. "How's it going?" She was in her forties, an elegantly attired hippie, and a woman who'd hung with the greats of that ephemeral era. Her presence was an homage to that moment in time when the stature of this firm was secured.

"I'm doin' great. Love the scarf." Madeline always wore extraordinary scarves.

"Thank you, it was a present from Jim Morrison's wife. She has fabulous taste."

"Pamela? I thought she was dead."

"Oh no, he never married Pamela. I meant Patricia Kennealy Morrison, the writer, a very respected rock critic. She worked for our parent corp. for a while. She's a Witch you know, a good Witch."

I almost dropped the bags I was carrying. Madeline had turned to pick up a large flower basket filled with purple hyacinths and I managed to hide my shock. Does she know? I wondered. How could she?

"I hear Witches are actually good. A bad Witch is someone who doesn't know what they're doing. Or why."

She nodded, chuckling approval. "These arrived for you." She handed me the basket, and I pulled out a small white card nestled between the flowers.

"Keep up the good work."—John Hadus

"An admirer?" asked Madeline.

"Professionally speaking, I guess so," I grinned. "Oh, I stopped at the bakery on my way in—Greenberg's sticky bun anyone?"

"You're evil," Madeline grabbed one of the white bags I was carrying.

"The devil made me do it."

"Your messages." Madeline handed me a thick pile of pink slips.

Since I'd started working at the firm, I'd been besieged with calls from old friends from the Music Building, friends of friends, and unknown referrals, all of whom wanted the entree and expertise my position now offered. I was on the fast track to the American Dream, and, finding that success was sweeter when shared, I was happy to help. Carrying my trophy, I made my morning pilgrimage through the hallowed halls of the music business. Phones were ringing, typewriters were clicking away, and music, all sorts of music from show tunes to punk rock, was pouring out of the partners' offices.

"Good morning. Would you like a Greenberg's sticky bun?" I put the offering on Sharon's desk, hoping to win a sweeter attitude from her by what Nonna called "sympathetic magic." She'd been Hadus's secretary for ten years and she'd seen associates come and go. But her longevity belied a temperament that was as erratic as the stock market, shifting from bull to bear in the blink of an eye, and with as little discernible cause. It was a characteristic I was beginning to think she learned from Hadus.

"I'm done redlining the McCarthy agreement and Hadus said he wanted the revised copy today." Resting the flowers on her desk, I pulled the voluminous document from my new Mark Cross briefcase.

She shifted her gaze from the flowers and snapped, "I don't have time for it. You see this," waving impatiently at a pile of papers on her desk.

"I'm just telling you what he told me," I said quietly but firmly, falling back from the barrage of electric staccato as she attacked the keys of her typewriter. Don't let her get to you, I told myself, she's just overworked.

Sharon was strategically positioned outside Hadus's door at the edge of the shared space occupied by secretaries, file cabinets, and equipment. No wonder it was called a pool, I thought, they live in a fishbowl, a gray fishbowl. I could understand Sharon's rebellions. Corralled within the office's center, and devoid of natural light, or privacy, the secretaries weren't even allowed to decorate their desks with family photos. Such cozy clutter might detract from reflecting our clients' otherwise uninterrupted glory, and we were streamlined for success.

The outer ring of offices, with sybaritic comforts and panoramic park views, belonged to the partners. The associates were on the opposite side of the secretarial pool. Our offices were small and spare with views of the buildings across the street. Still, they were *our* cubbyholes, with doors that were not supposed to be closed unless we were in conference, and with an implied superiority over the pool. The hierarchy was clearly demarcated in the geography of the firm. And I couldn't help but notice that this hierarchy had very specific gender distribution. The partners, with exception of Jessica Dutton, and the associates, with the exception of myself, were entirely male. The secretaries, however, were female.

I turned away, bumping right into Hadus, who was standing behind me, too close behind me.

"Well, I see you got my thank-you." Hadus smiled.

"They're lovely. Thank you, but it was quite unnecessary." Caught off balance, I stepped delicately sideways. "McCarthy's done, just waiting to be retyped." I could feel Sharon's eyes like a thousand little thorns in my back.

"Good. Leave those here and come inside." Hadus was in fine form this morning, jovial and relaxed, and I sensed it was because some particularly impressive client was sitting in his office.

So far I hadn't had any personal contact with clients other than my own. Hadus had me doing paperwork—masses of it, mostly redlining and comparing contracts with advances for record deals, rights to songs, books, and merchandising, in dollar amounts that were astronomical, enough to feed a third world country for a year. I smoothed my hair back, knowing that whoever was behind that door it had to be either an all-male band or a male singer/songwriter, who would inevitably check me out as the token female in the room. For some reason, the big acts were always male and they always had better deals than the women, even the few top women artists. Rock and roll was a man's business, and I was beginning to see how few women wielded power at the decision- and deal-making levels. I was determined to be one of the few who made it.

I followed Hadus into his office and there, recklessly and deliberately attired in torn jeans, old T-shirts, and Armani jackets, were the lead singer and the bass player who had just been serenading me in the reception area. Both swiftly stood as I entered. My pulse was racing. I wondered if my palms were sweating as the lead singer gripped my confidently extended hand. But it was the bass player who stole my slipping composure, elegantly bowing and kissing my hand. We took our seats and Hadus took control, explaining that I would be assisting him with the details of the movie deal they'd just been offered. Any discomfort I had with Hadus's irascibility, Sharon's backstabbing, or the grueling hours, was immediately forgotten. I was in the presence of rock and roll gods.

I went back to my office, willing to work as late as I had to. But that night was circle night, the one evening I tried to keep free. Just a few more pages, I told myself. The next time I checked my watch, I realized circle had started hours before. Exhausted, I decided to head home. There was a worried message waiting for me from Nonna. I knew why she had called; this was not the first circle I'd missed because of the demands of my glamorous new job.

I was sure not to miss our next meeting. When I arrived, the women were already sitting in circle. I quickly kicked off my shoes and dropped onto a pillow next to Jeanette, who was leaning like an odalisque on the old Persian carpets. I barely had a moment to catch my breath when Maia rang a small bell to quiet the conversations that always preceded circle. There were now eleven of us remaining from the original seventy-five. We were getting to know one another, exchanging books and music, and most important, sharing our dreams, visions, and experiences. I could only describe it as magical. This was a sanctuary, a haven where we could talk freely about the amazing psychic perceptions and magical synchronicities we all seemed to share, but were afraid others would not accept or understand. It was empowering to discover I was not the only one who had precognitive dreams, flashes of telepathy, or synchronicities. I was no longer alone.

Each of us was unique in our adventures, interests, and talents. Still, the support and encouragement we gave each other seemed to nourish our nascent psychic gifts. And although Maia was only a few years older than most of us, her maternal warmth, along with Bellona's disciplined focus, and Nonna's years of experience, reassured me about what lay ahead of us. The priestesses alternated with each other, and shared, in the running of our circle. Tonight was Maia's turn. While Nonna had been eloquent and regal, Maia was earthy and nurturing, with a flair for the dramatic as she fussed and purred over her brood.

"Sit comfortably, take off anything that pinches or binds. Alright now ladies, close your eyes and sit up straight," Maia began happily. "We're going to begin by breathing—it's the simplest movement of energy. It was the first thing you did when you were born from your mothers, and it will be the last thing you do when you pass from this earth. Notice how you're breathing. Now lengthen your breaths, breathing in slowly, inhaling deeply, and holding it. . . . One. Two. Three. Now exhale slowly, completely emptying your lungs. And again inhale, expanding the lungs, the diaphragm. Hold it: one, two, three. Exhale and relax. As you continue breathing deeply, feel how light you are becoming, as the pure clean energy of the air enters and fills you with life."

Within minutes, I was feeling buoyant, like a bubble that could float away. I heard Maia speaking, as if from a great distance:

"Keep breathing, slowly, and completely. Feel your body *relax*. Allow your mind to become *quiet*. Thoughts may float in. Just let them float by and *focus* upon the sound of my voice guiding you, focus upon your breath. . . . Feel how the air is filled with light and energy. . . ."

With each breath, the energy flowed through me more powerfully. I rode the current of feeling that her words, and my focused breathing, evoked. I was filled with light and power. It was exhilarating. Everything is energy and everything is connected, I observed myself thinking. I recognized the technique as very similar to yogic breathing. We were working with the universal life force that the Chinese call *chi* and the yogis call *prana*. All living creatures share this energy. I was delighted to discover Witches also used this ancient technique, which enables humans to consciously connect with this energy.

"We inhale as one, we exhale as one, we are becoming one, together with each breath, we become one circle, with no beginning and no ending." Maia's voice was rhapsodically hypnotic. She was joined by the other priestesses as they intoned a reverberating series of names:

"Isis, Astarte, Diana, Hecate, Demeter, Kali, Inanna."

A shiver of recognition ran through me. Gradually, a fourth voice, and then another, and still another joined in, so quietly they were no more than a gossamer breeze. I whispered the names, marveling at how familiar this chant seemed. And then we were all chanting, our timidity vanishing in a swell of gorgeous, full-bodied sound. The chanting rose and fell and rose again, the ambient energy growing as our voices lifted and carried each other. And suddenly, at the same unsignaled moment, we all stopped. We opened our eyes, stunned by a silence as rich in texture and dimension as the sound that had just resonated from the centers of our very souls. Looks of incredulous joy spread across our faces, and suddenly, we were all laughing.

Already I could feel the effects of these seemingly simple techniques—enhanced relaxation and concentration, the aligning of the group's energy, the growth of harmony and trust. I left each circle empowered and so alive I felt as if I could accomplish anything I set my mind to. This energy sustained me each day at work, where the pressures and tensions required more strength than I'd ever expected. At first the glamour and accomplishment drove me. But the demands of each work day required me to abandon more and more of my personal life and began to leave me feeling drained and exhausted. I used my magical energy to sustain myself, determined to succeed.

"What were we chanting?" I asked.

"Ancient sacred names of the Goddess." Maia told us in one of her rare explanations. Unlike Nonna, with whom I enjoyed such provocative discussions of the whys and wherefores, Maia taught us by simply imparting techniques, leaving it up to us to draw our own conclusions. I found her ways equally invaluable, for they moved me out of my head and into experience.

"I have a very important announcement to make," Maia poured red wine into the Goddess chalice in the center of the altar as she spoke. "It's taken several weeks to make our determination. You are the women we have chosen for training and initiation into our coven, the Mother Grove of the Sisterhood," Maia said with a loving smile.

With the word *coven*, a slight shock passed through me. I knew a group of Witches was called a coven, but I wasn't sure I was ready to call myself a Witch. I now understood why Sophia used the word Witch to describe herself—it was an act of defiance and reempowerment—as if by using the term she could force the world to confront its negative stereotypes, and the dark history and misogyny from which they had arisen. By reappropriating the word, she was reclaiming her power as a woman. I took a deep breath and stared up through the skylight. I could just make out the tiny sickle of a new moon, a time when, according to Wicca, new things began. I had begun to notice, and react to such things. Inexplicable excitement had filled me earlier that evening when I saw the slender arc of promise suspended above Manhattan. It *was* the time for beginnings. Was I ready for this beginning?

I had come to understand the Old Religion as a survival of the ancient Goddess religions. Living close to the earth, people's spirituality was a natural expression of their lives. But in this technological era of skyscrapers and computers, wonder drugs and hospitals, science and supermarkets, what did Wicca have to offer that could not be found elsewhere? Who would become a Witch? And why? Why would *I* become a Witch? What was the pull that had brought me back, week after week—was it the promise of a life filled with magic? Was it the energy that it gave me? Or a mystery even more profound?

"I know you've already begun to get to know one another, but let's go around the circle and tell each other about ourselves. Bellona and I are the High Priestesses of the Sisterhood, and Nonna is our Elder. I've been a Third Degree priestess for almost ten years." She began to pass cups full of wine and fruit juice. "We're retrieving the Old Ways, some of which we learned from the priestess and priest who taught us, some we learned from our Italian and Irish grandmothers. And we're creating new forms that make sense for the way we live our lives today. As you may have noticed, there are several other groups meeting in the temple—one is a traditional group of women and men, another is an all men's group. Our group will be devoted to women's mysteries, in addition to the traditional training." Maia paused and then turned to Bellona. "Want to add anything?"

Bellona nodded. "Some have criticized separate gender circles, but we think women need a sacred space in which to explore the full range of polarity and power within themselves. We'll also be working with men, and with the God energy, on occasion, but our primary focus is the Goddess because She, and you as women, have been neglected for so long. I also want to tell you how happy I am that you're all here tonight. Each of you is very special and we're looking forward to working with you. Maia and I are lovers, and I'm her magical partner." I could hear the urban edge of a Queens working-class upbringing in her accent, but she exuded a quiet confidence that would have been the envy of the finest finishing schools. "We'll work with you for a year, and then, those of you who survive," she smiled mischievously as we laughed in response, "and are prepared, will be initiated. At least two more years of training will follow. I'm thirty-two and I work for a construction company, managing the office."

Bellona turned to the woman sitting to her left. "We'll go deosil, that's clockwise, around the circle."

The women came from many different backgrounds. There was Annabelle, the tiny black-haired Southern beauty in her mid-thirties who'd shared my fears about Satanism, and was a romance novelist. She had small and perfect features with blue eyes that danced as she described her childhood interest in fairies and how it led to her discovery of the goddesses of Ireland.

Next to Annabelle was Marcia, in her early twenties; with dark brown skin, short curly hair, and a husky, muscular build. Born and raised in East New York, she was still living in Brooklyn with her grandmother and working as a hospital orderly. "I'm gay," she admitted frankly, "and I'm into the Goddess 'cause there isn't any other religion that respects women's power. I'm really into Artemis, she's a warrior goddess, protector of women. She's helped me find my own strength. So I'm really grateful to be here. O.K., that's it." She grinned and swigged her beer.

To Marcia's left was Mindy, a chiropractor in her mid-forties and mother of two, also from the South. Her father was a Methodist minister. Beside her was Gillian, whose "socially prominent" last name I immediately recognized. She was a magazine editor in her late twenties with her master's degree in Middle English literature and an astonishing knowledge of the Grail myths, which, she explained, was how she'd found the Goddess. Onatah, stunning, nineteen, and a college student, was working her way through school as an exotic dancer. Part Irish, part African-American, and part Native American, she described a lifelong relationship with the Virgin Mary.

"But I hated all that garbage about sin and women being responsible for man's downfall. And the fact that little girls couldn't be altar 'boys,' and that women can't be priests, and the idea that just one man determines God's will and no one can question him—people should question everything! Like the Pope's position on birth control—it's downright irresponsible when you consider that the most dangerous problem threatening humanity's survival is overpopulation."

"And the survival of the planet!" Gillian added, to my surprise.

"Right! So now I'm a recovering Catholic." We all laughed. "I'm also really into herbal medicine; I've been studying with a Native American healer. That's how I learned about Wicca. And I know it's a very special opportunity."

I could feel my heartbeat quicken as everyone's eyes turned to me. I took a deep breath and briefly described my background and how I'd found my way to the circle. "I can't tell you how much I look forward to circle. It's the best part of my week," I finished to nods of agreement.

Sitting beside me was Jeanette. She spoke slowly, with elegant reserve. "I'm Jeanette. I'm originally from Jamaica, so I was raised with Goddesses, though we call them ancestors or *orisas.* I work for the phone company, and let me tell you I hate it. But sometimes the Goddess sets a difficult path before us. I won't tell you my age, but I am older than most of you and I am a Capricorn, so I won't mince words with any of you. That's all, except also, thank you for inviting me." There was a precision about her words that was almost curt, but she smiled when she was finished, and that broke the tense formality of her speech.

Naomi was a sculptor from Ann Arbor who'd come to New York to attend art school. She chain-smoked as she described her Jewish mother and Episcopalian father. She had been exposed to both faith traditions, but much like myself, she considered her upbringing to be primarily intellectual and humanitarian. In her mid-twenties, Naomi had long, dark brown hair and was dressed in paint-splattered overalls and a velvet scarf. She, too, was gay.

Gillian suddenly spoke up. "There's something I'd like to add, if I may." Maia nodded. "I was raised in the Episcopal Church. The teachings of Christ are full of wisdom and beauty, and I adore the Gnostic Gospels—in fact, I call myself an Episcopagan, which shocks my family," she said, smiling. "But the religious institutions that have grown up around Christ's teachings are political. And the church's institutional misogyny simply turned me off. Wicca seems to be the only faith tradition which honors the divine as feminine—and I find that so empowering."

"What's misogyny?" asked Marcia.

"Hatred of women," I replied.

"Something that afflicts all three of the patriarchal religions," Naomi spoke up. "There just doesn't seem to be room for women."

"And one reason why so many women are finding their way to the Goddess and the Old Religion." Bellona added.

We all knew clergy and worshipers who were deeply spiritual and who respected women. And we had found wisdom and beauty in the faiths of our upbringing. But we also found all of us were dissatisfied with the teachings and practices of the religions with which we had been raised, and specifically, we felt alienated by their attitudes toward women: Marcia described how her mother had to kneel and beg the Catholic priest's forgiveness after she'd given birth to Marcia's brother. Gillian's sister had gone through a similar Episcopal "churching" ritual, and Naomi was forbidden to read from the Torah at the age of twelve because, though still a girl, she was considered a woman and "unclean." As for Naomi and myself, both raised in intellectual, agnostic homes, we shared an intangible hunger for something beyond the merely cerebral.

"Well, my dears," Nonna addressed us, "Wicca is a spiritual practice in which women play leading roles as priestesses, and its reverence for the divine as feminine, not just masculine, is deeply empowering for women. Our spiritual work embraces the balance between feminine and masculine; but this circle is going to focus on restoring the lost feminine because spirituality, and the world, and our own lives, have been so imbalanced without it. Then we'll work with the masculine energies, although many of these are also feminine qualities."

"Like being a warrior," Bellona added.

"And many qualities traditionally considered feminine, like nurturance and compassion, are shared by the God, and by men," Maia said.

Nonna nodded. "I think you all know me. Everyone calls me Nonna, and I'm the circle's crone, and I'm also not going to tell you how old I am, but I'm probably old enough to be your grandmother. I won't be coming every week, but I'll be checking in on all you Witchlets to see how you're progressing." We laughed at her title for us. "And you can always call me," she said looking directly at me, "and I will share with you all my knowledge and perspective. That is what a priestess is for. We do not intercede on your behalf with the Divine; we will not tell you what to believe or what to do. These are responsibilities you must fulfill yourself. A priestess is a teacher, and we will share with you all of the wisdom that has been passed to us, all of the techniques we have mastered. But your journey is your own. It is as unique as each of you and only you can understand and fulfill its purpose. But as a community, we shall travel in the same realm of the heart, the sacred landscape of the Goddess. Welcome and blessed be."

"What's expected from us in return for what we'll be taught? Is there a fee?" Annabelle wanted to know.

"No," Bellona replied quickly. "Priestesses might charge for classes, lectures, or for a reading. Until we set up a college, there is no fee for initiatory training, though you may contribute for various expenses. What will be required from you will be a lot more challenging—honesty, courage, compassion, creativity. We'll also ask you, when you've become priestesses, to teach others what you've learned."

Though no one had mentioned it, I knew there was one more crucial thing required from all of us: a willingness to travel beyond the limitations of our socially expected roles. Like the consciousness raising groups of the sixties, we were creating a place of safety and support by sharing our experiences, our fears and our dreams, by learning and working together. Our circle strengthened our confidence, our abilities, our faith in our instincts and intuitions, and our sense of community. We were delving into realms of consciousness even more empowering, and if the culture had no place for priestesses, we would create one.

Maia spoke up, her voice as maternal as her figure. "The most important thing you'll be asked for, and that you'll receive, is perfect love and perfect trust. These are the spiritual goals we strive for. On a practical note, if problems arise between you, please come to me and I will help you resolve them. Problems within circle remain within circle— this is where we work them out." I could hear the voice of a mother's experience speaking as she continued, gently urging us, "We ask that you try to leave your troubles at the door, but we know it isn't always possible."

"We also ask you to respect each other's confidentiality," Bellona added firmly. "Because of Maia's work at the shop, she's public and out of the broom closet, but the rest of you may not want anyone to know you're studying Witchcraft. Participation in a coven has been kept secret for a long time because people's lives were at stake. We can't be burned today, but people have lost their jobs, lost custody of their children, had their homes burned, and worse. So, until the world's prejudices change, secrecy must be honored."

Our conversation circled back to the experiences that had brought us to this hidden world: fascinations from childhood, a wonderful book on the Goddess, a friend who was a Witch. Strand by strand, story by story, we began to reweave the lost tapestry of women's spirituality. The patterns of unexpected similarities reinforced each other, the differences made the contrasting colors more vivid. As women had for millennia, we talked to each other. Retying our frayed heart strings, we made a silken cord of women's worth, and knotting its ends together, we restored the sacred circle, reuniting the world.

We were women seeking a spiritual home, a place where we would be respected and welcomed, where our souls would be healed and empowered, and where our experiences would be honored as a source of spiritual wisdom. We were seeking the Goddess—even I, though I still did not know why I was drawn to her. Perhaps it was She who had found us. I could already see how the diversity of our personalities and our backgrounds contributed to the vitality of our circle. In the realm of the forgotten, the suppressed, and the maligned, in the world of women and the earth, we were discovering our hidden history. With this new insight came a sense of freedom and tremendous strength. If the past was not as we had been raised to believe, the future opened before us as a vision of entirely new possibilities.

I might not believe in a Goddess, but I could not help but appreciate the feelings of sisterhood we were nurturing. I remembered Jeanette's observation that the Goddess wasn't something you believed in, but rather was something you experienced. This was a place where women could be fully and freely themselves, and there was nowhere else like it—not the Junior League, nor the gym, not even girls' night out.

On the way out, I browsed through the bookshelves, looking for information about the Goddesses in our chant. A title caught my eye: *When God Was a Woman* by Merlin Stone. There was something slightly shocking, something provocative about the challenge—even to someone who thought of herself as an intellectual. What would it mean if the world also thought of the divine as female, instead of just male?

I became fascinated with the idea of people worshiping a female deity and, as a lawyer, I wanted the facts: names, dates, and places. Who were these ancient people who worshiped the Goddess? Part of me was a bit skeptical about this new version of history I was learning from the Witches. How could the Goddess religion be practiced all over the world for so many thousands of years and then just disappear? Like a detective, I went home to the house I'd grown up in and scoured the shelves of my father's considerable library of classical history in search of clues to this mystery.

"Well, there's ample evidence of early matriarchal cultures." Brilliantly self-educated, my father responded to my inquiry about the existence of early Goddess cultures without the least bit of surprise. I was the one surprised to discover it had been a particular interest of his for several years. Even he knew about it! Why didn't I? Dad and I were sitting together on the front porch, sunlight pouring in and, though the light was too direct, this was where my father enjoyed painting. His canvas was set up before him and, as we spoke, he applied strokes of vibrant color with a thick paintbrush.

"Take the Willets book on Minoan civilization," he said. "You know it was a matriarchal culture. And there are several things you should look at regarding early Celtic culture—women were held in high esteem." He put his brush into a small jar of paint thinner, rubbed his hands on a rag, and we headed into the house.

"Here." My father reached to the top shelf of his library, an easy task for his six-foot-two-inch frame, and pulled down an old leather volume. "The women fought and ruled equally with the men. You should go to the sources—Herodotus, Diodorus, Hesiod, Plutarch. . . ." He began handing me book after book, all filled with scores of bookmarks between pages with contents of particular note.

I was amazed at the magic of finding what I was looking for right at home. Overwhelmed, I looked at the collection he was piling up for me. "Thanks, Dad."

"Take your time. Rome wasn't built in a day." He winked and left me to the books.

I followed the trail and quickly found my way through the vast array of archaeological, academic, and classical texts. These were not merely books—they were treasure chests of myths, etymology, and architectural and art history, all contributing irrefutable evidence of the existence of ancient Goddess-worshiping cultures.

Like most others, I'd grown up believing Western Civilization began with the historical Greeks and the development of Hebrew monotheism. I thought human history began with the "Good Book" and "In the beginning . . ." I was astonished to discover that there had indeed been a preexisting, extensive, and sophisticated religious worship of the Great Goddess. My reading confirmed that the Goddess religion of Europe as well as the Near and Middle East did indeed predate the three patriarchal Western religions—Judaism, Christianity, and Islam—by thousands of years. The first prophet of the Judeo-Christian god was Abraham, whom most biblical scholars agree lived around 1800 B.C.E., at the earliest. But I discovered that Goddess worship dates back to the Upper Paleolithic Age, about 25,000 to 30,000 B.C.E.

Sitting in a large cozy chair in my father's library, I read about the origins of the female figurines and statues I'd seen at circle, in the museums, and in my favorite browsing shop—an antiquities store that I'd recently come across on the Upper East Side. The figurines I'd seen were only 3,500 years old at the most—newly minted in comparison to carvings of female figures found in sites of small communities stretching across a vast area from Europe to Siberian Russia. Depictions of a female divinity accompanied the first signs of human civilization—art, agriculture, the use of tools, and construction of homes and other buildings.

As early as 7000 B.C.E., worship of the Goddess was at the heart of Neolithic agricultural communities along the northern course of the Tigris and Euphrates rivers, in the lands now known as Iraq and Syria, and in Anatolia, now known as Turkey. Goddess worshiping communities were also found in Canaan, which included vast territory now called Palestine, Israel, Lebanon, and Syria. In sites along the northern Tigris, more figures of the mother Goddess from the period around 5500 B.C.E. were discovered. Serpents, double-headed axes, and doves, all symbols of the Goddess, appeared with goddess figurines in sanctuaries called *tholoi*. And around 3000 B.C.E., the first writing, including sacred poetry to the Goddess, appeared in Sumeria.

Long before the people of the Middle East worshiped and battled over a male divinity, the people of Canaan paid reverence to a goddess called Queen of Heaven. The Goddess was the divine creatrix, law giver, mother, warrior, healer, bestower of culture and agriculture. As my father had advised, I turned to the ancient historians Diodorus of Sicily, Herodotus of Greece, and even Sophocles. They described the laws of Egypt, which gave preeminence to women as rulers, wives, and citizens. These laws were rooted in the worship of the Great Goddess Au Set, whom the Greeks called Isis. She gave laws to her people just as Yahweh, the Hebrew god, gave laws to Moses for the people of Israel. She also taught the mysteries of agriculture and healing. I recalled with annoyance a professor who, in his tight little bow tie and condescending tone, demeaned this pervasive and exquisite religious history, dismissing the Goddess religions as "primitive fertility cults."

I learned how the sacred site of the Great Goddess of Chaldea, Magna Dea, was marked by an enormous black stone, the same stone where Al-Uzza, one of the three aspects of the Great Goddess of Arabia, was also worshiped. This very stone is still venerated in the Ka'aba shrine in Mecca, the most sacred place of all Islam. A deep cleft that conjures images of a woman's vulva, and is called the Impression of Aphrodite, marks the stone. It is now covered and served by men who have usurped the divine role of the Great Mother's priestesses, men who are called *Beni Shay-bah,* Sons of the Old Woman. She survives, even veiled.

I marveled at how ancient worshipers honored the divine as both feminine and masculine, but the Goddess was as important, often more so, than the God who first appeared as her son, then as her lover. Priestesses of the Goddess, whose counsel and wisdom was sought by ruler and peasant alike, entered ecstatic states of consciousness and communed with the sacred, spoke its wisdom, and presided over their communities' rituals and celebrations.

In book after book I found evidence: Throughout the world, most of humanity once worshiped a goddess. In every area of the Near and Middle East, the divine feminine was revered, and it was from the womb of these early Goddess-worshiping settlements of the Fertile Crescent that Western civilization was born.

The ancient Goddess cultures generated the first writing, commerce, art, music, and religious ritual. Women played prominent roles as priestesses and leaders, status that was reflected with equal measure in the lives of "ordinary" women. They were peaceful cultures, engaged in agriculture and trade, and the archaeological evidence shows that they had no weapons, and no defensive structures such as battlements or moats. And in Germany, France (particularly Brittany), and the British Isles—in England, Ireland, Scotland, Wales—the Goddess-worshiping culture of the Celts (or Gauls, as the Romans called them) flourished, leaving countless shrines now buried beneath the churches and temples of the patriarchal religions that usurped Goddess worship. Throughout the rest of Europe, the Goddess in her many guises was also adored.

I was amazed to find common threads in the Old Religion of Europe and the Middle and Near East and in the other earth-based religions— Taoism, Shintoism, Native American, and other indigenous and aboriginal spiritual practices. In all of these traditions, the divine is known to be both immanent and transcendent. With the gentleness and strength of a mother's love, the Goddess spoke to the reality of most people's lives, for they lived close to the earth, which nurtured and sustained them. They farmed and hunted, and everything that existed in nature was an expression of the Goddess. She not only filled the heavens with stars, sun, and moon, but she was everywhere in the world around them—in the fruit trees that blossomed and nourished them, in the grain that grew in fertile fields, in the animals they bred and hunted, in the miracle of their own lives. They knew that everything was connected in a holy relationship.

. . .

It was a Saturday morning and I was searching for books on Goddess civilizations. I headed over to the used bookstores on Third Avenue. Completely fascinated with the material on these cultures, I nonetheless found myself wondering what any of it had to do with magic.

Light streamed into my favorite bookstore through a distant skylight. Countless specks of dust danced in the sunlight, and walking through the brilliant curtain of energy and particles, I was momentarily blinded. Emerging on the other side in the back of the store, everything seemed hushed. Slowly, my eyes adjusted and I began poking my way through the dusty tables. I heard a thud, and turned to see a brown striped tabby cat with beautiful yellow eyes staring up at me.

It purred, wove a lemniscate between my legs, and then walked away. It looked back over its shoulder, then continued deeper into the back of the store. I continued looking through the book tables until my neck grew sore, and then settled on a foot stool, nestled between stacks of aging wisdom, to rub my stiff muscles.

The cat brushed against a small pile of books which toppled across my feet. I laughed and began to restack them as she brushed against my leg.

"You're not very helpful, are you? Or maybe you are—eating mice before they can eat all these delicious books?" The cat settled between my legs as I casually opened one of the volumes. I had been looking for hard, cold facts. But today the universe had decided to begin teaching me one of its most profound lessons, by presenting clues encapsulated in metaphor.

There, printed on the flyleaf, was a poem. I began to read *Kubla Khan: Or a Vision in a Dream,* written by Samuel Taylor Coleridge in 1797 when he was twenty-five years old. A British poet, philosopher, Unitarian minister, and metaphysician influenced by the German philosopher Goethe, Coleridge introduced German philosophy and literature to England and was a close friend of William Wordsworth. Bliss settled around me like a charmed cloak as I read the haunting lines:

In Xanadu did Kubla Khan
A stately pleasure dome decree;
Where Alph, the sacred river, ran
Through caverns measureless to man
Down to a sunless sea. . . .

My pulse raced as I finished the intoxicating verses. What enchanted realm of prescient and symbolic mystery was he describing? I paid for the book and left, knowing with a strange and stirring certainty that this poem, so serendipitously brought to my attention, would be my treasure map, my guide to the hidden world of wonder I felt beckoning to me. I later learned this mysterious masterpiece was written while Coleridge was in an altered state, beyond the confines of space and time, as he emerged from an opium-induced dream. What was the meaning of the message he had returned with? I read and reread it over the days and years ahead, sure that once I deciphered its exquisite and enigmatic language, I would understand my magical calling.

I returned often to my father's library. My parents were delighted that I was coming to visit with such frequency—and I brought bookmarks of my own to tag all the passages that stimulated wonderful conversations with them. My alumni card granted me entree to one of the best academic libraries in the world, and I bought every book on goddesses for sale at the Magical Cauldron. Like a woman escaping the burning heat of the desert, I was thirsty for knowledge.

I sat in the great reading room of New York's public library, with sibyls presiding from the distant ceiling, turning the pages of dense academic tomes with their frequent untranslated quotations in Greek, Latin, or German. I found that throughout the world, and throughout history, goddesses and women who had been warriors, queens, priestesses, and scholars were proof of women's lost past, and inspiration for our future. As I read their stories and histories, I also discovered the powerful symbols and metaphors of the Goddess: trees and caves, animals and serpents, obsidian altars and the moon, poppies and wheat, bulls and labyrinths, birds and fruit, and more. Words and wonder turned dust into clay, clay into figurines, figurines into goddesses, and goddesses into women.

And then one sunny afternoon, I sat before my Libyan Sibyl at the museum, and reread *Kubla Khan,* my poetic roadmap:

A damsel with a dulcimer
In a vision once I saw:
It was an Abyssinian maid,

And on her dulcimer she played,
Singing of Mount Abora.

With each additional clue, the mystery, and the unknown force that animated it, became more compelling. I searched books looking for goddesses and heroines of Abyssinian descent. Turning the pages of an old encyclopedia, electricity shot through me as I learned that Abyssinia had been part of Egypt, and was now called Libya. My Libyan Sibyl was Abyssinian—a priestess of the Egyptian mysteries, a priestess of Isis! The world shimmered with enchantment as dreams and statues, ancient history and poetry, goddesses and my own life, magically converged.

Something stirred within me: a feeling of pleasure, a sense of pride, and a newfound desire to embrace these images of beauty and power. And though I did not recognize it, also stirring was the beginning of inner changes these ancient revelations would ultimately bring. A moon tree had been planted in the sun-scorched landscape of my heart and with every line, every image, a sylvan leaf sprouted, a ruby red fruit grew, a dove built a nest, a moon rested in its branches, an ancient serpent coiled 'round its trunk. I wasn't looking for an epiphany, nor a basis for conversion or belief. My original interest was intellectual and feminist. I did not have to believe in a feminine divinity to understand the implications for women: Here was a historical basis to challenge the limitations long imposed upon us and the justifications for those constraints. If we had created culture once, we could certainly do it again.

So the Witches weren't engaged in some sort of conspiracy theory or wishful thinking. Goddess depictions may once have been dismissed as nothing more than fertility objects and primitive tools to insure the continuation of the tribe. But profound wisdom lay buried in ancient metaphors, hidden in ancient poetry and myth, even between the lines of biblical passages. Something urged me to pick up my grandmother's Bible, which I would do again and again over the next months. As I stared at descriptions of violence and brutal sexuality, it was hard to imagine this book remained a touted guide to modern middle-class values.

Juxtaposed with its poetry and wisdom was a bloody record of battles, rapes, murders, and distorted information about the Goddess and her cultures: *"But ye shall destroy their altars, break their images, and cut down their groves, for thou shalt worship no other god, for the Lord whose name is jealous is a jealous God."* (*Exod. 34:13–14*). And on it went in ferocious manner: *"We captured . . . and put to death every one in the cities, men, women, and dependents; we left no survivor." (Deut. 2:34).*

The annihilation of the Old Religion began around 4000 B.C.E., when waves of nomadic, sheep-herding tribes moved down from the north into the Fertile Crescent and India, where goddesses had long been worshiped. The sun had seized the fertile earth in its fiery grasp and around 4000 B.C.E. a climactic shift stripped away much of the earth's green abundance in a harsh onslaught of desertification. Over the course of several thousand years, but with particular force around the second millennium B.C.E., relentless waves of humanity were moved by this shifting solar tide, pressed by force of arms into the fertile valleys of the Goddess. These tribes, referred to as Indo-Europeans or Indo-Aryans, were patriarchal, and they worshiped a solar, warrior god.

These nomads forged weapons instead of tools of cultivation, harnessed horses to chariots instead of plows, and honored the arts of war before those of love. At first, conquest mixed with cohabitation and the divinities and the customs of these two cultures coexisted. For a time there was a marrying of gods and goddesses, but this coexistence gradually deteriorated until the ancient Goddess cultures were almost entirely destroyed. The stories of the Goddesses became stories of conquest—the Great Mothers were vanquished and destroyed by sons, lovers, and husbands.

The mighty Taimat, ancient serpent mother of the generative abyss, was murdered by her son Marduk. Hercules killed Ladon, the serpent-dragon who guarded the golden apples of the Goddess. Yahweh, the Hebrew god, defeated the ancient serpent Leviathan, the "whore" of Babylon. Eve is "tempted" by a serpent, offered the fruit of the Tree of Knowledge, and disobeys God (following in the rebellious footsteps of Adam's little-known first wife, Lilith). In accepting the fruit, Eve damns mankind. The Old Irish folklore of St. Patrick driving the snakes out of Ireland actually recounts the driving of Goddess worshipers underground. I began to understand how so many of the ancient myths recast the Goddess, and her symbols such as the snake and the apple, in negative terms.

I finally knew why so many of the beautiful statues I'd seen at the antiquities shop and at the museum were mutilated, their noses and limbs knocked off. Temples had been destroyed and statues shattered as priestesses were replaced by priests and political power began to be held by military kings. With the military predominance of the Hebrews, worship of the Goddess was punishable by death, and a period of prolonged warfare led to the gradual destruction of neighboring Goddess cultures. The status of women declined precipitously. They were no longer independent citizens who could rule or own property. Not only were women forbidden to participate as religious or secular leaders, they were now chattel, the property of fathers or husbands, who had absolute power over them.

Violence enforced theology; stoning and other brutal deaths were inflicted on women who worshipped the Goddess, who refused arranged marriages, who were not virgins at marriage, who had sexual relations outside of marriage, or who were raped! In contrast to the increasing restrictions placed on women, the Bible simultaneously chronicled the rampant practice of polygamy by men.

Male power was so absolute that even today, throughout the Islamic world, the custom survives. Young women who defy arranged marriages are often murdered by their own fathers and brothers. Texts of the Koran and later appendages are interpreted to deny equal rights to women, who must have the permission of a male relative to go school, marry, name her children, or work. And she will inherit only half of what her brothers do. Women can be forced into marriage, including polygamous marriages; they can be beaten, killed, or repudiated—left without any support when a husband exercises his unilateral right to end the marriage—all without any recourse. Were any of these violations of fundamental human rights based upon race or ethnicity rather than on gender, they would not be tolerated by the world community.

But these abuses of freedom are not unique. Fundamentalist Christians cite biblical scripture to justify their requirements that women "submit" to their husbands, and Orthodox Jews prohibit Jewish women from praying at their most holy shrine, the Western Wall.

The roots of women's inequality and the destruction of the earth are to be found in this early religious shift away from the mother Goddess, who was immanent and present in the world, to the father God, who was transcendent and removed. I remembered what it was like for a friend of mine to grow up without her mother and realized that our souls and our culture suffered the same terrible loneliness and losses—of love, comfort, a positive feminine role model, nurturance, a sense of connection and safety, and so much more—because we lived without a divine mother. Here also was the tragic history of how humanity lost its connection to the sacred, how it came to lose its way in a maze of ultimate alienation, and how we have come to stand, now, at the brink of extinction.

The Goddess's sacred culture began to disappear from the face of Western culture. A male God assumed the throne of heaven, as kings seized the thrones of the earthly realm and religion became the sole dominion of men. Only they could become clergy, only they could interpret the divine, which was now entirely masculine: God the Father, and his Son, and the Holy Spirit. A masculine trinity now replaced the ancient Threefold Goddess of Mother, Maiden, and Crone.

These patriarchal religions had very different ideas about the divine and its relationship to humanity and the earth. In this new theology, the body was sinful, women were sinful, sex was sinful, and the earth itself was sinful. God, though having created the universe, had now removed Himself from it, although His name was regularly invoked by one "righteous" group to justify the slaughter of another. A hierarchical universe now replaced a circular one. Man paid obeisance to God, and all the creatures of the earth, including women, were to be obedient unto men, for man was made in God's image and God had given him dominion over the earth. Man stood between the burning fire of God and the world, which now now dwelt within man's shadow.

But since man had fallen from grace, the only way he could achieve spiritual union with God was by the denial of the flesh, of sexuality, and of the earthly plane. And women were held responsible for this fall from grace. It created a condition of profound spiritual alienation. But in the Old Religion, everything in nature and in the desire of humanity emanated from and was a part of the Goddess.

My studies led me to realize that Witchcraft, as the Old Religion is often called, and its modern renaissance, are rooted in the ancient Goddess religions from which Western culture was originally born. I didn't believe in a Goddess, but I was beginning to sense the vast shift in consciousness that accompanies a conception of the sacred that is feminine. I now had a historical mirror reflecting an image of myself quite different from the one my culture presented to me. The narrow restriction of women's lives has been justified by religious edict and secular statute. We have been labeled intellectually inferior, incompetent, depraved, dangerous, and in need of domination. Now I knew where these degrading and lingering falsehoods had originated.

The discovery of early Goddess cultures was profoundly liberating and empowering, a triumph for women. And as I reacted with unexpected emotion, with both excitement and anger to the lies which permeate our world, I found myself moving from the realm of the head to that of the heart, from merely thinking to also feeling, from the wisdom of intellect to that of the spirit. And I remembered my mother's early words about believing in the human heart. Just as physics had enabled me to accept and embrace my magical experiences, so this hidden history now led me further on my unexpected path.

A conception of spirituality was taking shape in my consciousness, and it had the sensate curves of something feminine, for I had eaten from the Tree of Knowledge and begun to dream of Paradise.

Magic

Magic (mǎj'ǐk) n. 1. The art that purports to control or forecast natural events, effects, or forces by invoking the supernatural. 2. a. The practice of using charms, spells, or rituals to attempt to produce supernatural effects or control events in nature. b. The charms, spells, and rituals so used. 3. The exercise of sleight of hand or conjuring for entertainment. 4. A mysterious quality of enchantment. adj. 1. Of, relating to, or invoking the supernatural. 2. Possessing distinctive qualities that produce unaccountable or baffling effects. (Middle English magik from Old French magique, from late Latin magicā, from Latin magic, from Greek magikē, from feminine of magikos Magian magical from magos magician, magus)

—The American Heritage Dictionary

Who's to say what magic is?

—JIMMY STEWART in Bell, Book and Candle

I arrived early to find the fluorescent lights in the temple on. The room appeared as I'd never seen it before. The paint seemed dingy with age, yellowed by the smoke of countless candles. The rugs were threadbare in several places, and the space seemed small and cramped, crowded with seats, podium, candelabra, trunks, bookcases, coats, and bags. A crumpled white paper used to wrap deli sandwiches, an empty juice bottle, and a brown paper bag filled two of the chairs.

I stood in the center of the room, turning slowly, surveying my surroundings. A wave of disappointment swept over me. Where were the tall pillars of marble, the jewel tiled floors, the diaphanous curtains? Where was the magic? Instead of sistra and zithers, I heard the thumping of bad rock and roll intruding from the rehearsal space in the basement below. The room seemed shabby and the whole effort suddenly preposterous. Magic. Who knew if it really worked? After all, if it did, why were these women still working in this obscure occult shop?

I'm outta here, I decided.

"What are you banishing?" It was Nonna, standing in the open door.

"Banishing?"

"Well, you're standing in the center of the temple turning widdershins."

"Widdershins?"

"Counterclockwise, the direction we use to make something diminish or go away. So what's going on?"

I shrugged. "Caught in the act, I guess."

"You're not supposed to act here, you're supposed to be as real and as present as you can possibly be."

Her unexpected bluntness was like a cold breeze from the ocean, clearing the fog from my mind. My sulkiness evaporated, but my doubts lingered.

"I was thinking how unmagical this place looks. And . . ." I paused, reluctant to offend her, "I was thinking of leaving, I've got so much work to do. . . ."

"You were thinking more than that. You were thinking that magic doesn't exist."

I felt myself respond to the way she seemed to read my mind, like a flower turning toward the sun. I listened with my heart, and not just my head, as she continued.

"It's difficult to look beneath appearances. We certainly treat the world as if it's the complete opposite of magical. In fact, we pretty much treat it like a garbage dump." She began to scoop up the trash. "Given what we've done to the world, it's difficult to see the divine is present in all that exists. Sometimes it seems downright impossible. But once you've seen it, you never forget. And once you've learned to treat the Earth as the body of the sacred, your world will be filled with magic."

"But what about all those people who treat it like a garbage dump?"

"People have to change on the inside before things can change outside. One person at a time. Then the world will reflect our inner beauty and peace, our spiritual wisdom. You know, in many indigenous cultures the shaman is called a 'wounded healer.' Do you know why?"

I shook my head.

"Because you can't heal others until you first learn to heal yourself. Now, why don't you put that briefcase down and help me get the temple ready? Start by cleaning the candlesticks. I'm going to remind our noisy neighbors that they're supposed to be finished in fifteen minutes."

Nonna handed me an old white-handled knife. "Use my curfane. And try not to think about anything but cleaning those candlesticks as well as you possibly can. Chop wood and carry water, as my Taoist friends say."

Sighing, I dug the sharp little blade into the melted blue wax. As I worked, my fingers became shiny with the aromatic oil that had coated the blue candles. By the time Nonna returned, I had finished all four candlesticks, and I was peaceful.

"Well, you certainly look more relaxed. I guess the peace and protection ritual they did last night is still working." She lifted my hand to her face and inhaled deeply. "Oh, I love that oil—High John the Conqueror, vervain, rosemary, and . . ." she sniffed again, "rowan."

"Peace and protection?"

She nodded.

"We need white candles for tonight, and a white cloth for the altar," Maia said, joining us.

"White," Maia explained to me in her nurturing way as I set out the candles and cloth, "is the color associated with purity, truth, and sincerity. Each color is associated with various qualities and different magical values or effects. Purple is associated with spirituality, green with prosperity, red with passion, blue with peace and healing, and pink is the color of the Goddess."

Colors, I also knew, are wavelengths of energy—violet is the shortest, red the longest. Psychological experiments had also established that different colors evoked different reactions. Green and blue are soothing, which is why the halls of so many institutions, like schools and hospitals, are painted green, while red and pink have been found to have a cheering and stimulating effect on people, particularly those who are depressed.

We would learn more about magic, color, and energy as our studies progressed, Maia promised. Suddenly, I remembered she had asked me to bring white flowers tonight, so I left the shop to buy carnations, lilies, and roses from the local grocer. And when I returned, the temple was bathed in the soft light of dozens of small white candles, the air was sweet with burning incense, the carpet covered with large pillows, and the room filled with the laughter of women. It had been tranformed, and I had helped.

Bellona led us through the group breathing exercises, and at first I found it hard to sit still and to keep my mind from wandering back to the events at work. But by the time she began the guided visualization, I was relaxed and focused and ready to concentrate on the images and feelings her words evoked.

Afterward, we stretched, drank water and wine, and whispered to each other. Annabelle turned to Maia.

"When are we going to do magic?" she asked.

Maia's eyebrows shot up and her lips pursed slightly. I was surprised at Annabelle's directness, but she was expressing what we'd all been secretly thinking. We'd been working for several weeks mastering exercises like the one this evening. After using our breathing techniques to quiet our busy minds, we had moved on to simple meditations, learning to focus on specific images and to visualize them with precision and clarity. We'd imagined apples and doors, letters and shapes floating in space. We'd imagined walking down spiral staircases and through heavy oak doors. We'd sat in arcadian glades and bathed in crystal pools. We'd even been given visualization homework, and I was able to hold the images clearly for quite some time. Gradually, I began to experience them with more of my "inner" senses, turning them three-dimensionally in my mind's eye, tasting the apples, feeling the heat of the candle, smelling the rain-soaked grass. We were all hungry for more complex challenges.

"What do you think we've been doing?" Maia replied, her usual maternal softness suddenly replaced with Sicilian spark. "Without mastering these basics, your magic won't work. It'll be like trying to drive a car without turning the key in the ignition, or steering, or being able to see out the window. Magic works, ladies, so you'd better learn to do it right, because you just may get what you ask for."

"But what *is* magic?" I heard myself asking. I still felt very skeptical and uncomfortable about "casting spells." It seemed silly and impossible. Who needed magic for love or money? Live your life, work hard, be a good and loving person, and all of that will follow. And yet, at the same time, the idea of having supernatural powers that could give me anything my heart desired was a childhood dream that I couldn't resist remembering. Who could? Despite my lingering skepticism, the only word to describe my spontaneous experiences and amazing synchronicities, even the principles of quantum physics, *was* magic.

I wanted the power to make these phenomena continue, and the wisdom to understand what they meant. These women had remarkable psychic talents, but what other powers did they have? Were they powers that I could develop and use?

"Well, isn't magic about casting spells? I mean, isn't it about power to make things happen, like money or love?" Marcia offered. She was sitting with her arm around Naomi. Though so different, they were obviously attracted to each other and had started dating.

Bellona answered, jumping in to soothe Maia's ruffled feathers. "Aleister Crowley said that magic is the science and art of causing change to occur in conformity with will. But I like Dion Fortune's version: Magic is the art of changing consciousness at will. Once you've changed your consciousness, you'll learn to change reality. That's what magic is."

She put it so simply, but the implications were astounding. I already knew that meditation clears the mind of floating debris, creating room for the sacred to enter. A noisy and confused consciousness cannot apprehend divine presence, let alone participate in the co-creation of reality. You must quiet the mind so the heart can hear, because it is when the sacred enters your heart that the mysteries begin to reveal themselves. I had begun to realize that was the magic my heart longed for.

"The exercises you're mastering will enable you to develop the skills necessary to do magic. You can't manifest a desire if you can't visualize it first," Bellona continued as matter-of-factly as if she were explaining how to drive a car. "You're learning to create a thought form on the *akashic*, or psychic, plane of pure energy. Once a thought form's been created there, you'll learn to animate or fill it with energy so it can manifest on the material plane." Could it be that simple, I wondered?

"I can certainly visualize the fella next door—now I just need a love spell so he'll . . . visualize me," Annabelle, our resident Southern belle, quipped.

"You expect us to believe you need magic to get a guy? Get over it!" Mindy pushed Annabelle teasingly. The circle erupted with laughter.

"Ah, a love spell. If you could bottle that, you'd be the richest woman in the world." Naomi snickered, "So where's the formula? 'Cause I need something to support me so I can sculpt all day."

"Magic works, make no mistake about it. And sometimes, some of it can be bottled." Nonna held up a small bottle of honey-colored oil that had been sitting on the altar. As she gently shook it, the color deepened to a rich amber.

"What's that?" Annabelle asked, her voice softening with sudden longing. She'd been divorced for several years and yearned to meet a man like the heroes in her books.

"An Aphrodite oil that I am preparing. It's for a love spell for someone who doesn't know how much she needs it." Nonna placed it carefully upon the shining copper pentacle in the center of the altar. An important magical tool, the round disk was inscribed with a five-pointed star that Witches use to charge and consecrate objects during magic. The disk symbolizes the earth and could also be used to invoke the earth's divinity. The star is the ancient symbol of the Goddess, representing the union of the four elements—air, fire, water, and earth—and the spirit, and a clue to the mystery of life itself.

Maia gently tapped the side of her bell and the side conversations that had suddenly cropped up quieted. Nonna spoke.

"Before we go any further, there are certain principles of practicing magic that every Witch must learn. Magic is *never* used to gain power over anyone but yourself. It's a grave violation of our spirituality to use power to control another, or to control nature."

"I don't understand," Annabelle interrupted, frustration creeping into her voice. "If you can't cast a spell, how can you do magic? How can you do love magic?"

Nonna spoke firmly. "You'll learn to cast spells—you're learning tonight, right this minute, but not in the way you think. This is one of the greatest misunderstandings about how Witches work. The great myth is that we cast spells over people, or try to bend nature to our will with supernatural power. That idea of magic has nothing to do with our practice of the ancient ways of the Goddess. It's actually a reflection of the patriarchal religions and their view of supernatural power, like when Moses parted the Red Sea. It reflects a very different spiritual world view from ours—one in which God placed man upon the earth to have dominion over it. We don't work with supernatural forces, we work with nature's divine energy."

Her simple words really struck me and I leaned into the circle, my attention completely focused as Nonna elaborated.

"Our spiritual work is about living in harmony with nature, because for Witches, everything that exists in the natural world is a form or expression of the divine. Through our spiritual practices, we learn to work with this energy, with its ebb and flow, not to control or alter it, but to transform ourselves and our lives, and to help others with the blessing of its sacred power," she added. "Magic is not about controlling another person, but about bringing your own divine power into fullest expression or manifestation. We don't seek to command, but to create. Magic, when done properly, brings you into alignment with the powers of the sacred universe, so that they may assist you in giving form to your true purpose, your reason for being. As you work, you will better understand all of this."

"There are two primary uses of magic," said Maia, her maternal calm returning. "The first is often called 'High' magic—this is the magic that has to do with being in the presence of the Goddess, or the God, to know Her within and to experience Her in the world that surrounds us. Then there's practical magic, which usually involves casting spells. This is the use of magic for necessities such as good health, prosperity, fulfilling work, or love."

"Nonna, you said you were preparing a love spell tonight. So how do you do a spell if you're not trying to control someone?" asked Gillian.

"It's not about making Mr. X fall in love with you," Nonna replied, "but about preparing yourself for love and drawing to you the person who is right for you, the person you're meant to be with."

"A soulmate?" I asked, my own longing closer to the surface than I thought.

"Perhaps. It all depends on the timing. You can't find your soulmate until you've found your soul," Nonna said reassuringly.

"And how do I do that?" I asked.

Nonna smiled, "Ah, well, that's the greatest quest you can make—some call it the search for the Holy Grail."

We pressed her for more explanation, but she would say no more.

Bellona closed the circle and Maia turned to us with a sly smile. "Don't forget, ladies," she warned us like a mother wrapping up her children before she sent them out to play, "be careful what you ask for, you're likely to get it."

I remained after everyone else had left. Each week one of us took responsibility for making the incense, preparing the temple, or cleaning up afterward, and now I learned that each of us would also be rewarded with this special time and magical tutoring with Nonna, Maia, or Bellona. I was delighted that tonight it was Nonna who had again taken me under her wing.

I absorbed the quiet of the temple as I carefully cleared off the altar. I dumped the charcoal and incense embers into a pot of earth, wrapped the copper pentacle in a white silk cloth, cleaned out the candlesticks, and returned the statue to the bookshelf in the north. Finally, I poured the wine and juice that filled the silver Goddess bowl into the sink while the cold water ran. Nonna explained to me that if we worked out of doors, the libation bowl would have been poured onto the earth or into a flowing stream, river, or ocean, as an offering with thanks and prayers. Here was another chance to make use of the visualization skills I'd been practicing, for it required much greater focus and concentration to practice this simple rite with its full measure of spiritual clarity when standing in a cramped bathroom.

All that remained on the altar were the white flowers and Nonna's love oil.

"May I smell the oil?"

"Of course, I made it for you." Nonna smiled at my apparent surprise and opened the little bottle. Slowly she waved it in three small clockwise circles beneath my nose. It was delicious and exotic, and I found myself leaning forward as she pulled it away.

"Umm yumm. What's in it?"

"Ambergris, patchouli, musk, orange, black narcissus."

"But why did you make it for me? I mean, I'm really O.K. being alone right now." Since starting my new job I just hadn't had much time for men. And I wasn't going to settle for a man who was anything less than magical.

"There are many kinds of love my dear. And one can never have too much love, whatever form it comes in. Right now, perhaps, you have too little. There is a lovely full moon coming up and it happens to fall on a Friday, the day of the week devoted to the goddess Venus, a powerful goddess associated with the powers of beauty and love. I want you to mark a pink candle with your name, with the astrological symbol for Venus, and with the word *love*. After it is marked, rub the candle in a clockwise direction with this oil. Once the moon has risen, I want you to put the candle in a safe place, like your bathroom sink, light it, and let it burn until it goes out by itself. After you light the candle, fill your tub with warm water and bathe in the potion we are going to prepare. Come."

A sudden thrill of excitement traveled up my spine as I thanked her. I tucked the little bottle in my pocket, remembering the results of the last magical gift she'd given me. I had begun to learn about the mysterious contents of the huge jars I now pulled from their shelves. When carried in a pouch, vetiver could break a streak of bad luck, if you slept with mugwort beneath your pillow, you would have psychic dreams, and High John the Conqueror would bring you money. I remained skeptical, that was my nature. Or perhaps my conditioning. The herbs, however, began to teach me otherwise. The ones with healing powers, like digitalis, St. John's Wort, echinacea, chamomile, willow, and eucalyptus oil, successfully challenged my narrow thinking, particularly as I learned that most of our medicines came from plants. If everything was energy, why couldn't the energy of plants have other uses?

It still sounded far-fetched, but what about all the other things people take on faith? Christians believe the miracle of Christ raising Lazarus from the dead and, later, himself; Jews believe the miracle of the lamp of oil that burned for eight days and nights at Hanukkah, and that Moses parted the Red Sea. And such beliefs aren't relegated to ancient history: Catholics believe in transubstantiation, millions believe in the power of prayer, and almost all faiths employ ritual in an infinite variety of forms including the lighting of candles and the burning of incense. Communion, which is certainly a magical ritual, might seem very strange if you weren't raised Christian. Beause we aren't accustomed to even hearing about Wiccan rituals, they feel twice as foreign.

In time, I would come to realize that spells are much like prayers— but a prayer asks an external divinity to intercede on your behalf because you are unable to effect some needed change yourself, whereas a spell draws up divine energy from within, as it also invokes exoteric divinity for support, to bring about change. And, most important, spells are accomplished in accord with the rhythms of nature.

Like many people in our hyper-rational world, I had difficulty grasping the idea of ordinary physical objects—candles, herbs, oils—having an actual physical effect on the universe. This shortsightedness is an old problem—and one of the reasons indigenous peoples, including pagans, are misperceived to "worship" rocks and stones in their "primitive" beliefs, a misperception which I now understood was a gross distortion of a profound spiritual insight. Western value judgments are made while blindfolded—while unable to see into the heart of the universe, to see that a rock, plant, or person, is made up of divine energy. But from a rational point of view, once I accepted the fundamental idea of objects as energy, a world of possibility began to open for me. And I could not deny the empowering effects our rituals had on me.

"These techniques we're learning seem very effective for relaxing, like yoga is, and it's great after a crazy day at work, but I still don't get what they have to do with magic," I said.

Nonna handed me a jar of dried roses as she continued explaining. "Relaxation is only the first step. Yoga does more than relax you—it opens you to the infinite divinity of the universe. It is an important means of changing consciousness."

"You mean literally altering brainwave patterns?"

Nonna nodded. "From the workaday wavelength of beta, to alpha, theta, and others."

I mulled over the implications of what she was saying as we carried the jars back to the oil office. From my reading I had learned that a number of neuroscientists theorized that transcendental experiences and mystical states—such as those brought on by yoga, meditation, psychotropics, and other ecstatic practices—might be the means by which we can gain access to quantum reality. My mind was racing and I wondered whether, in those moments when time seemed to stop and dimensions of astonishing experience opened, the human mind had some secret miraculous capacity to "travel" into the realm of quantum physics. Would these techniques remove the blindfold covering our eyes? Would they produce ecstatic states in which we could experience reality at its quantum level? Would we discover that the nature of reality was sacred? And was it possible that we had reached a moment of profound historical, evolutionary change, where metaphysics and physics could marry and generate an offspring of remarkable enlightenment and power?

The poet in me responded to the idea that the imagination could be a portal to divine revelation. Artists found inspiration through the imagination, why not spiritual practitioners, priestesses, and shamans? But the rational skeptic required verification. Physics had provided some of this; now, working within circle was contributing additional, precious proof through common experiences, perceptions, and interpretations. I was starting to see that "magic" did indeed work.

"The techniques you are learning are shamanic tools employed by Witches to activate mental powers, enter the spirit world, and reawaken latent spiritual powers," Nonna said as she searched the shelves for her next ingredient. "With these it is possible to initiate an entirely new relationship between oneself and the universe. To encounter your spirit guides . . . and your soul."

As she said these words, I felt my heart open and a world of possibility lay before me. I was being led by a force more powerful and mysterious than anything imaginable, into a realm where dreams quite literally came true. It wasn't some silly hocus-pocus, turning men into frogs, although I could certainly think of more than a few who deserved it. Instead, I was discovering an elegant spiritual practice, much of which was rooted in the lives of women, of European shamanism, which could heal and open the human heart. Magic was the art of unlocking the vast untapped powers of the human mind—powers to function in ways that seemed magical but were completely consistent with the new laws of physics where everything in the universe was interconnected energy. Could I learn to develop and use this kind of miraculous power? How would it change my life? And even before images of success and fulfillment could intoxicate me, I wondered how the universe would test my worthiness, for surely such an endowment was also a profound responsibility, one that could be earned only by the severest challenges. But what would these trials be?

The techniques we were learning *were* the means by which to open the doors of perception, to enter this multidimensional reality, and once on the other side, not only to navigate but to create. Aldous Huxley had written a book entitled *The Doors of Perception* about the spiritual ramifications of psychotropics. These were psychoactive plants, such as psilocybin mushrooms, peyote, and ergot, that could induce ecstatic states, alter consciousness, and reveal the divine. It was from this book that one of the most influential and literary rock bands of the sixties, the Doors, took its name, and that described the journey of discovery taken by Carlos Castaneda, who studied with Don Juan, a Yaqui medicine man. The use of psychotropics as a spiritual sacrament was an ancient and integral part of most shamanic and mystical traditions. But though they were popular during the sixties, even marijuana and organic psychotropics, such as peyote or psilocybin mushrooms, were illegal and, as an attorney and activist, I wasn't about to use anything that could compromise me. But I was thrilled to learn that there were keys to ecstasy and the world of the spirit that did not require the use of psychotropics and that were powerful, effective, and legal.

"There's a great deal for you to think about, and thinking is what you are most accustomed to doing, but now it's important for you to experience. And to come to know that you can trust the wisdom that comes to you from another way of knowing," Nonna gently tapped my heart. "Learn with that, and with time, you will begin to figure out why for yourself."

As I watched her assured movements, I felt that, perhaps, here was a community whose values might truly heal the wounds that haunted all of us, an ancient artistry that knew the body as a miraculous instrument through which the sounds of the Divine, if it existed, could reverberate into the world. It was an ancient system based upon the goodness, even more, the essential divinity, of the human heart. So far, everything I'd been taught resonated with the way I'd been raised, and did not contradict, but in fact, reinforced the scientific world view that most of us were simply unaware of. Rationalism and mysticism—it was a heady combination, a license for exploration in the next great frontier.

Nonna opened the jars, scooped out small handfuls of the fragrant herbs, and dropped them into a large mortar and pestle. "Now where's that oil I gave you?" I pulled it from my pocket, feeling its warmth. She took it from me, waved it beneath my nose, and added three drops to the herbs.

"You are to add all of these to three cups of pure spring water. Bring it to a boil, lower the heat, simmer for twenty minutes, stirring deosil, that's clockwise. As you stir, think about love. Strain the herbs from the liquid and pour the liquid into your bath water. Right before you get into the tub, add five drops of oil and the petals of three red roses to the bath water. Close your eyes, relax, and allow yourself to dream of love. But make sure to get out of the tub before the water gets cold. Put a drop of oil on your third eye," she tapped the center of my forehead, "over your heart, and beneath your navel. Place the rose petals between your pillow and pillow case and go right to bed. Oh, and be sure to write down your dreams in the morning. Now, grind these," Nonna instructed me as she handed me the mortar and pestle. "Thirteen deosil circles, and as you work the herbs, think about love."

I concentrated on the feeling of being loved, and giving love. Mother love, with its warm arms and soothing words, family love with its laughter and support, the love of friends with its shared secrets and discoveries. My pulse quickened as the grinding released an extraordinary perfume. I tried not to think about my unfulfilled yearning for a dark-haired, working-class poet, or kisses that awaken a soul from its chrysalis of dreams, or calloused fingertips like flint against skin, leaving trails of fire through the forest of night.

On the night of Venus's full moon, in the hour when it filled my window with silver light, I decided to set aside any lingering skepticism I had. I decided not to think, not to question or to doubt, just to do it and enjoy the experience of magic.

Look who's here! I've hardly seen you since you arrived—come say hello." Warm and jovial, Max Rosen had always struck me as a Jewish Santa Claus. But instead of red suits, he wore the best hand tailoring Italy had to offer. And rather than bestowing toys from a huge black sack, he made dreams come true with record deals. Of all the partners, it was Max Rosen who was an industry legend. More than just the senior partner, he was president of a very prestigious record label. Created with the birth of rock and roll, it had signed some of its greatest artists. The company was now affiliated with an industry giant. And my first record deal, my little single which had made its mark on the charts, was with Max. He was also brilliant, warm, and gracious. I adored him. And for reasons that remained a mystery, he seemed to like me.

Max Rosen's corner office was the color of money. The green walls had a lacquered sheen and were covered with gold records, posters, and photos that were astonishing for their equal measures of success, celebrity, and casual intimacy. I settled myself on the green leather Chesterfield couch. A huge mahogany desk filled the wall of windows opposite the couch, but Max always sat beside the couch in a matching Chesterfield chair.

"Would you like an espresso?" he handed me the tiny cup before I could nod. Max had the espresso machine in the coffee room sent over from Milan, and though it it made a terrible noise, it also made fabulous coffee. "So tell me what you think of what we're listening to."

A woman's plaintive, poetic singing, backed by a hard rocking band, filled the room. The tape reminded me again of my love for music and the reasons I enjoyed my job, despite its mounting pressures.

"I like it—she's got some real chops. And there aren't enough women in this business."

Max smiled. "So, Hadus keeping you busy?"

I nodded.

"He's a busy man," Max said with a tinge of disdain. His eyes came to rest on a photo of himself and Harold, his partner who had passed away a few years before. "Did I ever tell you about the time, this was in the deep South in the early fifties, we were chased by a truck full of men with guns? We'd gone into a black club to sign an act."

Max Rosen's friendship was precious and coveted by everyone, including Hadus—to whom Rosen, beyond passing courtesies, would not give the time of day. Basking in the warmth of his easy conversation, I was grateful he always had a few moments for me. We'd chat about music, or books, or philosophy and once in a while he would tell me stories from his remarkable life.

"We loved this business, God knows why—it's so full of pirates and cutthroats, and sharks. But with Harold there was such joy in finding the talent, in changing someone's life. He was a gentleman and he always treated everyone with respect." Max picked up the simple silver frame. "He was honest too—a rare quality. If he shook hands with someone, they had a deal they could count on. People knew they could trust him."

Max sighed and set the picture back on the table. "Well, it's not the sixties anymore, that's for sure." He sipped his espresso quietly, and then went on with his story. "The day he told me he was dying, we'd just been shopping at Pucci's, and I'd bought him a beautiful tie. We were at a little cafe off the Piazza Navona, and he turned to me, out of the blue and said, 'Max, the secret is you have to love what you do. If you love it, you'll treasure it, and everything the universe gives you. It's love that makes things grow, even in business, especially this business. Or at least it should be.' Life is rich; it's full of gifts—the more you have, the more there is to share. You know, it's men with small souls who think there isn't enough to go around. They fight to keep their little grasp on their tiny piece of the world and they're always angry because they're never satisfied. They're cursed with a hole they can never fill. They may get things done, but they can never keep what they've achieved." Max reached for his coffee, but we'd already emptied our cups. "So, is it still glamorous?"

I laughed, nodding. "Its pretty dazzling." I sensed Max had something else on his mind. He sat, waiting for me to continue, which I did. "I've brought in a lot of clients in the last few weeks, and Hadus always has plenty of paperwork for me to do."

"Not too busy to help me out once in a while perhaps?"

I was glad to have put the cup down or it would probably have shattered on the marble-topped table. Max laughed at my thrilled face.

"I'd love to! But I don't know if it would be a problem with Hadus. . . ."

"I'll talk to him. I won't need you very often, but once in a while I do need an associate—then it would be very helpful. And who knows, you might enjoy it." His eyes were sparkling.

"You mean I might love my work?" I smiled at him with unbridled gratitude, suddenly remembering Nonna's words about different kinds of love.

"You learn quickly, my dear."

"When I have a good teacher. Thank you, you won't be disappointed."

"I know that. I'll talk to Hadus later. You better get back to work—he's probably wondering where you are."

Hadus looked startled and then annoyed to see me emerge from Max's office. "I've been looking for you." He sounded sullen. I had no idea what the price of Max's cherished gift would be. I worked each day, and many nights, in a kingdom of uneasy alliances with hidden powers and veiled intrigues that I could only begin to suspect from Hadus's reaction.

Madeline handed me a pink message slip as I headed back to my office—an unfamiliar phone number and . . . "Jake called." I smiled with startled pleasure—how did he track me down? Born and raised in New Jersey, he was a black-haired, black-humored writer who made his living driving a truck. We'd met while I was working in D.C., falling immediately into an ardent affair that ended when I moved back to New York. Parting was inevitable in the face of our inherited habits of keeping distance. I didn't know the particulars of his family vacuum, but my work in circle was helping me to understand my own. My elegantly reserved mother and my Scandinavian father who'd never fully come home from sea, left me with an inherited habit of cool detachment. And so my heart remained restless and removed, yet in the center of my secret and enchanted garden, I longed for love to join me. We sensed that our abiding bond was friendship, and it was in this form we loved each other best. I couldn't wait to see him.

Nonna's love magic had worked, but in completely unexpected ways. I'd been thinking about a soulmate but the universe had brought me what I needed most—Max's words about loving my work, and the energy of Max's friendship, Jake's return, and most of all, a valuable, magical lesson: There are many kinds of love.

"She changes everything She touches
And everything She touches changes
She changes everything She touches
And everything She touches changes
Changes touches changes touches"

Over and over we sang the simple chant. Like Tibetan monks whose repetitive use of sacred sound was a famous meditational and consciousness-altering technique, with each musical reiteration I experienced a remarkable shift and cojoining of energies. I lost all track of time.

When the singing ended, evaporating like a golden mist into the black cave surrounding us, we sat for a timeless spell in harmonious silence. Someone finally stirred. Maia passed bottles of wine and water and grape juice. I realized how thirsty I was and how extraordinarily delicious the liquids were as they rolled over my tongue. We were quiet, speaking softly, moving slowly, the tranquillity suffusing and uniting inner and outer spaces.

"During our last circle we began to talk about magical power, what it is and how we can use it. There are two basic rules you must learn about magical energy. Every Witch uses these rules to guide her or his practice," Bellona began. "The first is 'And ye harm none, do what ye will.' The second is the Threefold Rule: 'That which you send out will return to you threefold.' This is true of both good and bad energy, and so we never send out bad. If you do not practice in accord with these ethical precepts, you are not a true Witch."

"Excuse me." I hated to interrupt, or to disrupt the extraordinary harmony we had just created, but dialogue was a part of circle, and I'd majored in Ethics and Political Philosophy. I couldn't let it pass. "The Threefold law sounds more like expediency: I won't do something bad because something worse will happen to me. That's more a model of deterrence than a truly ethical basis for people's behavior. It's like the morality of the Roman Catholic Church—if you commit a 'sin,' God will punish you with damnation and hell, so you'd better behave. 'And ye harm none, do what ye will'—well, that's an ethical norm. It's a moral statement about tremendous freedom and commensurate responsibility not to harm anything, not just people." I was enjoying using my philosophy training in this unfamiliar arena, and beginning to understand the inherent logic of Wiccan beliefs. "I guess it comes from the idea that everything that exists, at least in the natural world, is an embodiment of the sacred. So it's to be treated as sacred—with respect and care."

Nonna nodded, looking very satisfied with my statement, and Bellona didn't seem at all challenged or disturbed, but like she'd just been given something interesting to consider.

"And that is also how magic works—everything that exists is sacred and interconnected," Nonna said warmly. "But it's not an idea based on speculative or theoretical thought. It's a direct and personal experience available to everyone. The art of magic is about experiencing the sacred and working with it in an appropriate way. For Witches, when we use our various techniques to change consciousness, we are able to see and to experience the most profound spiritual truth: Everything that exists in the natural world is an expression of divine energy. Therefore, because everything is interconnected, we can have a positive influence on all sorts of events. When we do magic, we become one with the object of our magic."

"What you were saying, about everything being connected, that's what Chief Seattle said." Shy Onatah, who rarely spoke, took a book from the knapsack behind her. "May I read this to you?"

Maia nodded, and in soft, sweet voice Onatah began: "Every part of this earth is sacred to my people. Every shining fir needle, every sandy shore, every mist in the dark woods, every meadow, every humming insect. All are holy in the memory and experience of my people.

"We know the sap which courses through the trees as we know the blood that courses through our veins. We are part of the earth and it is part of us. The perfumed flowers are our sisters. The bear, the deer, the great eagle, these are our brothers. . . .

"Will you teach your children what we have taught our children? That the earth is our mother? What befalls the earth befalls all the sons of the earth. . . .

"This we know: The earth does not belong to man, man belongs to the earth. All things are connected like the blood which unites us all. Man did not weave the web of life, he is merely a strand in it. Whatever he does to the web, he does to himself. . . ."

Onatah cradled the book to her chest as we sat in silence, awed by the power of the words. "Seattle was a Suquamish chief when he spoke these words. He was being forced to give up his tribe's lands to the invading people of the United States in 1852."

"Wicca has the same spiritual sensibility, and the same understanding of our sacred connection to the web of life," Nonna said.

"It's a metaphor for the Divine energy which unites all," she continued. "The greatest Wiccan magical work is about connecting with this Divine force, allowing it to fill us, transform us, and make us wise. All magic flows from our connection to the sacred, therefore all of our work *must* be guided by the divine nature of the energy with which we work. Because the physical world is an expression of the divine, magic has always been used for practical purposes. But unless it is informed by the sacred, practical magic based on the projection of will alone rapidly deteriorates into selfish ego gratification. Ultimately, when magic is practiced only for this purpose, it soon ceases to work. As Maia said before, a car can't run on an empty gas tank. And all magic ultimately runs on our connection to the divine. There is a basic rule of magic that you must remember: The energy you put into a spell determines the energy that comes out of your spell. If you are angry, anger will return; if you are needy, neediness will return to you; if you are greedy, greediness will return to you. I think that is what most people think the Threefold law means."

Bellona nodded. "Yes, that's it. Our spiritual work is about learning to make the connection to the divine web of life and then giving expression to the sacred power that resides within each of us. When you have learned to do this, you will know when and how to do spells."

Do unto others as you would have them do unto you. Everything Nonna said seemed to expand this fundamental moral principle to a universe in which everything—earth, animals, plants, air, water, humans—was sacred and therefore to be treated with reverence. This was our first serious discussion of the underlying spiritual purposes of the exercises to which we had applied ourselves with such enthusiasm. We had simply trusted the priestesses, and willingly we undertook mastering the techniques which had enhanced our abilities to relax, concentrate, and visualize. The fact that these techniques had worked, not only for me, but for everyone else in circle, was one of the primary reasons I continued, even if I remained somewhat uncomfortable with the rituals. Like a major chord struck on a grand piano, the exercises seemed to foster harmony within the circle, respecting the expression of our unique energies while bringing these distinctive tones into a melodic resonance. These were important accomplishments, but it was now gratifyingly apparent that we had also been working to prepare ourselves for the sacred connection the priestesses had been describing.

"Enough talking. Let's see what you ladies have learned," Maia announced. "I think it's time to combine visualization practice with a very important technique we call 'grounding and centering.' Sit up straight, close your eyes, focus only on your breathing. . . . Feel yourself growing more relaxed. As the tension leaves your body, feel how strong and clear you are."

She continued. "Allow my words to guide you as you experience the images and feelings that arise."

I suddenly imagined a tall tree, with its bright green leaves blowing in the wind, and a thought entered my mind: The tree absorbed my carbon dioxide in order to live, and released oxygen into the air as its waste. As I was inhaling the tree's oxygen waste, the tree absorbed my carbon dioxide waste. I could see the exchange of precious gases, like radiant ribbons, flowing back and forth between us. We were joined in a mutual giving of life, a mutual recycling of energy. Maia's voice penetrated my thoughts and I smiled as her words echoed the images that had already come to me.

"Feel your body becoming the trunk of a great towering oak tree . . . from the bottom of your spine feel your roots descending into the earth beneath you . . . feel them spreading deeper and deeper into the rich, dark earth . . . feel yourself joined to the earth . . . smell the moistness of the soil . . . feel the nutrients that surround you . . . feel the earth's great powers of life moving up your spine just as it moves up the trunk of a great and ancient tree . . . feel it flowing through your body . . . opening your heart . . . filling you with strength and power . . . feel it flowing through you, cleansing and renewing you. . . ."

The images were clear, the sensations powerful. At first I felt something in the base of my spine, then it shot upward and spread like wildfire through my entire body. It was heat and electricity, it was joy and power. It was momentarily terrifying and completely exhilarating.

"You are the sacred tree of life . . . you connect spirit and earth . . . feel yourself making this divine connection . . . joining the two in the magical union of life . . . now concentrate the energy in your heart . . . feel your heart opening . . . expanding. . . ."

We each became a tree, and the circle became a sacred grove, a forest glade where arboreal spirits were sprung from that ancient wed-lock of heaven and earth.

"Now let us ground the energy. Exhale completely and as you do, return the energy you have received to the earth from whence it came. Give thanks and feel it flowing down your spinal column and back into the ground." Maia spoke slowly, pausing between each instruction, al-lowing us time to feel everything. "Draw your roots back up from the Mother Earth. Feel them curling and resting at the base of your spine. And when you are ready, open your eyes."

"Whew," Marcia let out a long breath. "That was amazing."

I looked around the circle. Jeanette still had her eyes closed, her head was tilted back and her round face, with its high cheekbones and full lips, was an immortal moment of explicit serenity and power. Annabelle's eyes were fever bright and she was fluttering about like a moth entranced by moonlight. Naomi and Mindy both sat with their heads bowed. Marcia looked sleepy and a little dazed. Gillian was run-ning her hand back and forth across Abremalin's fur, her body a reflec-tion of sensuous relaxation. I was keenly alert, invigorated and yet relaxed. I felt rested, revitalized, and a little giddy.

Only Onatah did not share our exhilaration and contentment.

"I'm feeling dizzy and kind of nauseated," she said, her long, golden fingers brushing damp curls from her forehead. "I couldn't feel anything at first, and then—it was too much."

Maia rose and moved swiftly to Onatah's side. She placed a hand on her forehead and another at the small of her back. "You need to ground the excess energy. Lean forward, slowly. That's right. Now rest your head on the ground. Put your palms flat on the floor. Now exhale, slowly. As you breathe out, let any excess energy drain out of your body, send it out and down through all the points where your body is in contact with the earth. Annabelle—" she looked up suddenly—"you should do this too, and any of the rest of you if you're feeling jittery or anxious. Let the excess energy flow out of you, from your third eye, your hands, and most important, from the base of your spine. Return the energy to the earth." Maia sat behind Onatah, one hand now on the back of her head, the other still at the small of her back. They sat for several minutes, joined in rhythmic breathing, Maia's body subtly slumping each time she exhaled. As I watched her, it was as if her features disappeared, her body metamorphosing from a voluptuous woman to the ancient, rounded hills of Tuscany.

Tenderly she stroked Onatah's head. "How are you now?" she murmured softly.

"Good, I feel O.K." Onatah replied.

"All right, sit up very slowly."

She was smiling, the tension drained from her face. "I feel fine now. Thank you."

Maia hugged her. "Hugging is very grounding," she said. "And so is eating."

"This technique is even more powerful when you're seated directly on the earth itself," Bellona offered. "You can use this whenever you're tired, or sad, or sick, or when you're going into battle, or about to do magic. But always remember to ground or earth the energy when you're done. Otherwise you'll end up feeling like Onatah, or worse."

Magic: It was once impossible for me to hear that word and not think of rabbits popping out of hats, card tricks, or women being sawed in half. But the magic I was experiencing was no illusion. It was powerful, physical, and psychic, and these Witches knew how to work with it at will. Would I?

When I got home I went straight to my bookcase, one of my own portals to the realm of magic. I reached up, moving my hand across my bookshelves, back and forth, up and down, without looking at the titles, using my breathing to keep my mind clear of thought, until a little voice that I always thought of as my library angel said: "This one."

I pulled the old book down from the shelf and resisted the temptation to peek at the title, allowing my fingers to simply open it. I looked down:

In the middle of the journey of our life
I came to myself in a dark wood
Where the straight way was lost.

It was the opening to Dante's *Inferno*. How perfect and beautiful. But frightening too. I thought I was discovering Paradise, returning to Eden, but was I unknowingly entering Hell? If everything was interconnected, what about that terrifying world of cruelty and greed, violence and despair that I lived in everyday? Was there enough magic in the world to change that?

Life seemed so simple at the beginning—a straight and simple path that society had laid out for us, that our parents expected from us, and that we ourselves, anticipated. Go to school, do well, get a good job, be well paid, well married, well taken care of. Conform and be well rewarded. Until you hit the wall, at thirty, or forty, or fifty, when the stock market crashes, or your spouse seems like a stranger, or the company downsizes, or there just isn't enough money, or the things that money can buy, to fill the gaping hole that swallows you at midnight. And the straight way is lost. But that, I began to understand, was when the magic of a real life began.

Dante's verse suggested a way of approaching life I'd never considered before. It was an unexpected, accompanied journey of self-discovery. Unlike the straightforward, phallic movement of our culture's expectations, forever growing larger and more distant from the earth, Dante's journey followed a path of primal movement, a sacred spiraling of energy. And although I was unaware of it, I too was moving like the serpent coiled and sleeping at the base of one's spine, rising and retracing its steps, retrieving and reintegrating the wisdom of the past, while perpetually moving ahead.

I was completely engaged by the idea that everything was divine energy. But abstract ideas were no longer enough. The possibility that I could *experience* the world as sacred seemed like the most precious gift I could ever receive, the kind of gift that could change everything. It also appealed to the open and wise child I nurtured within me. She remembered what it felt like to be surrounded by presence while walking, alone, in the woods, to have a butterfly land on her shoulder, to have a tiny field mouse climb into the palm of her hand. And she remembered how her best friend, at the age of ten, had stood on the highest hill on a sunny afternoon reading a rainmaking spell from her storybook about two little girls, one of whom was a Witch; how she danced on the hilltop as huge clouds gathered overhead and rain soaked her to the bone in a natural benediction of exalted recognition. And how she raced home in the deluge, convinced she too was now a Witch, a secret she shared only with me, and that she still carried within her heart to this very day.

I had stumbled into the Land of Oz, the realm of the heart's longing, following the spiral of the yellow brick road, a form I recognized as the very basis of life itself: the shape of our DNA. Again the connections between ancient, magical ideas and science were becoming clearer— the magical frame of mind we achieved in circle *was* the ecstatic condition opening the doors of perception not only to quantum reality but to a divine reality.

There was one thing I suddenly knew with absolute certainty: Magic is not just something you do, or make. It is something the universe does with you. It is our relationship to the divine. There is nothing more magical than the presence of the sacred in one's life. It changes everything. It is extraordinary, it is gorgeous, and it defies the limitations within which we lead our daily lives. Magic is the art of living a creative life that is graced with divine presence. It isn't something one does *to* the universe; it's what a living universe does *with* us once we have awakened to its divinity. It is the sacred dance we share. It is joyous, it is erotic, it is ecstatic, and when it happens roses bloom in the December snow, butterflies fill the trees in Costa Rica, and lovers find each other across a river of time. I thought about the last several years and my longing for love. Most people know intuitively that when you fall in love, the world is full of magic. What they don't know is that when you discover the universe is full of magic, you fall in love with the world.

Nonna's spell was still working.

CHAPTER 5

Between
the Worlds

If the doors of perception were cleansed,
everything would appear to men as it is, infinite.
—WILLIAM BLAKE, *The Marriage of Heaven and Hell*

I t was still chilly when the first robin reappeared in Central Park. I was diligently practicing the techniques I'd learned in circle, frequently combining them with hatha yoga, sometimes in the morning, other times right before bed. But my favorite time was lunchhour, whenever I could get away from the office. After several frozen failures, I knew it was warm enough for me to meditate outdoors when I couldn't see my breath in frosty clouds. I hurried to a huge old willow tree beside the pond in the park. I sat with my back against its silver bark, listening to the taffeta rustle of its golden branches, which, although leafless, seemed to screen me from passersby. And then, after asking the tree to help me, I practiced sending down roots and drawing up energy from the earth.

The ground was winter hard and even with a blanket to sit upon, it was difficult to sit still. But each day I remained in my business-suited lotus posture a bit longer, able to experience the energy moving more smoothly and powerfully throughout my body. When I was finished, I left birdseed for the sparrows, peanuts for the squirrels, and hot soup or a sandwich for the homeless man who had taken up occupancy in the gazebo nearby. All gifts of thanks to Mother Earth.

And then one afternoon, the robin appeared, not just as a sign but as a sorcerer of early spring. That was the first afternoon I heard the birds singing. The light was brighter, the breeze softer, and the unexpected warmth of the sun aroused some slumbering appetite that made people shed their thickened winter skins. Men looked at women and women looked back. And children, especially the youngest ones who were only just realizing they were alive, ran and skipped and played with the energy that would quadruple their weight and triple their height and double their joy if, years from now, they could just remember what this remarkable day was like.

That afternoon, as if summoned by the sun's insistent heat and the earth's awakening, the energy rushed up my spine, shooting upward and exploding out through the back of my head. I was sitting in a shower of sparks, the energy cascading over me and back into the earth.

When I finally emerged from beneath my bower, I was astonished by what I saw. People had a strange and vibrant glow of light around them: The young lovers on the bench threw off a soft yellow shimmer, an elderly Chinese gentleman practicing tai chi was bathed in lavender blue, and two men in suits walking too fast for their surroundings were joined in a blood red egg.

I floated down the path, marveling at the light show that encircled everyone I saw, past the slowly turning merry-go-round that began to spin faster and faster until the horses flew and the children screamed with delighted laughter. An explosion of kernels pushed the lid off the popcorn machine and flooded the sidewalk with a feast for pigeons and dogs that would forever form their dreams of heaven. The pushcart vendor smiled and as I passed his cart, the pinwheels began to spin and the huge bouncing bundle of helium balloons suddenly broke free and shot heavenward. The old man who sat every day, unmoving, in his wheelchair beneath his woolen blanket lifted his head and smiled.

"You're very pretty, miss." His voice was lively, as if he had just delivered the punchline to a story no one had heard before and all the women now adored him and the men wanted to be his friends. "Keep coming back every day. It gives me something to live for."

I stopped dead in my tracks, and we laughed. To his surprise, and mine, and certainly his somber nurse's, I kissed his grizzled cheek.

"Thank you," I said, smelling his aftershave that clung to my cheek.

He reached out a trembling hand and gripped mine tightly. I saw his thin skin stretched across long bones like an ancient parchment map of a vanished life; the brilliant blue veins were roads leading to the spice markets of Samarkan and the distant trading posts of Temujin, which his impatient children would think of only as brown spots and reasons to visit the doctor, who also could not see.

"Thank you," he said softly.

As I exited at Fifty-ninth Street, the carriage horses that lined the street, and to whom I fed sugar cubes each day, shook their powerful heads and whinnied. They danced sideways and backward, and several of them broke loose of their harnesses. Instead of cursing, their mostly Irish drivers stood back, nodding and muttering quickly to each other. One of them crossed himself, but the others laughed and passed a small brown bagged bottle of whiskey.

I walked back to work, a thin wand of willow in my hand, unconscious of the unleashed force of springtime and desire that followed me like my own shadow. Had I turned around, I would have seen a luminous reflection releasing every tether and restriction it encountered.

The willow is enigmatic, for its powers bridge opposite realms of being. It symbolizes death and the Underworld but has long been used in love magic, healing spells, divination, and for the conjuring of spirits. Since ancient times, it has been used to provide protection and deter evil, and now we use it as a source of aspirin. Willow was used to bind Witches' brooms, and magical wands were often made from its branches. Its bark was burned as an offering to Goddesses of the Moon, its leaves and wood used in lunar magic. By sitting beneath this tree, had I accidentally begun to join these worlds of death and divination, the Underworld and the Moon, the conjuring of spirits and love? What forces had I unknowingly unleashed by drawing upon the energy of the tree in the park?

The next day, the ground beneath my willow was punctured by thousands of sharp little spears of growing green and soon I sat surrounded by purple crocus cups whose orange centers glowed like the sun. As the earth reawakened, I found it increasingly difficult to return to the enclosed glass box that began to feel like a gilded cage. I'd never given a moment's thought to the idea of a soul, but something that would answer to no other name appeared like a speckled blue egg in a nest of willow leaves and river mud, close to where my heart beat, filling the space where my longing had lived.

As I returned to the office after my lunchtime meditation, Madeline handed me a pile of pink message slips and I handed her a crocus.

"Thanks, it's been a while since someone gave me flowers," she chuckled. "Hanson, and ICM, and . . . some other calls, and Hadus left this for you." She handed me the redlined contract I'd been working on, then leaned across her desk, staring at me. "Darlin', you're glowing. You look like you're having a love affair instead of lunch. Or like you're pregnant." Her voice reflected concern.

"Spring is in the air," I replied with a little smile. "And no—the only thing I'm giving birth to is myself."

"Looks like you're using more red ink than my third grade teacher," Hanley Pearson said, peering over my shoulder. He was the associate to Jessica Dutton, the only female partner in the firm. In his early thirties, he radiated the buttoned-down, well-scrubbed purity of the Midwest, but whenever he opened his mouth to anyone but Dutton, he exuded condescension. He reminded me of a perfect apple pie that had been sitting too long on his mother's kitchen counter. "He's got you running like a rat in a maze. How late were you working last night?"

"Mmm, I left around eleven-thirty."

"Ah, the bad old days—I remember working those inhuman hours. Keep it up and you'll be the new winner of our coveted trophy for fastest rat."

"Well, that's the problem with winning a rat race—even after you've won, you're still a rat."

"But you must admit, the cheese is superb."

"I'll admit it's tempting. But I'd kinda like to enjoy the race."

"You just haven't gotten used to being a rat yet. Give it time."

"That'll be the day," I laughed, oblivious to just how far into the maze I'd already run. I placed a small bunch of the crocuses, plucked from beneath my willow, on my office windowsill to dry in the rising heat of the radiator. Egyptians used dried crocuses as part of an incense that brought on visions. Witches used them in spells to attract love and nurture peace, both of which I longed for.

I spent the afternoon working on the contract Hadus had left for me, finally bringing it to Sharon for typing.

"Listen Bob, I don't give a damn," Sharon had her hand cupped around the mouthpiece of the telephone, trying unsuccessfully to muffle her conversation. Smiling, I held up the thick sheaf of papers. She answered my signal by turning her back on me.

"I hope that's McCarthy you've got there." Hadus was charging toward his office. "Do I pay you to talk to your boyfriend?" he snapped at Sharon. "Where's the revised contract?"

I handed him the untyped pages.

"Why are you giving these to me?" He took my papers and slammed them on Sharon's desk. "Finish it before lunch. Pretend it's a love letter to your boyfriend. You did have time to take my calls? Shit, Charlie Michaels." He crumpled the message slip and threw it into Sharon's wastebasket. "Sharks, they always smell blood in the water."

Sharon handed him a file.

"Don't give me this now!" He shouted at her as if she were a naughty child. I hated the way he talked to her, and lately he'd been talking to me in the same condescending tones. I felt my stomach tighten. "I've got ten minutes. Let's go over your billing file."

When I returned to his office with the file, Hadus pointed to a cup of steaming cappuccino. He had his tie off, his feet up and his cigar lit. It was seven o'clock on Friday, and the week was officially over.

"Enjoying it so far?"

"Very much," I said, relieved at his mood change. "Although I was hoping for a little less paperwork and a little more client contact," I added, trying to keep my tone upbeat.

He looked surprised at my directness. "You were, huh?" he seemed to smirk slightly. "We'll have to see what we can do about getting you a little more contact." His tone of voice and the way he ran his hand slowly down his tie disturbed me, but I pushed my discomfort aside.

"That would be great."

He nodded, smiling. "Hours a bit much?"

"Well, sometimes. But it comes with the territory, right?"

"Any other complaints?"

Was this a trick question, I wondered. "No complaints. But we did talk about my doing some pro bono work."

"Pro bono, eh?" He chuckled. "Well, sweetheart, if it'll make you feel any better, you can consider the work we do for half these young geniuses your contribution to making the world a better place."

"You mean they don't they pay their bills?" I was amazed.

"Oh, they pay all right—that's why we require a retainer *and* percentage agreements. But how many do you think actually make it?"

I knew what he was saying was true—over the last few months I'd watched one promising act after another unable to break into the business. Record companies had become like Hollywood, unwilling to take risks, willing only to invest in carbon copies or old reliables. Instead of financing young artists, they continued to pay enormous sums to a small number of megastars. The result was unproduced talent and a sluggish industry. But if I couldn't mix art with commerce, at least I could make some contribution with my pro bono work.

"There's a case I was working on at the foundation—it involves a teamsters local. No one's thought to use the RICO statute in a civil action to recover stolen pension funds and it could be groundbreaking." My enthusiasm was not catching his attention.

He cut me off. "We're up to our asses with this McCarthy business and I need your undivided energy right now. You'll have lots of opportunity to tilt at windmills once we've got this situation under control." He combined a skillful mix of reassurance and absolute control. Even though he was breaking his promise to me, there was no point in arguing. It wasn't like I had time on my hands—I barely had enough time to breathe. And he was the boss. "So what did you finish up this week?"

"The copyright stuff for the jukebox queen is done," I said. I handed him her file and the billing sheet. I picked up my coffee and barely had time to savor its expensive flavor when his mood took a seismic shift.

"I don't understand how you can bill out this much time to do her copyright work. God damn it—I can't charge her for this." Hadus threw my billing sheets back across his desk. I could feel the blood rush to my face.

"But that's what it took," I replied, startled by his unexpected attack. I had been dealing with my first "star," a woman whose songs had assisted countless seductions during the cocktail and swimming pool years of America's Camelot. It wasn't what I had expected. No matter how politely I approached her, she reacted as if I had been created solely for the purpose of annoying her. She had a lovely voice, but no more talent than scores of struggling artists who would have given anything for a fraction of the attention this woman commanded and abused. For all her glory and blessings, she'd lost her gratitude and her graciousness. Working for her left me perpetually frustrated and disenchanted. And even worse, it seemed her behavior was the too common

standard for many in the music business. The disillusionment of working with people who were less gods of music than they were gods of
arrogance was beginning to take its toll on my belief in the magic of
music.

"I keep having to redo this job. She gave me the wrong information
and then changed her mind about the material she wanted filed. And by
the way, she was very rude."

He began tapping his pen rapidly against the edge of his desk. It was
a sign I'd learned to watch for as his temper rose from its dark cave. The
frenetic movement stopped, and he erupted.

"I don't give a damn, you kiss her butt if that's what she wants. You
tell her she's God's gift to lounge lizards. All I care about is that I can't
bill for this amount of time. It's your problem, not mine. So when you
figure out what we're going to do about it, you let me know."

The phone rang and he picked it up, waving me out of the office. My
audience was over. It was my problem? I was so angry I could spit.

"These doors are thinner than they look. Next week you might want
to do your billing conference when everyone's gone home," Sharon offered as I walked out.

"Thanks for the advice. Next week I'll wear my asbestos suit," I
replied.

"You do look a little singed," she said with an edge of satisfaction.

"Take a deep breath, he's been like that all day." It was Madeline,
picking up the mail.

"Actually, he's been like that all week."

"Well, at the risk of having you quit, the truth is he's been like that
for years. Why do you think we call him the Volcano?" she whispered.

"Well, at least that means I don't have to take it personally."

"Right. And you shouldn't be upset by the diva either. She's really
very nice, she's probably just put out that he's not handling her personally."

I had a long way to go to master diva wrangling. And I did take
Hadus's remarks personally. As I headed back to my cubbyhole, I felt as
if I were turned inside out, my humiliation worn like a scarlet cloak for
all to see. It wasn't just that he was being unfair, or arbitrary, or dismis-
sive. It was the unnecessary brutality of his energy. I felt knocked off my
center, unsteady and insecure. Could I have taken less time to get the
work done? How could it be fair to hold me accountable for the behavior of a client over whom I had no control? Or was his anger about

something else entirely? Toxins of self-doubt and frustration coated me, and thinking about it was like scratching—it only made my discomfort worse.

I always worked as late as I had to, but circle night was the one evening I had managed to protect from my late night work requirements. It was my weekly vacation where the world opened in ways that money couldn't buy. But tonight I was chained to my desk. I was just beginning to be confronted by the challenge of balancing work and spiritual life—how could my two lives, with their increasingly divergent values and demands, coexist? My brain, which usually cut through the dryly efficient language like a shark through fish-filled water, was turning belly up. It was language that had a job to do, but it was beginning to sound like the possessed babblings of madmen. I felt a rush of annoyance when I finally checked my watch and discovered I had only half an hour until circle started.

I shoved the contract into my briefcase, threw on my jacket, and headed for the door. If I left now I'd just make it in time. The sounds of a woman's hysterical laughter leaked out from under the office door of one of the partners. It stopped abruptly and something pushed against the closed door with a dull thud. Standing in the dark, empty secretarial pool, staring into Hadus's cavernous office, I suddenly doubted the wisdom of my choice. What if Hadus piled more work on me and I couldn't get this contract done in time? Anxiety overwhelmed my desire, and I turned back to my office. Flipping on the light, I closed my door, took off my shoes, and opened the file.

The next morning I could hardly lift my head, so sharp was the pain from sleeping at my desk. The dawn was the color of burnished steel glowing from the fires of wounded Hephaestus, the gods' blacksmith and himself a god whose artistry was burnished on the forge of unrequited desire. My clothes were crumpled and my eyelids were sealed by the glue of overnight mascara. I felt flushed and feverish and I had missed circle, but the contract was done.

I washed my face in the ladies' room, discovering a tiny red rash covering my face and hands. Startled, I thought of the poison ivy my best friend got at camp one summer. I stared at myself in the mirror—the irritation I'd been carrying inside me was showing itself. It was magic of its own sort. Witches call poison ivy a warrior plant. Some say it's meant to keep you out of areas you ought not enter. You touch it only by accident, and even then it leaves you wounded with tormenting rashes that itch and blister, headaches that blind, fever that fills you with malaise. You may not have seen it going in, but its effects are indisputable proof of the territory you've now entered. The rash is a symptom and a warning, and surviving its assault can leave you so intoxicated that you madly think yourself immune. Madness is a quality that accompanies all of the ivies; some lead to suffering, others to ecstasy, for they are the plants of Dionysus, a god whose shadow form is thought to be the lord of the Underworld.

As I had since taking this job, I stuffed my briefcase with files to work on over the weekend. It was Saturday and the early morning streets were abandoned. I was relieved that no one would see me as I headed home. I should have been happy. I had a glamorous job. I had Jake. I had entree to a magical world of power and possibilities that most people only dreamed of. And, what a lot of people would think was most important of all, I had an affordable apartment in Manhattan. I had nothing to complain about, so why did I feel so uneasy this morning? When I got home, I put some calamine lotion on the rash and fell asleep to the sound of rain.

The following week I made sure I got to circle. The temple and the women in it were beautiful, bathed in the light of pink candles. A bouquet of pale pink roses and a basket of strawberries decorated the altar and everything was softened by a fragrant haze of floral incense that hung in the air. Maia, dressed in a deep pink silk gown, led us through our breathing and grounding, and I found myself seated again beneath my magical willow in the park. But her words drew me back to the little temple in Chelsea.

"Hand to hand I cast this circle," Maia said, taking the right hand of Bellona who sat to her left, and smiling as their eyes met.

Bellona turned to Jeanette, who was seated to her left. Clasping Jeanette's right hand as their eyes met, Bellona repeated, "Hand to hand I cast this circle."

The movement of energy was slow and went deliberately clockwise around the circle, received by each woman as she looked directly into the eyes of the woman to her right, listening to the magic words and opening herself to the gift of energy, then passed along to the woman who sat to her left as she, in turn, spoke the casting words. Around the circle went the invocation, and the encircling connection of hands and eyes and souls, something I was beginning to suspect actually existed, was made visible.

"Hand to hand I cast this circle." I spoke the magical words, taking Nonna's right hand in my left. As I looked into her eyes, a sense of joy and well-being, of tremendous strength and certainty flowed through me. Maia continued: "Circle is cast. We are between the worlds. Please close your eyes. In your mind's eye, one by one visualize the faces of all the women sitting with you in circle. As you inhale, draw the energy up from the earth. Hold the breath for a count of three, and let the energy fill your heart. Feel it opening as the energy flows into it from the earth. Imagine your heart is a red rose, and as you inhale, feel its petals opening one by one.

"Now, as you exhale, send the energy that you are feeling down your left arm and through the palm of your hand into the right hand of the woman to your left. This time as you inhale, draw the energy that is coming to you from the woman on your right through the palm of your right hand and up your arm into your heart. Let it fill your heart until you feel it opening and expanding, and then send this gift of energy to the woman on your left as you exhale. Please continue breathing deeply and fully using the movement of your breath to send the energy around. Inhale, draw the energy in. Exhale, send the energy around. Give and receive. Feel the energy moving around and around our circle. In your mind's eye, see the spinning circle of color and light."

My hands began to tingle, then my arms and chest as I felt the energy moving through me. I could sense it, see it, almost hear it like the crackling of static electricity. Round the circle it spun and I began to feel tremendous heat surrounding and filling me. With the heat came an upswelling awareness of enormous strength and solidity. Then, as if my eyes were open, I saw the faces of my sisters and felt not merely their presence, but their thoughts and feelings. Startled, I wondered if anyone else was experiencing this. And the answers came back swiftly—yes! There was delight, shyness, surprise, laughter. There were random images—of sculptures and the faces of older women; there were snatches of phrases and feelings long buried. And most of all, there was love.

"Gently release each other's hands," said Maia, "Now ground the energy: Place your palms upon the earth, your foreheads upon the earth, lie against it if you need to . . . let the power drain from your body back into the earth whence it came . . . feel it flowing down-ward . . . exhale and let the energy return to the earth . . . give thanks . . . and rest. And please be sure to eat something. You also need food to help you ground," she instructed us.

Plates of cheese and baskets of crusty breads, grapes, and apples, and the strawberries, were passed around the circle. Bottles of wine and juice were poured. We ate and drank and talked and joked about boy-friends and work and books and music. Being an only child, I began to understand what having sisters felt like.

From the moment I met her, I had felt I'd known Nonna all my life. And now, as I watched Maia chatting and laughing, I was beginning to know her too. She had a hot temper which I had seen flare more than once—at a rude customer, or the ceremonial magic group that would often leave the temple in disarray after using it. But her earthy warmth was as nourishing as her blazing anger could be frightening. Her educa-tion had stopped at high school, yet she was bright; her upbringing was clearly working-class, but her carriage regal. During circle, Maia was commanding and sublime, but before and after, she could giggle and chatter like a schoolgirl. She was fully human, embracing contradic-tions and embodying the rich complexity from which a life was created.

"The circle," Maia said, "is a way to contain magical energy for the purposes of doing spell work. It also keeps out external energies that can affect you while you're in an altered state of consciousness. When we work within a circle, there are a number of very important practices that you must all observe in order not to disrupt or destroy the energy within the circle. The first is that all movement is in one direction. Generally, that direction is deosil, or clockwise. This is the direction of increase. When we work with energy within circle, we want it always to move one way; think of it like stirring a pot—your mothers probably taught you that you should always stir in one direction. This is the same idea. So, we walk deosil, pass things deosil, offer libations deosil. Only when we are doing a banishing circle do we move widdershins, or coun-terclockwise, the direction of decrease."

"Once we begin working, you should try to remain in circle until we've finished," Bellona added. "To leave a circle, or reenter a circle, you must cut-out in order not to break the integrity of the container we've created." She moved her arm in an arc from left to right. "This is how we create an opening, and you must seal it behind you when you exit or reenter." She moved her hand horizontally three times across the space where she had made the arc.

"While a cast circle can be a barrier against external negative energy, it's also a means of containing sacred energy, which is very important to certain aspects of magical work. Think of boiling a pot of water," Maia resumed teaching. "When you boil water you create steam, which is a form of energy or power. Obviously, you can't boil water without a container. Similarly, in order to do magic, we must create or raise energy. And when we raise energy within a circle, by breath, chant, dance, or many other means which you'll learn, the energy must be contained within a cast circle. A circle is a cauldron of energy in which we may prepare spells, potions, and even ourselves for healing, love, money, guidance, transformation, or any number of life-enhancing goals."

Nonna picked up the silver bowl in the center of the altar and began to speak: "The magical circle is also a symbol of the Goddess. It's a profound symbol of interconnection, and an expression of how we experience and use power. In the Old Religion all are equal. The priestesses are teachers who share their wisdom and their skills so others can learn to make use of them for themselves. Priestesses are honored and respected as elders, but no one stands above another in the circle, no one has sole authority to interpret divine wisdom. That's a gift that everyone who practices the Old Ways experiences themselves. The Goddess assumes an infinite variety of forms and yet all are joined in the circle, just as we are.

"And as a symbol or form of the Goddess, the circle is an expression of the cyclical movement of divine energy, as well as the Goddess's nurturing and other feminine qualities. You will experience these as we continue to work together. In Western culture, most people are raised to believe that, at best, they have a weekly appointment with God at his place of business. They must go to a specific building at a specific time to worship him under the guidance of his particular executive representative—be it priest, rabbi, minister, or mullah. For Wiccans, everything is sacred, so 'worship,'" Nonna crooked the second and third fingers of both hands several times, making quotation marks in the air, "is possible anywhere and anytime. No building is required, only the casting of a circle to demarcate a sacred meeting place between the worlds where the Divine can be encountered."

And then Maia closed our circle, having us again take hands until she said:

"The Goddess is alive, magic is afoot. Our circle is open, but never broken. Merry meet, and merry part, and merry meet again. Blessed be."

I was running on the adrenaline of the day's usual intensity, fielding calls and plowing through paperwork, when Hadus suggested dinner with an important client as a reward for my efforts. It was circle night, a night that had become more and more important to me. This night, however, we would be starting later than usual and so I accepted.

When the cab pulled up in front of one of New York's most elite restaurants, I knew the reservations had been made weeks ago. But, as was Hadus's style, it was sprung on me as a last-minute surprise. An offer I couldn't refuse. And why would I want to? After all, this was a coup, an acknowledgment of how hard I'd worked, and how much I'd contributed. Or, I wondered as his hand rested too long on the small of my back while we walked to our table, maybe I was just window dressing, or worse, an implicit sexual trophy.

During the brief business conversation, I attempted to contribute legal strategies I had presented to Hadus only hours ago. My foreboding feelings worsened as Hadus swiftly appropriated one strategy and condescendingly dismissed another, which he had greeted with appreciation in the privacy of his office. Now, ignored and invisible, I sat quietly as Hadus and the client discussed their expensive watches, golf games, and parties in the Hamptons. The exquisite food and setting were spoiled by the sorrowful flavor of humiliation.

The evening wore on and my anxiety grew as the cocktails and bottles of wine began to affect Hadus. Though I sat with my spine as straight as my conversation, Hadus spoke to me, and about me, with an air of proprietary intimacy. Until this evening, our exchanges had been, as promised, strictly business, but now I couldn't help but wonder if dinner was a mistake. When the dessert menu finally arrived and they ordered brandies, I excused myself. Hadus kissed my hand when I stood to leave, his fingers moist and sticky. He was charming and drunk, but as he squeezed my fingers, I sensed he was seething at the frustration of his intentions.

I worried in the cab down to circle. Should I have refused to go in the first place? Was it unprofessional of me to leave? Was that familiar, frightening vibe I'd gotten from Hadus real or imagined? The musky smell of brandy clung to my fingers and with it I caught the scent of another obscure emotion I'd picked up—an unexpected weakness, a vulnerability he'd never shown. Shuddering, I wondered: Was it his vulnerability, or my own? Possession, control, domination—those qualities I remembered too well, but beneath his anger tonight I sensed a desperate and unfamiliar need. For what? I wondered as the cab stopped in front of the Magical Cauldron.

I rushed into the sanctuary, relieved to discover that circle hadn't started. It was the first full moon after the Spring Equinox and the women were laughing, intoxicated by the gentleness of the night air. I shed my work clothes and quickly slipped into the soothing silk of the long white dress I had bought for circle. Warmth and safety encircled me and, slowly, I began to relax.

The room was lit by lavender candles. A marble statue of a goddess holding a basket filled with fruits and flowers presided over the altar, which was covered with the flowers of spring—violets, crocuses, forsythia, daffodils, tulips—and the brightly colored eggs we had painted the week before. In front of the statue was a large silver bowl, and in front of that, nestled between the flowers, in a line from left to right, were representations of the four elements. First was the element of air, represented by a brazier from which billowed clouds of the sweet-smelling full moon incense, spiraling upward and filling the room with a delicious haze. Next to the brazier burned a yellow candle in a silver candlestick, representing fire. Two small silver bowls sat to the right of the candle. One was filled with water, and the other, lined with glass, was filled with rock salt, a symbol of earth.

Nonna was explaining the origins of Easter. "The word *Easter* comes from the name of the German goddess of fertility, Eostre, or Oestara, and the Slavic earth goddess Ostra," Nonna explained. "And why do you think we have Easter egg hunts, and bunnies everywhere?" She pointed to the colored eggs that decorated our altar. "These were the ancient symbols of the Goddess and her gifts of fertility at this time of rebirth. The Catholic Church timed the beginning of Easter to coincide with the first Sunday after the first full moon following the Spring Equinox, another remnant of the Old Religion just below the surface of the new. This is the time of year to celebrate the rebirth of life. And the circle, the egg, is a symbol of this cycle of sacred renewal. The very act of casting a circle, of sitting in circle, rather than all lined up in church pews, is an expression of the Divine Feminine Principle. The circle is not just a living symbol of the Goddess, it is an embodiment of the

Goddess. So let us begin." Nonna knelt before the altar. She wore a long dress of red silk that fell in folds around her like the petals of a great red rose.

Nonna closed her eyes and we followed her example, joining our breaths to each other, and our bodies to the earth we sat upon. A gentle *Om* rose and fell and we opened our eyes to see Nonna stand, wand in hand. She walked to the east, raised her hazelwood wand and pointed into the darkness. As she spoke, she walked slowly, gracefully yet commandingly, three times clockwise around the circle, her wand lifted before her, a small thin line of flickering blue light trailing from its crystal tip.

"I conjure thee a circle of art, I conjure thee a circle of power, I conjure thee a boundary and a protection between the worlds of the mighty ones and the worlds of mortals. I conjure thee a sacred circle to preserve and to contain the energy that we shall raise herein. And as I do will it, so mote it be."

As she encircled us with her words and her intent, we took hands, eyes meeting. The temperature in the temple soared, and little beads of perspiration slid between my breasts.

"Circle is cast. We are between the worlds." A thrill shot through me when I heard that magical phrase, which was always spoken at the conclusion of casting a sacred circle. It meant that through the use of magical ritual we had journeyed from one world to another. All magical work begins with the casting of a circle. No matter how it is accomplished—by the taking of hands or the traversal of a priestess using wand or blade, feather or bone, speaking traditional verse or the spontaneous wisdom of the heart—casting a circle is the ancient demarcation of sacred space, and it is the beginning of altering one's consciousness.

As our priestesses began to formally cast the circles, I realized I was ready to experience ritual as more than superstitious mumbo jumbo. I began to recognize that this final utterance marked the completion of a profound transition from the mundane world to the sacred. It was an essential part of the magic of changing one's consciousness, enabling us to see the sacred to which we were too often blind. I had discovered that ritual, as these wise women were teaching us to create it, was an enacted meditation. Ritual was a sacred art, like a living mandala—the symbolic, geometric diagram incorporating a square within a circle—which is used for meditation in Eastern mystical traditions of India and Tibet. As a focus for meditation, mandalas enlighten human beings to the presence of the divine in the world around us. And ritual, complete with gestures, poetic invocations, incense and other sundry props, was an exquisite tool to effectuate that enlightenment. All were part of a symbolic language that had begun to resonate in the depth of my being, speaking to an aspect of my mind that, until now, I barely knew existed. My unconscious was being given a vocabulary with which to communicate to the conscious me. I was learning a language that spoke to my heart. And to what my priestesses referred to as "the Goddess."

We took hands as Nonna began singing:

"We are a circle, within a circle
With no beginning and never ending"

It was a simple chant and we picked it up quickly, swaying gently as we sang, over and over again. The sound grew and subsided, then grew again, mesmerizing us. Utterly average voices blended into exquisite harmony, then broke apart into a round that spurred the sound into a dizzying circle of energy. Words disappeared into syllables which broke into fragments of sound that hung suspended like feathers floating in the air, then suddenly they began to spin back together, taking shape again like a bird of paradise. Finally, our voices disappeared into an unknown vanishing point in another dimension of reality, and together we stopped, all at once, as had become our frequent though utterly mysterious practice. My entire body was vibrating from the effects of the sound. We sat in silence.

"Please lie back, breathe, and relax," said Nonna.

The Persian carpet was as soft as cat's fur against my shoulders, my fingertips, the rounded backs of my calves. I lay on the floor of the temple, deeply relaxed. My mind drifted and I smiled to myself, feeling as if the carpet and I could lift off at any moment.

"Tonight you will take an important step in the art of magical visualization. Your eyes and your minds are filters which alter your perception of reality. . . . You will learn to remove the blindfold and see the Paradise in which we live . . . to open yourself to the presence of the divine. . . . Feel the blindfold that covers your eyes . . . remove it. . . . As you open your eyes you find you are no longer in the temple. . . . You are lying in a green field, white clouds float in the blue sky overhead. . . . As you sit up, you see a flaming blue star burning brightly before you . . . this is a portal into the realm of the Goddess. . . . It grows larger and larger as you approach it. . . . You step through it, feeling its power as if you had stepped through a wall of electricity. . . . Look down at your hands, your arms, see the dancing energy which is your body . . . look up, you are in the field, at one with grass, clouds, sky, sun, all are a radiant dancing play of movement, of shifting light waves and colors, combining and breaking apart. . . ."

Nonna continued, leading us into a sacred dance in which matter became particles and particles became waves of energy which returned to particles and then to clouds and grass and women. And when Nonna was silent, images appeared spontaneously and delightfully, summoned by our own individual nascent powers. Finally, she brought us back through the flaming blue pentacle, back into our bodies, back into the temple.

It was a lovely and curious exercise, and I wondered about the images that had floated in and out of my mind. Stretching, I noticed Gillian sitting with her head bowed.

"Are you O.K.?" I asked her softly. Perhaps because we seemed to share so much—background, education, professional jobs—we had become confidantes, calling each other on the phone, lunching together at restaurants near our offices, double-dating. She looked up at me and there were tears in her eyes. I put my arm around her shoulders. "What happened to you?"

Tears ran down her cheeks. "I'm all right. I'm just—I don't know . . . at the end, before she brought us back, I thought I saw it."

"Saw what?"

"The Grail, I thought I saw the Grail," she whispered.

"A grail? You mean like a goblet?" She nodded. "What did it look like? Was it silver, sort of floating in the air?"

"You saw it too?"

I nodded, a rush of goose bumps flying across my skin. "It was filled with light, running over the sides like water."

"Yes, like glowing water. It was as if the sun was rising out of the top of it." Gillian and I turned, startled to hear Onatah's gentle voice. "I don't remember Nonna describing it, do you?"

"No, she didn't."

"I saw it just before I came back through the flaming star. It appeared and then disappeared just like that." Marcia snapped her fingers.

By now the rest of the circle was listening to us. Jeanette had seen a large cauldron. Mindy had seen just the shining water, and Naomi had seen the sun rising over the ocean. Annabelle had also seen a goblet.

The priestesses exchanged looks and Nonna explained, smiling like a proud grandmother. "The goblet you saw is the legendary Holy Grail. It is an ancient Celtic symbol of the Goddess Sovereignty, the spirit of the sacred earth. The cauldron is another form of the Grail. It's called the Cauldron of Cerridwen. These visions are signs of your progress. We're ready to move on," she said with a nod to Maia and Bellona.

As the laughing conversations swirled around me, I remembered the story of Cerridwen's cauldron—a magical cauldron into which the bodies of slain warriors were placed in order to be given new life. Cerridwen is an ancient Celtic goddess, and her cauldron is the symbol of the Goddess's mysterious powers of rebirth. She lived on an island in the middle of Lake Tegid in Wales. There she lived all alone but for her two children, a beautiful daughter named Creidwy and a son named Afagdu who was so ugly that no one would play with him.

The Goddess grieved for her son's misfortune and so she thought to herself, I will make a magical potion for my beloved son and though his form is hideous, his soul will be beautiful, for I will bestow upon him the gifts of wisdom and intelligence.

And so Cerridwen set about to make the magic potion. She brought out her cauldron, huge and black and round. She filled it with sacred herbs and precious liquids, with chervil and vervain, with the songs of birds, and the laughter of children, and the stories of heroines and poets. She brought jars of water from her sacred wellspring and finally, when the cauldron was full, she lit a fire beneath it, using huge logs of oak and ash and thorn.

Thirteen full moons and a day would pass before the potion would be ready. The day approached, and Cerridwen knew she would have to leave the cauldron to find the last ingredient: the first narcissus to bloom beneath the last full moon. Whom could she trust who would not steal the precious liquid?

She chose a little boy named Gwion and warned him not to touch the cauldron's contents, for not a drop could be lost or the spell would be broken. She gave him a huge broom handle and told him to stir it carefully. And stir he did, standing upon the hewn trunk of an ancient oak. But a log broke in half, and the fire, escaping its wooden prison, leapt upward, making the cauldron's contents boil and bubble and splatter. Three drops flew from the great black vessel and burned poor Gwion's fingers. He howled in pain and quickly stuck his fingers in his mouth.

His eyes grew wide and he trembled where he stood, for suddenly he heard everything in the world and knew the mysteries of the ages. He saw the future and understood the past. And with his sacred vision he knew that when she returned Cerridwen would be furious that a mortal now possessed the gifts intended for her son.

He dropped the broom and fled, changing himself into a hare so Cerridwen would not find him. But though he ran and though he hid, Cerridwen knew and pursued him. She transformed herself into a greyhound, her red jaws snapping just inches from his white tail. He changed into a fish and jumped into the river; she became an otter, and swam swiftly in pursuit. He became a mourning dove, and she became a hawk; he became a grain of wheat, and she became a hen.

She fell upon him, and gobbled him down, but as she returned to her form as the great Goddess, he became a child within her. For nine months she carried him and finally, when he was born, she could do him no harm and so set him afloat in a magical cradle upon the shining waters.

He was found by a prince, who named him Taliesin and raised him as his son. Even as a young child he was a poet of such gifts that wise men and fools traveled from all over to hear him. His poetry sang the struggles of humanity, the sweetness of the land, the journey of the soul, the mystery of death and rebirth, the eternal turning of the wheel and the infinite shifting of forms, and the poet's initiation by the Goddess who is the Muse and from whose cauldron all blessings flow.

As we were gathering our belongings, putting on our shoes, and saying our good nights, wrapping each other in loving hugs, I pulled a Tarot card from a display deck at the front desk. The power of divine confirmation electrified me as I stared at the Ace of Cups—the perfect image of the Holy Grail floating above azure waves, radiant water flowing over its sides and a sun rising from its center. I would use this image for my meditations and visualizations during the next cycle of the moon.

The essential quality of the circle we had cast was its equality and interdependency. But it was much more—I could see that when we combined our energies in a circle, we were far stronger than when we were alone, and we could experience the movement of energy in astonishing ways. I felt myself joined to the earth and to the other women and profoundly empowered by these connections. I knew what the earth and the circle gave me, but I still wondered what I gave in return. I came to know the circle as an organic and feminine form, as the meeting place where two worlds unite; it is where the unseen is seen and the seen reveals its true and sacred nature. I was beginning to realize that all that exists is sacred, and I also realized that we were not "creating" sacred space, so much as revealing to ourselves the sacred nature of the space we occupy. I was learning to move between the worlds.

Though it was almost dawn, I decided to walk home. I was struck by the simultaneity of darkness and light, of the tall buildings and the long shadows they cast at sunrise, of the homeless on the street corners where limousines awaited their well-heeled occupants, giddy after a night of partying. I witnessed the polarity but I sensed within it an extraordinary wisdom. Everything in the world was far from perfect, but there was something enlightening about the energy inherent in this chiaroscuro contradiction: The darkness defines the shape light assumes, negation expresses the possibility of what *should* be. In knowing this, I realized if we are ready to see the unseen—if we have the courage to face the shadows we normally seek to avoid—we can create what *could* be. In the face of everyday tragedies, the very possibility of healing and of transformation made my heart sing.

The universe responded to my shift in consciousness with magic of its own: As I rounded the corner, heading toward home, I found in the dirty window of an old antique shop, barely noticeable for all the years of collected city soot, a silver chalice, the symbol of the Goddess. I bought it as soon as the shop opened the next day, and it became my first magical tool.

Air & Fire,
Water & Earth

Where shall we get religion? Beneath the open sky,
The sphere of crystal silence surcharged with deity . . .
The midnight earth sends incense up, sweet with the breath
of prayer—
Go out beneath the naked night and get religion there.
—SAM WALTER FOSS, **Nature and Religion**

I believe a leaf of grass is no less than the journey-work of
the stars.

WALT WHITMAN, **Leaves of Grass**

Bellona stood before the altar clasping her athame, a ritual double-hilted dagger, to the hollow between her breasts. The six-inch blade pointed down and the black handle was marked with symbols—Witches' runes, Nonna had called them. I didn't know what they meant but I knew the athame was a symbol of the air element and the powers of the mind—both logical and intuitive—and was used to point and direct energy. It was dramatic and a little frightening but Nonna had assured us that it was never used to harm or to take life. And as I watched Bellona handle it with easy confidence, it seemed also to be a symbol of power retrieved and redeemed by the use to which it was now being put by a woman.

Swiftly she raised the blade, decisively cutting the billowing smoke above the brazier. "I purify and consecrate this creature of air, that all good may enter herein in the name of Nike, winged goddess of victory."

Again she carved the air in an indecipherable gesture, this time over and through the flame that drew itself into a long thin yellow line struggling to lick the point of her blade.

"I purify and consecrate this creature of fire, that all good may enter herein in the name of Amaterasu, goddess of courgeous illumination."

Next she dipped the blade into the shining bowl of water. "I purify and consecrate this creature of water that all good may enter herein in the name of Yemanja, goddess of nurturing waters."

The little grains of sea salt in the bowl rattled as she moved the blade through them. "I purify and consecrate this creature of earth that all good may enter herein in the name of Brigantia, goddess of the sacred land."

Bellona lifted the brazier by its long metal chain and walked to the eastern quarter of the circle, facing away from us and outward to the enveloping darkness of the surrounding temple. She raised the brazier aloft and began to walk deosil, clockwise, around the circle.

"I purify and consecrate this sacred circle with the power of this sweet air, blessing us with the gifts of imagination, wonder, and laughter."

She circled around us once, leaving a ring of shimmering smoke behind her. I inhaled the fragrant air, stretching the movement of each breath so time slowed and my mind cleared like a shining mountain lake. Bellona returned the burning incense to the altar. Maia handed her the candle and Bellona again walked to the east where she held the burning flame aloft. Slowly, commandingly, she encircled us with the dancing flame.

"I purify and consecrate this sacred circle with the power of fire, blessing us with the gifts of passion, courage, and will." As she passed by, I felt a wave of heat envelop me. The temperature in the room seemed to climb as she returned the candle to the altar. Maia then handed Bellona the silver water bowl. Again Bellona walked to the east, then raised the shining bowl to some unseen watcher and again, walking slowly, speaking carefully, she carried it, clockwise, around the outside of the circle of seated women.

"I purify and consecrate this sacred circle with the power of these gentle waters, blessing us with the gifts of healing, love, and compassion." She dipped her fingers into the water, sprinkling each of us. We jumped and giggled as the chill struck us. Bellona grinned and I enjoyed how easily these women mixed joy with solemnity. It was their willingness to laugh that enabled me to accept their seriousness. Without it I would have probably succumbed to the discomfort I had felt whenever they began to ritualize. Laughter and poetry and all that they implied about freedom, spontaneity, and truth, were my keys to the castle where the Grail was kept.

"I purify and consecrate and ground this sacred circle with the power of earth, blessing us with the gifts of fertility, creativity, and form." The salt pinged against the wooden floors as Bellona cast it decisively before her.

I felt the solidity of my body and sensed the strength of the women who sat with me.

All four elements had now been carried once, clockwise, around the circle, beginning and ending in the east. Bellona again took her athame from the altar.

"Please rise and face east."

She walked, deosil, to the east and we all stood with her, facing outward into the darkness waiting for some unfamiliar light to illumine our slumbering psyches. The sun was about to rise.

Bellona raised her arms and, in a voice filled with confidence, she summoned forces I had never realized existed until that moment.

> "I summon, stir, and call ye up
> Mighty ones of the east,
> Ancient powers of air,
> Powers of wonder and imagination,
> To witness our rites and guard our circle
> In the name of Nike, winged goddess of glorious messages
> Hail and welcome."

As she spoke her knife carved the air. Her gestures spread grandly before us and I realized that she was drawing the shape of a star. In five swift, decisive movements with her flashing blade, she carved a portal through which the ancient airy powers of the east would now enter our circle and our minds, stirring them, teaching them, opening and challenging and enlightening them with images and questions, ideas, and inspirations from a realm of magic that had patiently awaited our invitation.

Bellona moved next to the south. She raised her athame and began to speak. We too faced south and, following her example, raised our arms upward. Some raised just their right arms, hands outstretched; others raised both arms, palms up. I was most comfortable with my right arm upraised and my palm up as if to receive the hand of a friend, and my left arm down but slightly angled, my fingers pointing earthward. In this way I felt myself somehow connected to both heaven and earth, the "other" world, and my "own." I later learned that this was the traditional posture of the magician, who unites both realms in her, or his, being.

Bellona sliced another opening between the worlds and again she spoke the archaic yet stirring words, this time declared as a warrior's challenge:

> *"I summon, stir, and call ye up*
> *Mighty ones of the south,*
> *Ancient powers of fire*
> *Powers of courage and passion,*
> *To witness our rites*
> *And guard our circle*
> *In the name of Amaterasu, august goddess of the sun's rapture*
> *Hail and welcome."*

As she spoke, I envisioned a flaming red star appearing before us and through it I saw a vast and burning desert. A tawny lion, her muscles rippling, approached us. The sun was an enormous orange fire ball in a white sky shimmering with heat. A surge of determination ignited within me and I felt the strength of my convictions like a blazing star to guide me.

Bellona walked next to the western quarter of our circle, and we turned with her. Again she carved a starry portal in the darkness, but this time her gestures and her tone of voice were gentle, soft, and welcoming.

> *"I summon, stir, and call ye up*
> *Mighty ones of the west,*
> *Ancient powers of water*
> *Powers of love and compassionate healing,*
> *To witness our rites*
> *and guard our circle*

In the name of Yemanja, voluptuous goddess of the dreaming
waters
Hail and welcome."

Through the blue star before me I saw an emerald ocean where whales and dolphins, tortoises, and otters played together. I saw a woman, standing in the waves, her belly full of life, waters pouring forth from between her legs, and in the waters were carried forth all the life that lived upon our miraculous planet. I thought suddenly of my mother, who was struggling each day to care for my ailing father, of her love and strength, her nurturing and good humor. I tasted salty tears as they reminded me that we have all been born from the ocean womb of what Nonna called the Great Mother.

Bellona had already begun her invocation in the north. I turned, joining the others, as she finished speaking:

"I summon, stir, and call ye up,
 Mighty ones of the north,
 Ancient powers of the earth
 Powers of fertility and form,
 To witness our rites
 And guard our circle
 In the name of Brigantia, sovereign Goddess of the fertile earth.
 Hail and welcome."

The feelings that had overwhelmed me in the west ebbed as I stared through the green star. Visions raced before my mind's eye: rich brown fields filled with golden wheat, orchards of ripe apples, a huge bear lumbering down the side of a pine-covered mountain, two cubs ambling at her side, a herd of buffalo thundering across a vast plain. I found myself suddenly aware of the tangible power of my body, and the simple and exquisite pleasures it gave me through all of my physical senses. I realized that my body not only housed my intelligence and courage, it had intelligence and courage of its own. It was the temple of my soul and my soul's form. My body had been born and had the extraordinary power to give birth, to create and to sustain life, like the earth itself. Like the Goddess.

Together, we turned once again to the east for a final salutation. Bellona then turned to us and said:

"Our circle is cast. We are between the worlds."

I felt alert, powerful, filled with love—and I had a bear's appetite. We were starting to become very creative with our post-circle feasts— the flavors, the textures, and colors were as extraordinary as if prepared by the finest chefs. I suspected it was because my senses were heightened by our circles. We all ate heartily but I noticed that Jeanette would take small portions of the sweetest and most fattening foods, then refill her plate repeatedly, as if no one would notice how much she was eating, or wonder what emptiness she was struggling to fill.

Nonna wasn't with us tonight, and I missed her, but as we feasted, Bellona provided tonight's lesson: "Casting circle, where you fully visualize and meditate on each of the four directions—the qualities, powers, animals, or totems, and wisdom of each—is a very powerful act of magic. You should practice invoking, visualizing, and meditating on each element. Set up an altar, in the appropriate quarter of your home, using the colors, symbols, tools, images, and goddesses for that element."

The experience of being in circle had become more intense since we'd begun to purify the elements and invoke the four directions. While it took longer to formally cast the circle, it also facilitated an aesthetic and effective shifting of my attention away from the chores and cares of the day to the sacred undertaking at hand. The words, gestures, symbolism, and the repetitive use of all of these, quickened a change in my thinking: Ritual was becoming an effective technique to change my consciousness at will, making me more aware of the magical and sacred nature of the world.

I was being given a mystical compass that would guide my magical journey, and in the casting of the circle and the invocation of the four directions, I found the model of our spiritual course: beginning in the east, the realm of airy inspiration, moving to the south with its fiery will of power and passion, then to the west, where we learn to temper our power with compassion, love, and feeling for others, and then to the north, where, having traveled the circular road, we can now give form and expression to our lives. Moving clockwise, we return again to the east, the direction of wisdom, to learn from our travels, our travails, and our changes, and to set out again, just as each day the sun rises anew, on another circular journey of discovery. And in the center of the circle, where the priestess stood before the altar, was spirit.

Harmonizing all four, and ultimately five, aspects of our humanity—

mind, will, emotions, body, and soul—is essential to the holistic integrity of our character, for in the Old Religion, all are equally valuable. Each quality needs to be developed in relation to the others so the personality is one of dynamic, not static, balance. This work is the heart of ancient "alchemy," something most people today think of as the impossible, magical practice of changing base metals into gold. Alchemy is actually an ancient metaphor system describing the spiritual work of transforming the dross, or base metal, of an unbalanced, spiritually disconnected personality into the gold of a spiritually enlightened being. Through this process, the individual participates in her, or his, own metamorphosis, and is awakened to her, or his, role in the divine co-creation of the world.

Unfortunately, our culture has dismissed the religions and metaphors of Native Americans, aborigines, Witches, and other indigenous earth religions as primitive pantheism in which trees, and rocks, and springs were superstitiously worshiped. Oblivious to its own prejudices, our Western world demeans their religion as an idolatrous, frightened inability to know the one "true," transcendent God. Erroneously dismissed as godlessness, paganism is actually just the opposite: It is a spirituality in which everything in the natural world is experienced as holy. *Pagan,* I had learned, comes from the Latin and simply meant one who lived in the country. *Heathen,* a term so often and pejoratively applied to Native Americans, originally referred to someone British who lived on the heath. These were people who lived close to the earth, intimate with her changing seasons, her generosity, and her mystery. It was from this familiarity, not fear, that their knowledge of the sacred arose.

The metaphors for the divine used by these ancient earth religions were often those of goddesses, the symbols of seed and sickle, flower and fruit. But these symbols were more than mere metaphors, for the sacred wisdom of these forms, and their changes, was experienced—seen, heard, smelled, touched, and tasted—as the infinite manifestation of the divine. The people of the earth beheld and revered the body of the sacred in wind, wolf, river, wheat, and moon. They knew they lived upon hallowed ground and that, as an embodiment of the divine, nature was a spiritual teacher of infinite wisdom. Contrary to the old Western patriarchal interpretations of the divine as transcendent and the earth as fallen from grace, they believed that the body and the earth were sacred, so neither required conquest or denial. The body, and the earth, are not only temples of the spirit, but its living manifestation. The wisdom of the body and the earth is the spirit's wisdom, and therefore to be revered.

With each circle, each day that passed, I was traveling deeper into a sacred landscape and learning the language of this realm. The elements were an important part of that vocabulary; they were a metaphor system that described the nature or characteristics of energy as it took form in the world around us: Air was the gaseous state, water was liquid, earth was solid, fire was energy. Spirit was the point at the center where all of these combined; it was the nature of reality at its quantum level. The elements also described aspects of ourselves as beings of energy.

In a magical circle, each direction or quarter corresponds to an element and a range of human and natural qualities. Specific colors, animals, magical tools, and powers are also associated with each direction, as are times of the day, positions of the sun, and seasons. These correspondences describe a sacred relationship between humanity, nature, and the divine, and were the vocabulary with which I was learning to express my experiences and perceptions. Through the beauty of poetic metaphor, I was discovering that one could truly understand and appreciate the world, not merely through science and logic, but through aesthetic response. These metaphors were portals into the realm of the numinous.

In this world of sacred revelation, winds are the bringers of messages. They contain the last breaths of all who have gone before, and rush to greet the newborn and carry her cries, and her laughter, to her parents' waiting ears. They foretell the Goddess's seasonal transformations, carry forth a young man's songs of struggle and faith, and whisper the secrets of a yearning heart. They bear messages of prophecy sent by a living universe and, when one is ready, they blow open the gates of Paradise with an invitation to enter.

Ancient Phoenicians, renowned as astonishing sailors, offered saffron to the sylphs and zephyrs of Ashtoreth, goddess of fertility, and to the moon, silver orb of the unconscious that rules the tides of wind and sea, of women's bodies and humanity's soul. Witches still use saffron to summon these airy spirits, which will respond to the subtlest summonings of the heart, the aspirations of the soul, and the viscerally wise demands of the body. If you pay attention, they will tell you which path to take when a fork appears in the road.

On the brink of summer, pale and shimmering, the sylphs flew between steel-gray towers, lifting skirts and reminding women who had been married too long or not at all, that they were beautiful. Zephyrs sped through the canyons of the city, ripping the financial pages from the wintery grips of anxious businessmen and filling their tobacco-stale nostrils with the arousing scent of apple blossoms, lilacs, and women. Magic was in the air.

But our offices, of course, were airtight. Skyscrapers had windows you looked out of, not windows you opened. We were safely ensconced in our bell jars, while processed air was filtered into our cubbyholes through the metal grates of hot-air heaters and air conditioners. It had no scent, no moisture, no message. Like the fluorescent lights with their unworldly glow, this trapped oxygen was lifeless. Despite the adrenalizing pressure of phone calls, contracts, and meetings, I began to feel as if some unknown tranquilizer accompanied the funneled air into our offices, and my mind would grow hazy after several hours in the enclosed space. Something vital was missing from this man-made environment.

It was late in the afternoon and I yawned and stretched, impulsively deciding to take my work and my belated lunch out of doors. It was late in the afternoon by the time I settled in beneath my green willow in the park. I thought back to the day's frustrations—Sharon's increasing hostilities, a client's temperamental airs, Hadus on the brink of some explosion. Something was wrong in this business paradise to which I devoted so much of my life. There was a tightness about almost everyone in the office, a strange mixture of anger, fear, hunger, and sadness. Something was missing and no matter how hard they pushed, they couldn't find the missing piece. There was always exuberance when a deal closed, or when an important new client was signed, but the high seemed to evaporate almost immediately, replaced by an appetite that never seemed satisfied. Rapacity always reasserted itself.

Let go of it, I reminded myself. I closed my eyes and settled into the sultry cushion of sun-warmed air filled with the music of the park—a mother singing with her child, the merry-go-round calliope in the distance, the boom boxes that rose and fell as they passed on adolescent shoulders. And the songs of the trees—their perfect unintended harmony of catbird and cardinal accompanied by the rustle of leaves. I opened my eyes and opened a file, but a sudden gust of wind seized the pages, lifting them aloft like doves exploding from a cage. I ran, frantically trying to snatch them up before they disappeared. An old woman stooped gingerly to help me and a small child joined in, laughing with delight at this new game. Breathless and sticky with early summer sweat, I collapsed on a bench, holding the disheveled, disordered pile.

"Can we do it again?" the little boy asked.

"Not right now." I had to smile. "Maybe tomorrow. Thank you."

"Thank you. Bye." And he ran off.

Meticulously I began to place the contract pages back in their correct order. The section on warranties and indemnifications followed by the stipulation of state law followed by . . . I nearly dropped my hard won mess. The universe had sent me a message, a magical message: A blue-lined sheet of notebook paper had been added to my pile. Carefully handwritten were the final lines of the cryptic poem *Kubla Khan*. Its obscure and exotic references held me fascinated and I remained convinced they were clues to my journey. The lines were followed by a student's interpretation of the artist's poetic visions received in an opium dream, marked by a teacher's oblivious red reminders about punctuation and spelling:

Weave a circle round him thrice,
And close your eyes with holy dread,
For he on honeydew hath fed,
And drunk the milk of Paradise.

Had the winds heard my heart? These magical lines seemed like an invocation of love, but it wasn't love waiting for me when I got back to the office. My calm and clarity were instantly shattered by Hadus, appearing in the doorway of his office.

"Am I paying you to chitchat?" he snapped at Sharon, who quickly got off the phone. "Inside," he directed me. "I want you to sit in on this negotiation. And you," he pointed to Sharon, "if you can find a moment to steal from your important private life, call Harrison, then get in here and take notes."

He was ransacking his desk as I took my usual seat facing him. The room was suffocatingly close, and it seemed too small to contain his overwrought figure. His eyes darted wildly over papers and files that he threw to the floor in frustration. "Where's the McCarthy partnership file?" he hissed at me. I grabbed it from Sharon's desk and handed it to him.

He tossed the unopened file onto his desk and leaned back in his chair, furiously tapping the desk with his pen as he picked up the phone. His negotiating technique, used by many in the business, was simple and straightforward—loudest wins. I was learning that in Hadus's world, all that really mattered was who had the power and how much they were willing to pay, or give up, to get it. He'd mastered the art of illusion—in this business, an artist, an actor, a song, a painting had value only if people thought it did, regardless of any intrinsic value. And without the power to dominate, there was no value at all. Hadus's game started with seduction but almost always ended with sheer force.

Even though Hadus had me working interminable hours redlining drafts, he'd never really explained what the deal was all about, or rather, what the power positions of the parties really were. As far as he was concerned, as an associate, I didn't need to know. I was supposed to learn by example, by doing. But what I was required to do at work taught me very different lessons than those I was learning in circle. If survival of the fittest, in the worst sense, was required of me, I wondered how I would ever fit in. Worse, I wondered whether in my drive to succeed, I would start behaving the same way, adapting to the demands of my surroundings and playing the game by their rules.

Wasn't there another approach that could accomplish the same goals? I wondered how our lone female partner had made it, though I'd heard she was worse than Hadus. When I arrived, it never occurred to me how much I would appreciate a gesture of support or solidarity from her. Months had passed and, as the difficulties of being a young woman in such a highly competitive and aggressive field accumulated, I realized how valuable that fellowship would be. In law school the women professors had warned us that we would have to be twice as good as the men to be considered half as qualified. I was also learning that it meant we had to be twice as tough.

"So, that's where it stands," Hadus was barking into the phone. "At the eleventh hour you're telling me that unless we bend over the deal is dead. Well, maybe you've forgotten it doesn't work that way." He was at top volume now, which signaled that he was drawing to a conclusion. I watched as anger flowed out of the receiver, jumping onto Hadus's face, running down his arm, coating him with little red sparks that jumped off his body and crackled into the room. Sharon stirred in her seat and her dress snapped with electricity. It seeped under the door and we heard a crash and cursing as something shattered on the marble floor outside.

"If your boys think we're gonna roll over, tell them they've picked the wrong gang to screw with. We'll see you burn in hell first." He slammed down the phone and turned to Sharon. The room was blistering hot and I realized the air conditioner wasn't working.

"A letter goes out now to that scumbag. I'm gonna rip his heart out and feed it to him for lunch." Sharon and I sat frozen in our seats, watching his chair hit the wall as he flew out of it. "Let's go. I mean now. You," he snapped at me, "call McCarthy. Tell him to get down here." I dashed to my office like the hounds of hell were at my high heels. Beneath the adrenaline rush, I was shaking. The abusiveness of the whole thing was awful, and his ferocious rage frightened me. What was I afraid of—that he would turn it on me?

We were in the season of fire, and summer had already scorched the concrete skin of New York with the blast of a dragon's furious warning. When the work day was finally over, I couldn't bring myself to enter the redolent hell of the subways so I tried to hail a cab. Standing on the corner, my arm extended, I noticed a man in a wool suit near me, smoking a cigarette and sweating. Why didn't he take off his jacket, I wondered? The city was dissolving into a mirage of shimmering heat as a cab careened around the corner and screeched to a halt in front of me. In the moment I shifted the shoulder strap of my briefcase, the sweating man crossed in front of me, throwing his burning cigarette into an overloaded garbage can, and grabbing the cab door.

"Hey," I cried out, stunned. "I was here first!" Fury engulfed me. And this, I suddenly suspected, was what Hadus had been trying to elicit from me, the killer's instinct that gorged on rage, fear, and humiliation.

"Shit!" The cab stealer cursed, shaking his hand which he'd burned on the blazing metal handle. He got into the cab and slammed the door behind him.

"You bastard!" I exclaimed.

The cab sped off and a strange odor warned me as the garbage can burst into flames. Old newspapers, a baby's dirty pink shoe, and stained brown paper bags fueled the fire. I jumped away, hearing the angry blaring of horns and shrieking of tires and then the doomed thunder of colliding steel. I looked and there was my abducted cab—its radiator smoking into the crushed trunk of another. The drivers jumped out, screaming foreign words that everyone understood the meaning of. The asphalt melted and passersby peered curiously at the businessman sitting slumped in the backseat. The street smelled infernal and a sudden wave of nausea left me dizzy. I stepped backward into the park, leaning against a tree, waiting for the trembling rage to leave my body. I inhaled the sweet air slowly, feeling my blood cool with the tears that suddenly came to my eyes.

"Are you all right dear?" An elderly Chinese lady with soft white hair and sneakers stood next to me.

I nodded.

"This heat is ruthless. Take this, it will make you feel better." She held out a small paper folding fan, the kind that opened like a peacock's tail. It was brightly painted, and as I squinted at it in the glaring sun, I saw the figure of Kuan Yin, goddess of compassion and mercy.

"It's very kind of you, but I can't take your fan."

"Nonsense." She pushed it into my hand, the lines around her eyes deepening like the mysterious patterns of fallen yarrow sticks as she smiled at me. "I always carry several," she said, another fan appearing in her hand. I blinked and rubbed the water from my eyes—she hadn't pulled it from her pocket or her purse; it was simply there, already moving faster than the wings of a hummingbird, its breeze turning my perspiration to beads of crystal that floated to the grass below. A squirrel dashed between us, seized them up and, his tail twitching, he leapt onto a nearby bench to nibble on them.

"I guess he likes the salt," I said, laughing with surprise, which doubled when I turned to my companion only to find she had disappeared. But the beautiful fan was in my hand.

Feeling restored, I left the park and climbed into the cab that appeared the moment I lifted my arm. Some people just don't get it, I thought, as we passed the overheated calamity. I fanned myself, then rolled down the windows and let the wind blow through my hair.

Maia had told us our astrological charts would give us detailed elemental portraits of ourselves, and so I'd had mine done. I was an Aquarius, an air sign, which made perfect sense: I had studied philosophy in college and loved the rarified realms of thought. I loved to read, I loved music and poetry, and I was a lawyer—I made my living with words and logic, argumentation and persuasion. Maia was a Leo—a fire sign. And she was certainly fiery—passionate, dramatic, quick to anger. A fiery disposition needs the temperance of cooling waters—the capacity to experience compassion and love, as well as the ability to think before speaking or acting impulsively. Bellona was a Cancer, a water sign. And indeed, Bellona always had a calming affect on Maia. I realized, suddenly curious, that I didn't know Nonna's sign.

I knew Hadus was a Sagittarius, a fire sign. The image of a desert came into my mind, and I realized that without water, fire will burn out of control, scorching and laying waste to everything. So too, a person's willfulness can destroy everything around him if his drive for power is not tempered by compassion. Without love, his life was a wasteland. I also suddenly realized that fire is fueled by air, feeding upon it as it does wood. I had been careful not to give Hadus any ideas about the possibility of resuming our personal relationship. But was the idea of my unavailability spurring him to rage? What could I do to make my life at work easier?

I followed Bellona's suggestion to begin casting circles at home, slowly meditating on each of the four elements. Unable to recall the exact words of Bellona's invocation, I remembered simple things like the colors, the animals, the qualities of being, and I focused on the feelings and the insights each evoked in me. I found myself uttering spontaneous, poetic invocations of each of these directions—invocations that were simpler, stripped of the archaic language, yet rich with personal meaning. And that, I knew, was most important of all. Every day for weeks, if only for a moment but longer when I had the time, I stood in my studio, four candles glowing in each of the quarters—yellow in the east, red in the south, blue in the west, and green in the north. I had no altar, no tools, only myself—but that was all I needed.

I began in the east, throwing open my windows and breathing in the cool, early morning breeze. I burned carefully prepared incenses of fenugreek, meadowsweet, mugwort, sage, and the leaves of singing aspen and sacred bodhi trees until visions floated before my shuttered lids and the veil between the worlds was lifted by breezes of sacred insight. I listened to the music of Miles Davis, Mitch Ryder, and Mozart, and braided feathers of swan and seagull in my hair. With my grandmother's pen I wrote in a small leatherbound book on pages of pearl-colored linen. I wore long scarves of silver and lavender and chose my words carefully. On my way home from work I walked past playgrounds to hear children laughing and, after days of these meditations, when I felt my mind was clear, I turned and faced the south.

In the season of fire, I gave myself over to its wisdom. In the center of a circle of red candles, dazed by the heat and the brilliance created when so many tiny flames were brought together, I remembered the power that grew each time we met in circle—so many small, bright flames combined. My skin was too hot to touch and I burned on the outside until I found the fire burning within. I rose each day to greet the sun's return, climbing to the roof of my building, raising my arms, and yelling like the ancient baboons from the temples of Isis who sat beside the Nile at dawn and greeted their god's rebirth. I wore red to work and would not take no for an answer. After days of working with fire, when I felt the flame of passion rising within me, when I wondered if its scorch would ever accept the offering of my soul and answer my prayer with rapture, I turned to the west.

Each day for a week, I bathed in a deep porcelain tub filled with cool water and herbal potions of angelica, comfrey, deer's tongue, galangal, goldenseal, heliotrope, and peppermint to soothe my work-wearied heart. I wore palliative blues, and spoke in even tones. I danced in a necklace of conch shells, spinning round and round until sweat flew like rain from my body. I drank eight glasses of water every day and visited the rivers that flowed past the island on which I lived. I cried salt tears when suffering crossed my path, and I longed to heal the wounds that I was first discovering. I began to trust my feelings the way I trusted my intelligence and when I was ready, I turned to the north.

I bought jewel colored Italian suits of Chinese silk spun by magical silk worms and I offered some of the fruits of my labor to others in need by writing checks, small but useful, to groups that cared for the earth or for humanity. I filled my room with plants and fed them with minerals to help them grow. I filled a small brown gourd from Africa with blue corn from Arizona and I rattled for the ancient ones to come to me. I watched for flowerpots on windowsills and treasured my visits to the park. I went dancing and made love with Jake, but of all the directions, the power of the north, of the earth, seemed the most elusive. A full cycle of the moon had passed since I'd begun my meditations, and so I turned to the east, to understand what I was learning. My circle was cast and some part of each day was now spent between the worlds.

The countless simple things of daily life were filled with radiant texture and my heart filled with gratitude for the warmth of the sun on my skin, the music of children laughing, the strength of Jake's embrace. But as I learned to sense the sacred in the small things of the world, I also began to see its absence in the way we had ordered our lives, for there were contradictions everywhere. Working each day in a high-powered business, traveling in overcrowded trains beneath the earth, living and working in climate-controlled spaces, always cut off from the beauty of the earth, I realized the only alchemy most people were interested in today was the translation of their own powers, and the generous gifts of the earth, into the gold of accumulated wealth. And I couldn't help but wonder if people were hardened by the relentless media chronicling of daily acts of horror that crawled from the abyss left by humanity's lost soul. In just the short distance from subway entrance to elegant office lobby, I watched as the well-dressed and busy turned their eyes to avoid the underworld we accept as ordinary—the homeless and the dying in residence upon our streets and the steps of our churches.

These were the unnatural, man-made consequences of a cultural shift that began thousands of years ago, away from the sacred earth, to a distant sky god. The religious beliefs of a culture define its values. Its cosmology has tremendous impact on social and economic institutions, culture, history, the status of women, sexuality, and countless other facets of daily life. We have become disconnected from the divine, from the feminine, the earth, and from each other, living a millennial alienation from the sacred. God was separated from man, man was separated from woman, and all were separated from the earth. For too many centuries, each has existed in painful separation from the others, and the world we have created expresses this terrible alienation. It also expresses our longing for reunion.

In circle, and in my daily practices, I learned how the Old Religion of the Great Mother Goddess honors and expresses a connection to the earth, the moon, the sun and stars, and the animals and plants that share the planet with us. Its rituals reinforce and give expression to the constant awareness of sacred relationship to all that is and to the divine as it is embodied in all that exists. Perhaps here in the scorched wasteland beneath the burning warrior sun, deep within our culture's shadow, I had finally come to a source of insight, to a wellspring where the sacred flowed in healing waters.

The alchemy of spiritual transformation remained protected and hidden by country clans and urban magical orders who secretly practiced Western mysticism. The Masons arose from this magical and intellectual lineage and it was their revolutionary brotherhood that founded the United States. They believed in the brotherhood of man, the existence of a divinity, and the immortality of the soul. Many of the treasured, secret rituals of the Masons reflected those of the Goddesses at Eleusis and Delphi, and the most overt symbols of those beliefs decorate our flag, dollar bills, and seals of high office. So often these days, as right-wing politicians and conservative Christians appropriate history for their own exclusionary political ends, they assert that we were founded as a Christian country. In fact, we were founded by magicians as an astounding political experiment, reflecting their equally insurgent, and ancient, spirituality.

As I visited the Metropolitan Museum, I found alchemical and pagan symbolism throughout Renaissance painting; and I began to discover how writers such as John Donne, Samuel Taylor Coleridge, William Wordsworth, Walt Whitman, William Butler Yeats, Henry Thoreau, even the young T. S. Eliot, George Bernard Shaw, John Steinbeck, and many others, composed their poetry and prose with this spiritual vocabulary.

I had only begun to understand and experience the power of these ancient symbols and archetypes. Under my priestesses' tutelage, I was learning an ancient symbol system which, as Jung discovered, was a vital language for communication between the conscious and unconscious aspects of my mind. Even more exciting, this system was also a vocabulary for dialogue between ourselves and the divine.

In the time of rebirth that was spring, I was beginning to sense the meaning of immanent divinity. Our work in circle now encompassed a variety of magics that further opened my eyes, my heart, and my mind to this wondrous discovery: The Goddess was alive, the earth was alive, and finally, I too began to feel alive in ways I'd never suspected possible.

Every day I sought a quiet moment of beauty, which I cherished, for the demands at work were increasing and I barely had time to do my laundry, let alone cast a circle regularly. I had no time to see Jake, and when I did, I was either too tired, or too wired, to enjoy our relationship. My life was out of balance and I was accumulating a tinderbox of anxiety and fear as Hadus's temper ruled each workday. The timing couldn't be better, I thought to myself, as Bellona announced that tonight we were going to learn how to use elemental magic to do a banishing. We were going to rid ourselves of negativity, to drive away and expel unwanted energies and influences, to cleanse and purify. I yearned to immerse myself in cool water, but we were to work with the season's power of fire.

A small bottle of oil was passed around the circle. I dabbed a pungent drop on my third eye, all of my chakra and pulse points, my heart and breasts.

Bellona looked like a lioness as she stood in the southern quarter of our circle. Four red point candles burned brightly in each quarter and on the altar, which was decorated with red poppies. She raised a beautiful wand of blossoming almond, and as she spoke, she drew an invoking pentacle of red fire which danced before us in the darkened temple.

> "I summon, stir, and call ye forth,
> Mighty ones of the south,
> Ancient powers of fire,
> Powers of the desert lion,
> Powers of the fiery hawk,
> Powers of the ancient dragon,
> Powers of courage,
> Powers of will,
> Powers of passion.
> Attend our rites and guard our circle
> In the names of Sekmet and Horus
> So mote it be!"

She continued through the rest of the circle and came to rest where she had begun, in the east.

The statue of Sekmet sat upon our altar, a large black cauldron before her. In it burned a blue flame. Bellona threw something into the cauldron and the flame exploded, crackling and sparking, sending tongues of leaping fire into the darkness in which we sat. Startled, we jumped, frightened as Bellona moved around the circle like a caged cat. She stopped in front of me, snarling, "What do you fear? Where is your courage? You will need it for the journey ahead."

I stared into her extraordinary face, and saw the eyes of Sekmet staring back at me. She seized my wrist and poured her magical concoction into my hand. Rough sand rubbed against the soft skin of my fingers and palm.

"Find your answer in the fire." She pushed me toward the center and I felt everyone's eyes on me. What was I to say, to do? I looked into the deep black cauldron, and I thought of hell. Hell was not knowing. No, hell was the fear of not knowing.

"I fear fear. My courage is found in facing it, whatever it looks like." I surprised myself with the certainty and the determination I heard in my voice.

Bellona smiled. "Feed your fears to the fire, and nourish yourself with its heat," she commanded.

Into the flames went the herbs and saltpeter in my palm, and with it went some of my fears. As the flames rose, so did my courage. I stared into the blazing cauldron, strength rushing through me like crimson lava running through the earth's veins.

My focus was drawn from the leaping fire by the sound of Jeanette's words, so similar to my own.

"I fear those who use my fears against me. I fear that weakness in myself but I know my courage grows with my freedom."

I watched as she tossed the handful of magic into the fire. When each of us had banished our fears in the flames, we took hands and began a slow chant:

"Air I am.
Fire I am.
Water, earth, and
Spirit I am."

As always, the singing was soft and tentative as we listened to the priestesses and tried to remember words and melody. But soon we were singing with the freedom and confidence with which our fire ritual had filled us. Our bodies swayed, shoulders bumping, hips colliding, until the sound and rhythm had swollen to such force that we began to dance. Faster and faster we circled, pushing beyond the first wave of exhaustion, accelerating past the shortness of breath and parched tongues, no longer dancing but running instead. Relentlessly we chanted, now in gasps and raspy mutterings. But we kept on. A rush of energy hit us, our voices soaring in unexpected harmonies and power. And from an unknown place within, I heard my own voice rise in joy.

Finally, the chant dropped to a delicate whisper, like a soft summer breeze in the early morning, slowly fading into silence. The dancing stopped and Bellona stepped into the circle's center. She threw a handful of herbs into the burning cauldron and the flames leapt heavenward. Smoke spiraled through the skylight and I felt my fear travel with it into the night sky.

"So mote it be," she declared. Bellona picked up her wand and stood in the east, her shoulders squared, her chin lifted with a victorious pride. She raised the wand and drew a banishing pentagram and as she gestured she spoke:

> *"Mighty ones of the east,*
> *Ancient spirits of air,*
> *Ere ye depart for your fair and lovely realms*
> *We bid thee thanks*
> *Hail and farewell!"*

And with these ceremonial words, addressing the spirits of each quarter, she circumnavigated the circle for the last time that night. Returning to the east, she turned and faced us, a satisfied smile filling her face.

"Our circle is open, but never broken. Merry meet and merry part, and merry meet again!"

A great whoop of joy filled the room, as a burst of release and freedom swept aside the broken terrors that had constrained us. Where a dolorous knot in my heart had been filled with unspoken fear, I now felt movement and possibility. I stepped out of the circle, changed by the fire magic we did that moonless night when the dark orb was in Cancer and the sun was in Leo.

The banishing ritual had worked its magic, but I knew I needed more strength to cope with pressures at work. I also needed strength to deal with the grief that I too often felt at the world's great miseries. I decided to spend the weekend in the country. It wasn't until I finally escaped the city, crossed the river, and traveled to the woods that I began to understand the power of the fourth quarter, the power of earth. I was breathing hard from a climb up the ridge that ran alongside the Delaware River. As I surveyed the landscape before me, I felt like I was traveling back in time. Old farmhouses stood next to rich brown plowed fields, their orderly rows awaiting the green life that would soon grow there. But the houses, and the people, and even the cultivated fields, were few and far between. The earth had a vitality and peacefulness that the small population did not damage.

I sat with my back against a large, old tree. A great wind whipped about me, wildly lifting my hair, my scarf, and my spirits. It was as if the trees were singing to me. I grounded myself and began to feel the earth's energy fill me with more power than anything I'd experienced in the city. And then I felt the energy of the tree. It was astonishingly familiar, reminiscent of the sacred tree circle we had done, but so much more vital, alive, and connected, beyond even the extraordinary experience of the energy in circle. What was the tree telling me?

Feeling the earth's power coursing through me, I knew the answer: I needed to work with the earth to attain balance in my life, to find a means of expression for my ideas, passions, and dreams, and a way to give them form. I needed to learn the wisdom of my body and my heart, not just the wisdom of my mind. The ideas coming from my mind were like the blowing winds—here and then gone. But the wisdom that moves upward from the earth remains rooted in the earth and connects it to air, water, and fire.

I sensed how the tree itself, like any living thing, connects spirit and matter. The tree *is* spirit and matter, I realized. It would take years for me to fully experience and understand this, not just with my mind, but with my entire being—mind, body, and soul. It would be like planting the seed of a slow-growing oak in the soil. Patience was what was important, not just the destination, but the journey. The goal is not just being full grown, but learning to grow. I knew I had to learn the wisdom of the earth for my life to take form.

I filled myself with the earth's power and then, finally, I stood, stretching slowly, enjoying the movement of my fingers, my arms and legs. The countryside was bathed in honeyed light as the sun descended and I realized the moon had risen before the sun had set. I stood between the two spheres that faced each other from opposite sides of the horizon, spellbound by the beauty that surrounded me. Carefully, I emptied the bag of birdseed I'd brought along, a small offering for the gifts the tree, and the land, had given me.

My body was aching and exhausted by the time I got back to my rented car. But already it was teaching me lessons I needed to learn. It required better care. My body was not just some biological machine designed to carry my consciousness around. I was beginning to understand that, contrary to a culture which called the body sinful, it had intrinsic value, intelligence, and spiritual wisdom to offer me, if I would honor it. It was time for me to inhabit my body. I began a regime of simple exercise and better eating. I began to listen when my body spoke to me and it was my body that taught me that ideas, and visions, and dreams require not only courage, but action in order to come true. I could never have guessed what those actions would be.

CHAPTER 7

Magic Mirrors
and
Altered States

*The real voyage of discovery consists
not in seeking new landscapes,
but in having new eyes.*

— MARCEL PROUST

R ed sky at night, sailors delight; red sky in morning, sailors take warning," I murmured the prognostic verse my father had taught me. It was a red dawn, but this morning I was happy for I greeted the sky after a night of magic. I sat on my rooftop watching the world awaken. I'd never realized how many birds sang as the sun rose— almost enough to drown out the roar of garbage trucks making their early rounds.

The interpretation of signs and portents is a lost and misunderstood art. If you lived close to the earth, you understood when nature shared her wisdom with you. With her guidance, you could see the invisible and foretell the future. You could learn from her other creatures and you would know that when the wolves began to howl in the northern woods in August, winter would arrive early. You would know that when the orange oriole arrived, summer flew in on her wings.

It is still possible to know the meaning behind the earth's mysterious movements, to see the patterns in her portents. You can read the clouds, the ripples on the sea, the flight of birds, and the color of the night sky to see what waits ahead; or you can shoot the stars and lay your course by them. All of these my seafaring father had done. But what of the more mysterious portents? At circle, we were learning many ways to gain the sight. It used to be said that when a bird landed on your windowsill, someone had died. When the moon is in Venus, an orrisroot hung by a silken thread will make a pendulum for dowsing or for love. Burn bistort with frankincense and you will have the second sight. And camphor, some yogis and Buddhist priests may tell you, when burned in the right amount, will open your third eye. Mugwort and lemon balm, gathered at the full moon and brewed as a tea, bestow the gift of visions. Romans made a divining rod from the forked branch of the magical hazel tree to find lost treasure or subterranean springs. The Egyptians used the branch of a pomegranate, the Chinese preferred the willow, the Celts cut blackthorn or rowan, but even ash would twitch and bend when the prize had been found.

Today we dismiss folk wisdom as mere superstition. And, like most people, I had dismissed it too, but as I mastered the correspondences of elemental magic, I began to understand how the universe speaks to us using poetic symbols—such as the bird in the window. The bird was a spiritual metaphor for the flight of someone's soul, a metaphorical ripple of the actual event in the energy field. These signs were magical mirrors into which we could look to bring a distant world into view.

Still, I wondered, was it really possible to know by such strange means the longings of one's heart, the mysteries of the universe, or the future that awaits us? Could I see outside the laws of space and time, beyond the constraints of linear logic and old-fashioned cause and effect? Was it possible that I could know the truth by other means? Was it really possible to reenchant the world, I wondered, when, with each passing day I grew more disenchanted with the world in which I worked? And could such strange means provide the guidance I yearned for as the path I now walked grew more difficult?

The stresses at work were accumulating—the long hours, Hadus's hair-trigger temper, Sharon's surliness, the imperious manner of the attorneys I dealt with. Instead of feeling confident and empowered by my glamorous job, I was feeling increasingly anxious and uneasy. I had been delighted at the possibility of working in the arts, but this world of the rich and famous seemed so often to be driven by greed and fool's gold. My fears that Hadus's tantrums would be directed at me were coming true with distressing frequency. And when he was not in a fit of temper, he had begun to indulge in sexual suggestiveness despite my icy boundaries. Was this pervasive uneasiness and rapaciousness the price I had to pay for financial success and security?

Reluctantly, I came down from the rooftop and got dressed for work. Heeding the warning of the dawn, I dressed in blue, the color of peace and healing, hoping for a day without rage or innuendo.

I was very disappointed that you didn't join me for dinner last night." Hadus stretched his long arms, pushing past the ends of his expensive French cuffs. I observed him carefully as his fingers curled and his fists clenched. His body grew taut, then suddenly it slackened. He removed his glasses. He stood up and casually closed the door to his office. There was no reason to feel the sickening tightness in my chest, I lied to myself. I clicked my pen and turned to a blank page of yellow legal paper.

"So what's up today?" I asked, trying to redirect his attention to work and stave off my sense of forewarning. My intermittent psychic impressions seemed more of a burden than a blessing in these tension-filled offices.

"I think you should have dinner with me tonight." A shudder rippled through me as I felt him standing behind me. "I want you to know, I'm very impressed with the clients you've brought in, and I've been thinking about giving you a few of our more high-visibility clients to work with." I felt his hands on my shoulders. He moved them slowly back and forth, and I shifted in my seat to avoid them.

"I'm sorry. Did I make you uncomfortable?" He lifted his hands and moved in front of me, leaning against his desk. "We used to have such a good time. . . ."

I cut him off. "You know you're making me uncomfortable."

"You should be flattered. After all, we're old friends, more than friends actually." He smiled and leaned toward me. I could smell the garlic and stale coffee from his lunch. I leaned back but the chair restricted me. "We're terrific together. I know you've felt it too. Why shouldn't I think about more?"

"Our deal was strictly business."

"Promises were meant to be broken."

"Not that one." I was angry and anxious but I tried to sound cool.

"No need to get upset. You want business, you'll get business. I'm a patient man. Who knows, maybe you'll change your mind." He sat down behind his desk and my tension eased. I breathed a sigh of relief, but too soon. "I've been talking to Matt Klein."

I felt like I was in a falling elevator. Matt Klein was a client I'd brought in. Why was Hadus talking to him without my knowledge? I'd worked relentlessly to get him a deal and he was about to sign with a major label. It was a decisive career boost for me. And that, I suddenly read in his mind, was why.

"Matt has the greatest respect for you, but he's a little concerned about your . . . lack of experience. I assured him that you were a top associate, more than ready to handle this negotiation. As far as I could judge, you've done a splendid job. I assured him I couldn't have done better myself."

Stay calm, stay calm. I knew exactly where this was headed.

"But he says he'd just feel better with a lawyer with more . . . years and more connections. And I think," he winked and I wanted to punch him, "just between you and me, he feels a male lawyer can fight just that little bit harder. You understand."

"He wants you to represent him."

"Precisely." I wanted to reach across the desk and strangle him, but I sat still, trying to contain my anger. "I want to take him to another label. So what do you think?" said Hadus. "I mean he is *your* client."

The way he emphasized *your* made me want to scream. We both knew my opinion didn't matter. It was a *fait accompli*. I'd just have to deal with it. I was in a business that was all about power and when you were in the junior position, being taken advantage of was to be expected. I was lucky it didn't happen more often. But there was more going on here. I struggled to ground myself and as I sat there, I heard it as clearly as if Hadus had spoken it aloud: He meant to remind me who had the power in our relationship, whether business or personal. By bringing in so many clients, I was stepping out of his shadow and beyond his control, which he now reasserted.

I felt as if I were choking as I swallowed my powerlessness. Slow your breathing, I reminded myself. I sensed fear—but it was his, not mine. For a moment, it came into view: I realized that his desire for me made him vulnerable to feelings he could not, nor would not admit, feelings that he felt weakened him because of the needs it aroused, for support, for nurturance, for emotions he had long ago decided to live without. Feelings that he sought to control by controlling me.

"What can I say? It'll be good for you, and fine for him, but I can't say it's going to make me happy. Or the record company I've been dealing with." I struggled to be diplomatic, to sound mature and businesslike. This was my chance to show how aggressive I could be—was it a test? Either way, I had already lost. If I kept my cool I was being passive. But if I was assertive I'd be called a hysterical bitch.

"Trust me. They'll still do business with you." Despite my determination to keep a poker face I could feel my jaw tighten. Hadus's voice changed to a soft, slightly patronizing purr. "This deal isn't that important. Don't let it get to you. Besides, we're a team. Think of it as me just giving you a hand."

"You're not really giving me any choice here, are you?" He smiled, knowing he'd gotten exactly what he wanted. "So what about my fee?" I asked coldly, barely concealing my anger.

"Bill him at two hundred dollars an hour for the time you've put in so far, and I'll even kick a piece of my hourly to you for the, uh, referral. You'll make out O.K., maybe better." He leaned back in his chair, a satisfied grin on his face. "O.K. that's settled. So, I'll need the file. Now let's talk about dinner tonight."

I shook my head. "I thought we'd already discussed this."

Hadus frowned. "That's your choice?"

"Yes," I said firmly. "It is. I'll get you Matt's file." I left his office as if sleepwalking in a nightmare. My power abducted, anger whirled about me like storm clouds rolling down from the mountains. I composed myself, hoping no one would notice the effects of my defeat. The phone rang as I stared out the window.

"Hey you, how 'bout meetin' me for dinner?" It was Jake, and I thanked the universe for reminding me that not all men were like Hadus.

All week long I had been devising strategies for dealing with Hadus. Could I master him? I laughed at the question, remembering his wild eyes and nervous ticks. I considered resigning, but I knew it was myself I would have to master. I was determined not to be driven from a job that still held so much promise for my future. But how could I cope with such regular disempowering?

As I would have in ancient times, I turned to the Goddess's priestesses for guidance. I couldn't wait to get to circle, where I knew that Nonna, Maia, and Bellona could teach me their ancient arts of divining. The priestess's gift of sight had once guided the greatest nations. No decision was made in ancient Athens, birthplace of Western civilization, until the oracle at Delphi had been consulted, for it was she who uttered the messages of the divine. Her words of counsel were sought by kings and politicians, warriors and poets. Odysseus consulted her about the Trojan War and Oedipus sought her aid as well. Socrates swore by her wisdom, and it was at her temple that Homer composed his immortal epics dedicated to the Goddess.

At the temple dedicated to the Great Earth Mother Gaia, this prescient priestess sat upon a cleft in the rock, called Delphys, which meant "vagina," the opening to the Goddess's womb. Here inspirational vapors were said to induce a trance for the priestess Pythia—the Pythoness, she of the ancient serpent of wisdom and creative coiling which slept beneath her throne. Plutarch, like Pythagoras, was a priest at her temple, and wrote that the oracle was a thousand years old, describing the priestess's ecstatic catalepsy and divine communion.

The Greeks called this trance-speaking by the Pythia *entheos,* meaning "within is a god," from which comes our word *enthusiasm.* Priestesses from Asia to Egypt, from Libya to Iceland, spoke with the wisdom of an altered and expanded consciousness that apprehended and expressed the Divine. They taught the epiphany of music, song, and dance; they descended into caverns and knew the earth's mysteries of death and rebirth, and, like the Scythian shamans, about whom great legends grew, they knew about the ability to fly.

Signs came from the gods to guide and direct us, and the capacity to interpret them and to speak with the Divine was an ancient gift honored in women. But when the Goddess's oracle was rededicated to Apollo, women were forbidden to inquire of the oracle, though it had always been a woman who spoke the coveted prophecies. The temple at Delphi was closed in 529 C.E. by the Christian emperor Justinian, who could neither read nor write. He also closed the schools of philosophy, most of which had been located at the Goddess's temples and were taught and attended equally by women and men. And the Goddess's temple at Eleusis, the center of her mysteries for over two thousand years, was closed. These and other assaults banished the Goddess and her priestesses to a netherworld of demonization.

Women in Greece were forced to wait for over a thousand years before they would again be allowed an education. Throughout the Fertile Crescent, women could no longer receive an education nor speak the wisdom of the Great Goddess. However, if you traveled north, you would find that reverence for women as interpreters of the sacred remained.

The Celts and the Gauls honored women as bearers of spiritual wisdom. One famous shaman, a Druid priestess named Veleda of the Bructeri, from the Rhineland or from Brittany, for both laid claim to her, was renowned for leading the war against Rome's invasion of Gaul. She was an arbiter when a peace agreement was made between the Romans and the people of Cologne. She correctly foretold the destruction of the Roman legions in 69 C.E. and was a captive of great prize to the Romans, who executed her after she condemned their imperialism and their brutality.

Farther north, women were great shamans. In Iceland the priestess was called *spakona,* from the word *spa,* which meant to prophesy. She conducted rites of sacred song and sat upon a raised platform, which symbolized her ability to see beyond the ordinary. It was said that Odin himself consulted a seeress seeking to know his destiny.

Traveling east through Europe, in field and forest, by the trance-inducing powers of drum and psychotropic, you would see that people worshiped the Great Goddess of the animals. Farther east, across the sea as far as your sails could carry you, you would find in Manchuria women shamans who wore a copper mirror in which one could see the soul, and into which a counseling deity would come to rest or focus. In Korea they used beads to summon the divine. They too worked in trance within a sacred circle. For thousands of years in Japan, women were *itako, okamin, kannagi,* or *kuchiyose*—titles of wise women who spoke the wisdom of Ogamisama, the Great Goddess. They were *miko,* daughters of the gods, who advised emperors and villagers. They underwent traditional training, rituals of initiation, and worked with magical instruments such as the bow, the one-stringed lute, and the drum. They lived and traveled freely until the end of the nineteenth century, when their practices were outlawed. Then they practiced secretly, discreetly, until the arrival of General Douglas MacArthur in 1945 who ended the prohibition of the Shinto traditions which these women founded.

Travel west and you would find the medicine women of the Turtle Island, the Americas, as they came to be called. Grandaughters of Nokomis and daughters of Spider Woman, of White Buffalo Woman, of the Great Mother Earth, they knew the ancient healing songs and prayers. They spoke with the plants and knew which were helpers and which could harm. They knew the wisdom of the seasons, the animals, the earth, the sky. They kept the mysteries of the Moon Lodges and presided over births, deaths, initiations, marriages, and the rituals of the seasons and the community. They traveled between the worlds, returning with lost souls and secret wisdom. They were elders honored by their people and, in some tribes, they chose the chiefs for times of peace and times of war.

Journey south and you would find the priestesses of Africa, who were taken captive and brought to America, where they disguised their ancient ways: their dances of the Orisa, possession by the spirits, prophetic throwing of the bones, the magic of Yemanja and Oshun, goddesses of the sacred waters, and many others, hidden in the garments of their captors' church. Santeria and Vodou are descendants of the Yoruban religion, and though profoundly misunderstood by Western culture, they remain rooted in the shamanic wisdom of their past.

The world had been filled with women who knew there was another way, an inner way to the truth. This was the wise artistry of the Sibyl, ancient prophetess and priestess of the Goddess, who had first summoned me in dreams, and then appeared to spur my journey by the serpentine route I now traveled. I sought not just her aid, but the mastery of her gifts. I had visited her often at the museum over these last months, and tonight, I hoped to have an opportunity to work as this hidden sisterhood always had. I wanted to know what the future held for me, what challenges of self-mastery were ahead, and what tools I would need for the journey.

"You look like you need a hug." Nonna stretched out her arms. I hadn't seen her in several weeks and just the sight of her radiant smile reassured me.

"I've missed you. Where've you been?" Feelings of vulnerability and exhaustion weighed on me like a mantle of lead and I wasn't sure if they were mine, or hers. "Are you O.K.?" I asked her.

"I haven't been feeling well lately. Nothing to worry about, though— you do too much of that already. Just what happens with age." She chuckled. "It may be natural but that doesn't mean I have to like it. So, how is your job going?"

Her hands trembled as she poured oil from a large brown bottle into a smaller blue one. She had lost weight and her face seemed drawn and ashen. I wanted to ask her what was wrong but I sensed she would only avoid my questions.

"Some of it's wonderful," I responded with forced cheerfulness, my own concerns suddenly seeming petty. "I've met some major stars, which is definitely fun. And some of the work's interesting—I'm not saving the world or anything, but it's good to be challenged. Everybody thinks it's glamorous, and I guess if you're a partner with star clients it can be."

"Ah, glamour. You know glamour originally meant the magic of illusion. So, you're seeing through illusions—that's an even greater magic, so what's the matter?"

I smiled. Nonna always knew. "Nothing," I lied.

Her eyebrows went up.

"Well, all right, you're right. . . ." I was still hesitant about burdening her with my fears. "I've just been having this uneasy feeling, as if something were very wrong. Maybe it's because everybody seems so, well, unhappy. They never seem satisfied. And so many of the lawyers have this terrible energy—they're so pretentious and condescending with each other, with me, even their clients. It's not just that I have to listen to them—I can *feel* them, psychically." I sighed. "It's really true that you have to be twice as good and twice as tough when you're a woman." Just talking about it made me feel better. "Anyway, it's silly to complain, I'm incredibly lucky to have this job. I'm just going to keep making the most of it."

Nonna patted my arm. "There's a lesson in everything, my dear. I know you'll get what you need to from this experience."

Bellona opened the door to the temple, waving us to join the other women inside. The cares of the day slipped away as circle was cast.

Maia took a small leather pouch from the pentacle in the center of the altar. Slowly, she turned it round and round, passing it back and forth between her hands. "Ladies, in this pouch are runes. They are the first Scandinavian alphabet, and every letter has a magical meaning and power. They were given to Odin, husband of the Goddess Freya, after he had gone through a journey of great sacrifice and transformation. Tonight, they'll help you to know yourself better."

My heart leapt. I had just discovered that the name *Odin* came from the old Norse words for "wind" and "spirit." The intricacy and depth of meaning of these pagan symbols, and the way they infiltrated one's life to deepen *its* meaning, amazed me. And now, here were Odin's tools, his gifts, which would allow me to see with my inner eye, to see things that had been hidden.

Maia gave the little sack a last tumble, then closed her eyes and held it to her heart. "The use of divination requires honesty, courage, and a willingness to face things about ourselves we've always been afraid of or that we've kept hidden. As you pull, ask what you need to know."

One by one, we each pulled a rune stone. I reached into the pouch. The stones were cool and smooth, and they made a lovely sound as my fingers stirred them round. This couldn't have come at a better time, I thought to myself.

Suddenly I felt a stone push itself into my fingers. I pulled it out and in the center of the opalescent pebble was a strange marking:

```
┌─────┐
│  X  │
│  X  │
└─────┘
```

I copied it onto a small piece of paper and returned the stone to its companions. The pouch traveled around the circle, and when each woman knew the moment was right, she pulled a rune. I watched as Jeanette sat with her eyes closed, clasping the pouch to her heart. We waited patiently, for we were learning to give each other the spoken, and unspoken, support that we all needed to make this journey with openness and trust. Jeanette opened her clenched fist, and as she gazed down at the little stone in her hand, a shadow crossed her beautiful face. She quickly returned the rune to its pouch and handed it to Marcia.

When everyone had pulled a rune, and written it down, Maia began.

"Before you is a symbol of spiritual insight. Let's see what you can learn about your runes while in trance. Sit comfortably and relax."

I sat holding the image of my rune, breathing deeply and slowly. The movement of breath was the movement of the life force, and a sense of connectedness and well-being flowed through me.

After a few minutes, Maia continued her visualization: "Now look at the rune you've copied. Stare at it. Don't look away, no matter what. If your concentration slips, use your breathing to return your focus to your rune."

The circle was, as always, lit only by seven candles, one in each quarter and three on the altar. The candles created pools of golden light in the surrounding darkness. We sat, and stared—interest gradually replaced by boredom, then impatience. The priestess was persistent and certain as to her method, and my concentration shattered and refocused with startling clarity. I continued staring at the paper, when suddenly the little *x*'s disappeared. I blinked, and they momentarily came into view and then vanished again! I was about to look up when I heard Maia's voice coming from very far away.

"Keep looking at your rune. You are entering a light trance state in which you'll find yourself feeling very peaceful. You'll also find that you have visionary powers. I'll guide you to a place of power that will enhance your abilities. You may close your eyes as you listen to the sound of my voice."

I closed my eyes and soon I saw two cave-black *x*'s against a vivid red background.

"Before you is a large wooden door marked with your rune. Open the door and enter. You're standing in a large circular room. The ceiling is high above you, capped with a skylight of crystal. Light pours through it and fractures into millions of dancing rainbows. You see a spiral staircase in the center of the room, leading down through the floor. As you begin to walk down the stairs, you see that the first steps are red. The stairs curve to the right, and you must hold onto the banister as you descend. The steps are now orange. Continue walking down the stairs. They are turning bright yellow. Walk down the stairs, which are turning green . . . now blue . . . and finally you see they're violet. At the bottom of the stairs is another wooden door—again marked with your rune. The door is heavy but it opens for you. Pass through to the other side. Here you'll find your place of power."

Before me stretched green and golden fields rich with grain, vineyards, and orchards. A simple dirt path with a stream running beside it wound through this flourishing landscape, leading to a circle of standing stones on a green hilltop. I set out on the path, astonished that I could feel the cool breeze and the hot sun against my skin. I heard birds singing and smelled roses. I had gone some distance through the fields when an old woman stood in the path before me. Dressed in white, her hair was long and silver, her skin pale, her eyes bright. She smiled and turned away from me and I saw that the path forked behind her. The path to the left led to what appeared to be a great city. I wondered why I hadn't seen it before. To the right, the path led up the little hill to the stone circle.

"Which way should I go?" I asked.

When she turned back to me, her face was younger, like that of a woman who might be her daughter, or my mother. Again she smiled, but she did not answer me.

"Well, I know what cities are like," I said. "I've lived in one all my life. They're certainly places of power. But I've never been to a stone circle." I looked up at the hill, and when I looked back to my silent companion she had changed yet again, this time to a woman younger than I. Knowing she wouldn't answer, I didn't bother to ask. I took the path to the circle. I'd gone just a short distance when suddenly I tripped. Looking down, I found myself tangled in a rope of words—warnings about danger, risk, and self-doubt, money, conformity, status, and power.

"Be a good girl." It wound around my ankles.

"Be polite." It snaked up my legs.

"Do what you're told. Do what you're told. Do what you're told." It wrapped itself around my waist as I struggled to pull the words away.

I panicked—what was I doing wrong? This was supposed to be a place of power, but I was helpless! I struggled desperately, and they wrapped themselves more tightly around me. My mind, the power is in my mind. I'm smart—I can figure a way out of this. I stopped struggling and looked at the twisting strands of language. Had my mind created them? Was it a warning that I'd chosen the wrong path? The more I thought, the tighter they twisted. Suddenly I remembered the lesson in the woods: I needed the wisdom of the earth, not just the air. In the instant I wondered what that might be, music surrounded me and the ropes exploded into a thousand pieces. A wild wind whipped around me, sending letters flying every which way. The air was filled with the humming of honeybees. And I was laughing. The mind writes a good joke, but the body knows what laughter feels like.

I raced to the top of the hill, pausing outside the great henge. The sound of a woman's laughter filled the air as I passed between the stones. The woman from the crossroads was standing with her back to me in the center of the standing stones. She reached down and gestured over a low granite altar. And then, without showing me her face, she vanished. Carefully I approached the altar. The ground felt as if it were charged with electricity, racing up my legs into my heart. It began beating like a drum in my chest as I looked down to see the double x's, placed within the center of an eye carved into the rough stone. Three times the symbol had appeared to me. Light leapt from the stone into my outstretched fingers and shot up my arm. Every molecule in my body danced with power. And then, from far away, Maia called us back:

"It's time to return. Give thanks for the insight you've been given. Walk back to the door." She spoke slowly, allowing us time to experience our return clearly. "Pass through, and return up the staircase. See how the color of the steps changes as you climb . . . from violet, to blue, then green . . . then yellow . . . now orange . . . and finally, red. Leave the room, closing the door behind you, and return to circle. When you're ready, open your eyes."

The room was silent.

"Let's go round the circle. Tell us what you experienced, what you saw with your inner sight," Maia encouraged us gently.

Each of us described her experiences and when we finished, Maia provided the traditional interpretation of our runes. Only Jeanette would not share what she had pulled, nor what she had seen. She asked to see the *grimoire,* Maia's book of spells and rituals, prophecy, and interpretations, including explanations of the runes' meanings. We all sat quietly as she found what she was looking for. Her face was a mask of mystery but hidden behind its stoic passivity I thought I saw a familiar pain surfacing in her eyes. I felt a terrible wave of grief radiating from her and I wanted to hug her, to reassure her that whatever she'd seen, she had friends who would stand by her. She sat silently, allowing no one near enough to offer anything except respect for the distance she clearly required. She handed the book back to Maia and we continued around the circle.

My rune was called *Ingwaz.* Ingwaz is another name for the Goddess Nerthus, the primeval Great Mother Goddess from whom all life comes. The rune is a symbol of her vulva, like that of the Irish Goddess Sheila-na-gig, carved on Irish churches, and dating back over thirty thousand years to rock carvings found in France. It means fertility, a new path by which the heroine, or hero, comes to the Goddess. It is a symbol of the all-seeing eyes of the Goddess and her magical powers of rebirth, emanating from her womb. It is, therefore, a symbol of the gift of second sight. This rune is also an emblem of feminine sexuality and the power of creating life out of the abyss. It signals the need to free oneself from past constraints and from the limitations imposed by culture and upbringing. It is a secret sign which, when posted on a home, means that a priestess dwells within. I thought of the priestesses of Delphi, and the Sibyl who had led me here.

"And the old woman at the crossroads?"

"You met the Goddess of the crossroads," Nonna replied. "She's an old friend of mine. The Greeks called her Hecate, the Crone. She's an ancient goddess, older than the Titans. She refused to move to Mount Olympus when Zeus arrived with the rest of the Greek gods, and traveled freely between all the realms. She's the Goddess of magic and wisdom and she accompanied Persephone on her journey through the Underworld."

"Why did her face change?"

"You saw the Goddess in her triple form: Maiden, Mother, and Crone. The Romans called her *TriVia*. That was a powerful revelation."

So I'd finally encountered the Goddess. Somehow I'd expected more drama—like a bolt of lightning or a burning bush. But there was a feeling, radiating outward from my heart—of peace and self-confidence, like nothing I'd ever experienced.

"Are you O.K.?" I asked Jeanette as we were cleaning up after circle. She looked away, but nodded.

"You know, if there's anything I can do to help. . . ."

She looked back at me and I saw, beneath the cloak of dignity that she always wore, a moment of vulnerability, a brief connection of our hearts. And then it vanished as swiftly as it had appeared.

"Thanks. I'll be fine—I always am. It's just something I thought was over and done with long ago."

I didn't want to let go of that momentary intimacy. But I didn't know what to say. I'd never had sisters, and my mother, though deeply loving, was a formal person. In my awkward silence I thought of the evening's oracle. The runes helped us to see ourselves, our strengths and our challenges. And with the runes' reward of self-awareness came the capacity to change. With them, as with other mirrors, we could courageously and wisely undertake the work of spiritual transformation. And, perhaps, as the ancient Sibyls had, we would have the power to help others do the same. But I wondered if such a complicated world—colored by history, other people's problems, our own deeply rooted patterns—could be changed merely by pulling some ancient letters.

"Do you think it's possible to leave our past behind? Or is it always with us, turning up to haunt us when we least expect it?" I asked myself as much as Jeanette. She looked startled, as if I'd seen too far into her silent soul. I pressed on. "I mean, the past is what's made us what we are today. And the world we're living in now is what it is, has the values and the problems it does, because of events that happened in the past. The status of women is a perfect example. I'm treated like a second-rate citizen because of past attitudes toward women that are still forces in today's culture. And just on a very personal level, we are our parents' children. My rune told me to break with the limitations of the past—but I wonder if it's possible."

"I don't know." Jeanette shook her head. "People say we're responsible for the life we lead and, mostly, I think we are. But there are enormous forces at work—history, economics. And other people. So much seems beyond our control. If we have a warning, can we avoid disaster? Who knows? But I do know that how we handle hardship is up to us— we can be beaten down," she swiftly brushed the hair from her forehead, "or we can fight back. I believe when we fight back, we find our strength."

"And our clarity. It takes terrible pressure to turn a lump of coal into a diamond." I hugged her and she returned my hug. "Anyway, call if you want to talk."

She smiled, but as we parted I could see the shadow still veiled her face.

At home that night, I stood before the mirror, wondering at the mystery of life before me. There was far more to the person who looked back at me than I had ever imagined. I had thought of the mysterious universe I had first encountered as a presence "out there"; but now I was discovering how much of that hidden yet ever-present spirit also existed within me. She had only begun to emerge from the shadows. I needed mirrors to know myself. We all did, though in this day and age mirrors were used for perfecting what we saw on the outside, rather than seeing the truth of what lay within.

As I drew the rune in my diary, and wrote down my vision, I marveled at the mysterious power of the mind to "randomly" select a symbol of precise personal meaning and to discover its meaning using our "sixth" sense. I marveled at the message the rune had carried between the worlds. But how was I to act on its advice? Much as I might want to, I certainly wasn't going to quit my job—how would I make a living? But I accepted the rune's counsel that by devoting myself to my work in circle I would find the answers I needed.

These ancient techniques for altering consciousness and enhancing perception allow us to see our true motives, into the darkest recesses of the heart, into the spirit world. Like an oracle, into dialogues with the Divine. And the power of the unconscious, or the "presence," or the Divine, to move matter and to communicate by the sophisticated manipulation of symbols, was pure magic. Whether I used the runes, the *I Ching,* or the Tarot cards, they all provided guidance, self-discovery, and, most important, discovery of a living, conscious, interactive universe. And the inherent wisdom of these oracles strengthened my growing sense of a presence I had begun to see as sacred.

I used to think Witches cast spells over people. Now I understood that true Witches work only to gain power over themselves. They work to accomplish self-mastery—to achieve healing, wisdom, compassion, and freedom, and to liberate themselves from the constraints that the world, or their upbringing, have trapped them in. Magic is part of this process of self-awareness and liberation. To do sacred magic, we must first come to know ourselves. And to see ourselves as we truly are, we must have a mirror. Among their many spiritual arts, Witches had long used a variety of mirrors to see into the deepest parts of their own souls, and those of others. They also looked into the heart of the universe.

Over the months and years that lay ahead, I was introduced to many methods and tools of divination. Some were easier to use and master than others, and they varied in the depth with which they could see into one's soul, into the future or past. The *I Ching* and runes revealed the infinite wisdom of the moment; the Tarot stretched further ahead and back in time, and astrology charted the most distant course. They are indeed mirrors into the soul, and the distances at which they focus upon the soul's journey, the vistas they reveal, vary like the lenses of a camera.

Insight can also come through dreams, the interpretation of signs, numerology, journeying, and other altered states including trance. There is also a method that Witches call "scrying," which involved the use of a crystal ball, or round black mirror, or bowl or body of water, into which one stared until visions appeared. Initially, the use of divination techniques such as the *I Ching,* Tarot, and astrology gave me a sense of life being preordained. But as I became more proficient in their use, I began to see that the idea that life was predetermined, or already lived, is simply untrue.

These oracles, these divining tools, are like a lighthouse to a ship at sea. They tell you where the shore is, where the rocks lie, offering guidance in a storm or on a dark and starless night. But, ultimately, the decision as to how to chart your course is your own. Do you sail or motor, tack or run for a long haul? Do you head for port or push on? Your choices, your free will, your expectations, fears, longings, beliefs, all affect the outcome of events. A divinatory tool provides you with information regarding forces, possibilities, and probabilities so you can make wise decisions. Most important, awareness, courage, compassion, and growth come from making your own choices and learning from them, not abandoning your responsibility to some mechanistic prediction. This was the real magical journey to maturity and to the divine.

Using techniques I had mastered, I was entering a realm of consciousness where the symbol was a portal to something numinous on the other side. In circle, we honored the Divine in its myriad expressions, and I was learning to open myself to the sublime beyond the metaphor. I wanted to fully explore religious metaphors and rituals and so I attended services of various faith traditions and interfaith services. I met many deeply spiritual and wise people, and came to a greater appreciation of the brilliant diversity in humanity's experience of the Divine. Each tradition had meaning and wisdom, and I gathered these many figures of divinity from an array of religions—Mary and Jesus, Kuan Yin and Buddha, Kali and Krishna, Al-lat and Allah, Spider Woman and the Great Spirit, Shekinah and Jehovah, and countless others, finding the pairs even where they were not acknowledged—in the winnowing basket of my spiritual harvest. I also realized I could not accept the limitations of any religion that demands adherence to literal interpretations of its myths and metaphors to the exclusion of all others. Nor was I satisfied with any that denied the feminine. I needed a spirituality that opened my mind, rather than one which sought to narrow it.

The emotional stress at work had begun to take its toll, and I found it increasingly difficult to deal with what I picked up psychically from people. Sometimes it was a specific thought; but, more often, I felt people's emotions, picking up related images. The stronger the emotion, the quicker I read it. Especially with Hadus. But I noticed that I was also beginning to shut down and was often unable to sense anything at all. I worried that my psychic sensitivity would disappear as it had when I went to Washington, but I also sensed that my shutting down psychically was some sort of instinctual protective mechanism. I was relieved to discover that by using various divinatory techniques, like wearing glasses when you become nearsighted, I was able to regain much of my "second sight."

In a sense, our use of a magic looking glass can be compared to Alice going through the mirror into another dimension. Contemporary anthropologists who have studied shamanic cultures call this dimension "nonordinary reality," most easily "seen" or entered while in an altered state of consciousness. It is the destination of ecstatic practices. Shamans call it the spirit world. Physicists might describe it as the fourth, or "other" dimension of space-time, or the "frequency realm," or quantum level, to which we are generally oblivious because our daily mindset is focused on survival. Once our attention is fixed on not getting eaten by a tiger, hit by a bus, or yelled at by our boss, we're not paying attention to the myriad magical connections and events that actually make up the fabric of our lives. We are locked in the literal symbols and actions of our lives, and are unable to grasp the mythical pattern that animates them.

With divinatory tools and altered states, we can see the deep archetypal and sacred forces at work in our lives, and most important, we can see their meaning, rising from the depths of our unconscious to the conscious light of our daily vision. Meaning cannot be quantified in the manner required for scientific "proof." We find it instead in context, symbols, patterns, myths, stories, cultures, rituals, poetry—all are maps of insight into the nature of our sacred field of being. It is up to us to discover and to create meaning. As physicist William Keepin said of meaning and quantum reality—which I now understood applied equally to the existence of the Goddess—"It's like trying to prove the beauty of Mozart's music using chemistry. Music is beautiful to those who hear."

And I was also beginning to see that without the Goddess, without an appreciation for those aspects of being which we think of as feminine, without nurturance, compassion, intuition, connectedness, beauty, and the uniquely feminine creative, generative, *and* destructive powers, it is impossible even to begin to fathom the fullness of sacred meaning.

I was learning to see the world with my inner eye—to apprehend the sacred presence that animates it, its beauty and therefore its truth. Witches, and other shamans, know that nonordinary reality coexists with everyday reality, but is rarely seen, or heard, by most people. It is in this unseen, shadow realm that the laws and principles of magic rule. In an altered state of consciousness, we are able to step through the mirror and draw from the Goddess's sacred well of meaning. We enter the other dimension and become aware of connections. We step outside of time and relive the past and foresee the future.

As I had already discovered when we began to practice elemental magic, we can invoke or invite energy in the forms of angels, spirit guides, power animals, wraiths, and aspects of the Divine which we call "gods" or "goddesses," into our routine lives. When we have cultivated these long-lost capacities, we are able to see the connections, and the forms of the sacred, which have been with us all along.

But, for all the wisdom I'd been gleaning, all the techniques that brought me peace and wonder, when I looked at my life I had to admit I felt as if I stood in the midst of chaos. Chaos: from the Greek *xaos* and *xa,* meaning "to yawn, to gape," like the great vulvas of the Celtic Sheila-na-gigs or the symbol of *Ingwaz.* Chaos is the void, a yawning gulf, an abyss, the formless void of primordial matter. The expectations I'd had of satisfying work now seemed in doubt and I was confused. What had Jeanette said? It's how you deal with what's been handed to you. She looked like she knew what she was talking about, like a woman staring back into an abyss from which she'd only just begun to emerge.

What could magic offer in the face of the world's chaos? Magic was the art of changing one's consciousness, one's point of view. So perhaps my thinking about chaos as destructive was mistaken and reflected the limited thinking of the past. Perhaps chaos was not what we thought it to be. Perhaps chaos was, as the rune from circle had instructed me, part of the energy of liberation and creativity, the energy that would move us into the future.

Hesiod, one of the early Greek poets, wrote a creation myth telling the tale of the origin of the gods. Chaos appears, not as disorder, but as the source of all creation. With Chaos appears Gaia, as the created universe, and Eros as the creative energy. But the goddess Chaos preceded the Greeks in her origins, traced back to earlier written records in Egypt and Sumer as the goddess Tiamat, who battled with and was conquered by the sky god, Marduk. And this was our history. It was the history of Father Sun, science, and the church as institutions of domination and power. The ancient defeat, and subsequent disparaging of the meaning of Chaos, was a critical part of our ancient history in which the masculine overcame and suppressed the feminine, order replaced spontaneity, control subjugated fecundity, sun dominated moon, god surpassed goddess, repression strangled sexuality, and chaos came to mean disorder rather than the generative womb of the universe. The abyss is not empty—it is full of creative energy, and meaning.

By pursuing Chaos Theory to its outermost frontiers, scientists have discovered that within the seemingly chaotic lies an astonishing pattern of order and beauty. They have come to label this new insight "String Theory," marveling at how the universe appears, exactly as described so many years ago by the Goddess's priest Pythagoras, as harmonically vibrating, circular "strings" of energy: the music of the spheres. Science has now realized what the Goddess traditions have long known—that enlightenment is to be found in coexistence with the presence of chaos, the spontaneous and unexpected, the serpent that awakens behind a rock to startle us from our unconscious meandering. How we deal with the world's challenges, what we decide to do, is what determines who we are.

Past and present do not dictate the future but merely bring us to the point from which we will travel forward. The choice would be mine. What would it be? Would I have the courage to take unthinkable risks? To journey into unknown realms with no maps but the stars to guide me and no eyes but the one with second sight?

The tools of circle would be my compass and my sextant. I would learn, as my father had, to shoot the stars, to chart a course into realms of wonder. I realized that, in addition to altering our consciousness, divination enables us not only to see into ourselves, and into the heart of another, but into the archetypal patterns at play in our lives. It frees us from the constraints of the stable, linear worlds so we may enter the realm of nonordinary reality. It empowers us to discover the meaning of our lives.

At circle tonight we had combined a simple trance technique with an ancient method of divination. The results had impressed us all. By staring only at the rune I confined my attention to the symbol before me and thereby entered an alpha meditation state. Through my experiences, I was beginning to understand that an altered state of consciousness—whether created by divination, ritual, yoga, chanting, breath, rhythmic drumming, or other means—is actually expanded consciousness. It's like removing a blindfold to see what has surrounded you all along. Nonna had referred to it metaphorically as the lowering of the veil of Isis.

Certainly, like everyone else, I wanted to see my future. I wanted to know if I would find my soulmate and if my job would work out, despite these recent challenges. I was becoming more comfortable with the new vocabulary and techniques of circle. But what I wanted most was to experience communion with the Goddess. I sensed I was drawing nearer to her, and I knew instinctively that in her presence I would find the ultimate magic mirror, the revealer of truth and the truth itself.

A current of connection, of peace in the face of the unknown, courage in the face of ancient fears, traveled through me. I promised myself I would learn to see the truth as Odin had, as the priestesses of the earth had, with my inner eye. But would these techniques alone really be enough to lower the veil? And once it was lowered, would I see the Goddess—or would I see just myself, staring back empty-eyed and fearful?

CHAPTER 8

The Guardian at the Gate

Between the desire
And the spasm
Between the potency
And the existence
Between the essence
And the descent
Falls the Shadow. . . .

—T. S. ELIOT, *The Hollow Men*

The only devils in the world are those running in our own hearts;
that is where the battle should be fought.

—GANDHI

S elf-protection is a basic survival skill. You can't live in this city without knowing how to defend yourself," declared Bellona.

"So how do we start?" asked Gillian. Behind her cool blond exterior of boarding school breeding, I'd learned that she nurtured a passionate devotion to the Goddess's mysteries. With each circle her spirit was becoming more evident.

"You must find your center, and remain there, no matter what attack or provocation may come," Bellona replied. "Tonight we'll show you how to create a psychic shield that'll protect you from all sorts of malignant energies, human or otherwise."

The word *malignant* provoked nervous glances, but Maia reassured us. "The more attuned you become to the energies around us, the more you'll have to learn how to protect yourselves. Ladies, you're going to start picking up on other people's thoughts, their energies, and you're likely to pick up on a certain amount of etheric garbage that floats around out there."

I knew she was right—though I'd been shutting down, I needed a shield.

"You'll find it helpful to invoke a warrior goddess," Bellona continued. "She'll help you find the warrior within yourself."

"The Celts had a warrior goddess, didn't they?" asked Gillian.

"Celtic women were respected warriors," Bellona nodded. "And they had quite a number of warrior goddesses—Morrigan, Macha, and Scathatch. There was the Roman goddess Minerva, the Hindu Kali, the Yoruban Oya, the Egyptian Sekmet, a lot of others. The Greeks had warrior goddesses too—Athena and Artemis, not to mention an entire race of warrior women—"

"The Amazons!" exclaimed Marcia. She'd been practicing martial arts, and she was clearly enthusiastic about tonight's circle.

"Women have always been warriors, as well as mothers."

"Like Joan of Arc," Marcia added.

Bellona nodded. "Burned as a Witch. But the male energies are also important in learning the ways of a spiritual warrior—gods like Odin," I smiled as she continued, "and Mars. The warrior's path is a noble one; people have mostly forgotten that to follow the warrior's path is to become a spiritual warrior, not a mercenary. It's not a path of warfare with others, but confrontation with one's self."

"You said the fight was with ourselves—so what about our own internal rubble? Stress, insecurities, negative patterns," I asked, thinking of the battles I fought each day and the toll they were beginning to take. My parents were fighters and they'd raised me as a warrior, to fight for my principles. But these daily battles seemed increasingly removed from my ideals. I wished Nonna was with us, for I had wanted to talk to her, but she had battles of her own to fight and Bellona seemed well suited to lead our foray. "And what about other people's demands on us?" I added.

"They're all shadows," said Bellona. "You have to learn to get rid of the garbage, one step at a time, your own and other peoples'. Start with purification. You can use the elements for this. Bathing in water is one that everyone already uses. Native Americans and Wiccans use sage smoke to cleanse energy, thoughts, and feelings, what people call the aura."

"Like my smudge stick," Onatah said, pulling out a bundle of tied herbs from the huge shoulder bag she always carried. "My Native American teacher gave it to me—we burn it before working."

Bellona nodded. "Right. Why don't you light it and pass it around? You can also drink sage tea, or bathe with it, or sea salt, or other purification herbs. Fire itself is cleansing—remember the Sekmet ritual we did. You can also use the earth for purification. When you use herbs for purification you're using the earth. An ancient way to purify a magical tool is to bury it. You can lie on the ground and let the negativity flow from you into the earth, where she'll transform it. But always remember to give thanks."

"Once you've cleansed, you need to protect yourself from invasion by negativity, whether it's toxins in the environment or toxic energy from other people." Maia picked up a beautiful mirror from the altar. Its handle was carved in the figure of an Egyptian woman. She held it in front of her heart. I leaned forward with interest. "One technique is to imagine a concave mirror between you and your opponent. Whatever they send to you is reflected, or deflected, back toward them. This way you don't have to do anything more than 'return to sender.' Another method I like is to create a sphere of protection around myself, sometimes referred to as a shield of 'white light.' With practice you can learn to create one that'll act like a filter, allowing only the pure energy to enter, which you can put to good use, but keeping out any negativity that's been sent at you. That's what we'll work on tonight." Her reassuring warmth made it seem easy and the results certain. I hoped she was right.

I was seated, as always, in the east. Jeanette sat to my left, Gillian on my right. Maia looked over toward us as she spoke.

"Please sit comfortably. Close your eyes, ground and center."

Minutes passed. I could feel a terrible sadness and a tremendous determination radiating from Jeanette as she held my hand. I sent her love and then refocused my thoughts upon my breathing, allowing my mind to become quiet. I felt the weight of hands on my shoulders and I shuddered. What was that?

"Now send down roots, draw the energy of the earth up. . . . Feel it filling you with power and strength . . . Feel it pulsing through you, radiating outward, forming a glowing white energy field all around you. Inhale and draw the energy up from the earth . . . exhale and send the energy out into a radiant shell of power that surrounds and protects you. The shell is porous. Like a net of light, it allows in only healthy, pure energy, but it protects you from anything bad. Inhale and feel how you can absorb the cleansed power without taking in any negativity. . . . Feel yourself growing stronger. . . . As you grow stronger, feel this protective barrier of radiant light grow stronger. . . . Now concentrate the energy in your heart and your solar plexus. . . . Send it outward from yourself. . . . Seal yourself within it. Remember, you will take in only pure energy, which strengthens and renews you. Feel the energy stored in your heart and solar plexus. It's available to you whenever you need to create this shield of light. . . . Open your eyes."

We blessed the wine and cakes, and as we began to partake of them, suddenly, in a quiet voice, Jeanette asked, "What do I do with my anger?"

"It depends on what caused it," said Bellona, easily opening a juice bottle none of us had been able to open. "It can be a healthy reaction to an unhealthy situation—a messenger warning you to pay attention. But it can also poison you if you ignore its warning, if you don't take action to protect and take care of yourself, to honor yourself. Then you need to cleanse yourself."

And remove the cause of the anger, I thought to myself, little knowing what that thought was about to set in motion.

Maia continued. "A simple way to get rid of anger is to place both hands in a bowl of water. You can add salt, sage, a few drops of eucalyptus oil, ground vetivert, and pine needles to the water. Visualize your anger, like a black sticky fluid draining from you into the bowl. When you feel cleansed, pour the water into a river or the ocean. Or down the drain. As you pour it, you ask the waters to transform the negativity and you say:

"*Away, away*
 Be cleansed this day
 With water and earth
 Return to mirth
 Pure heart bind it
 Never mind it"

"And then you break the bowl and bury the pieces. And clean out your sink, if that's where you poured it."

"Is that how you stay so calm?" Bellona joked. Even Maia laughed, for she knew herself. Maia often flared just like a Roman candle, and when she did we were learning to stay out of her line of trajectory. It certainly wasn't the visage of a pacific, contemplative, saffron-robed mystic. It was dramatic, like fire raging up a brush-covered hillside, scorching everything in sight. It was like a force of nature, yet because it was never ill-willed or cruel, I found that it didn't upset me. Certainly not like the vitriolic explosions at work. I wondered if I could use the energy filter and Maia's anger purification at work.

"Beats a hundred dollars for a therapist's couch and it sounds a lot quicker," laughed Naomi, our resident jokester.

Everyone laughed with her, except Jeanette, who was carefully writing down Maia's instructions. As I watched her, I remembered our conversation after the rune readings when she'd said that life's hardships can strengthen you, depending on how you respond to them.

"But don't forget, anger can be a sword that saves your life." Bellona's voice had the hardened edge of someone who knew the toll of battle.

Jeanette looked up, her attention speared by Athena's lance, as was mine. Would Jeanette turn her mysterious, unspoken fear into a warrior's sword of righteous anger? For all of our differences, we suddenly seemed so like one another—I too kept my troubles to myself, and I too needed to turn fear to anger and anger to action. But how?

Well, this is a nice surprise." I settled back into the sybaritic comfort of the limousine.

"Slim, it's the only way to go. It gives you the right point of view when you gotta deal with scumbags. I'm gonna enjoy this," Tony Pagano laughed with obvious anticipation. He was one of the business's best record promoters—a short, swarthy bundle of nonstop energy. We'd done a number of deals together and had become friends. I'd been schooled in the high road, and he was teaching me the low. "So he doesn't know you're bringing me along?" Tony asked.

"Of course not, that's the whole point: shock value. We want him completely knocked off guard."

"Well, this is gonna do it. He's gonna shit his pants when you walk in with me."

"That would be gratifying, but I just want him to back off this hardass position he's been taking."

"If this doesn't do it, nothing will."

We were on our way to see Don Marshall, a very well known manager whose stadium-packing band had passed its heyday. He needed clients and I had one he wanted—a fabulous group that had opened concerts for some major stars. It was pure coincidence, or maybe a whole lot more, that the band had found its way to me, that Don Marshall had approached them, and that Tony had been partners with Don for years before they'd had a falling out. Tony knew every move, motivation, and misery of Don's professional and personal life, and that knowledge was my secret weapon.

Don had offered a deal that amounted to slave labor; it was more than unethical, mixing contracts for producing with managing and a record contract. I knew that when he saw Tony walk in with me, he'd blow a fuse. And that was what I was counting on—my hope was that once he was off balance, he'd cut the crap and offer us a real deal.

The office was shabbier than I expected—pine paneling covered with old concert posters, photos, and a few gold records, filing cabinets, Xerox machines, boxes, too much stuff in too little space.

A pretty young woman nearly jumped out of her skin when Tony walked through the door behind me. He put his finger to his lips and she threw her arms around him. "God, I've missed you. It just isn't the same. How've you been?"

"Good, good. I'm great. So's the great man in?"

She grimaced and nodded.

"Can you please tell him I'm here?" I asked. "But don't mention Tony."

"No problem." She smiled conspiratorially and ushered us into Don's office. He was on the phone with his back to us. We sat down. He kept talking, a ploy to annoy me that only heightened my sense of enjoyment. It was just a matter of time. He hung up and started to turn.

"So, I assume you're ready to—" He looked like I'd punched him in the stomach. It was so satisfying.

"Never assume," I smiled sweetly. "I know you know each other."

Tony smiled his best rascal's grin.

"What's he doing here?" Don glared at me.

"Well, he's part of the team. Now the question is, are you?" The power had suddenly shifted. I could feel it in the room like the soft thick air of a gorgeous summer day, and he knew it. I thought I detected a little bead of sweat on his upper lip.

I laid out our terms and he argued, but I'd driven a wedge through his steely armor and it was just a matter of time until we reached a point of agreement. Tony excused himself to call the band, and Don came out from behind his desk.

"Clever, aren't you? Get what you wanted?" He stopped inches away from me and his hands shot out like rattlesnakes striking and grabbed my breasts. It happened so quickly I couldn't think. But I did react, with equal speed. I took a step toward him, reached around, and grabbed his ass. And I squeezed as hard as I could, using my nails so that the message would clearly be one of pain, not pleasure.

He recoiled from me as if he'd been bitten.

"It's not as big as it should be, but it will do until something better comes along," I said calmly. I tucked my briefcase under my arm and slowly walked to the door. "I don't think we'll need any more personal meetings. Or, you can meet with Tony next time." And before he could reply, I walked out the door, closing it on his stunned face. Exploding in a fit of laughter, I pulled Tony from the office, and we headed for the Russian Tea Room.

I laughed the rest of the day. And I learned something about sending energy back from whence it came. It wasn't my mind that reacted—it was my body. It knew how to protect me, to respond in kind. Just a few months ago, my mind would have been paralyzed with embarrassment and confusion, which was exactly what Marshall intended with his crude attack. But my body had known what to do. It now had its own warrior's wisdom and a capacity to take care of me in ways I'd never suspected. That was good. In fact, that was worth the entire frustrating, ridiculous encounter. My mind had plotted the strategy, but in the final moment it was my body that brought me to victory.

There were very few women in the music business back then, and on this day I'd had only a brief brush with the reality women too often had to deal with. Today I'd won what I wanted for my clients, and I hadn't succumbed to humiliation. In fact, I'd handed out a fair dose right back, and frankly that had felt pretty damn good. I'd been clever and strong, played by the rules of the game—I'd won. I'd been as tough as I'd needed to be. But, finally, as I sat in my living room with nothing but candlelight and the play of dancing shadows on the walls, I became aware of an entirely different emotion: I felt violated. I was proving that I had what it took to win. But I was becoming someone I didn't want to be.

I lit a small bundle of sage, slowly breathing in its cleansing smoke. As I grounded, my mind became quiet. And then the insight came: I had grown up learning to fight for others, to fight for noble causes, but I'd never really learned how to fight for myself. I was naively unprepared for what I was encountering in the work world, mistakenly thinking my mother's generation had fought, and won, the struggle for women's equality in the workplace. It began to dawn on me that my own life had become the battleground of my ideals. I remembered Nonna's words that I could not heal others until I had healed myself—perhaps it was also true that I couldn't fight for others until I'd learned to fight for myself. But how?

Was it always going to be like this? Was I going to have to grow a skin so thick that nothing could penetrate it? Then what? Would I have power, money, respect? I knew, as the clock struck midnight, that there was a price to be paid in this game. When I had what now lay within my grasp, I was afraid I would be like all the others—indifferent to, or even the cause of, the suffering of others, trapped in armor that could not be shed, and no longer able to feel the wind's soft kiss, or the touch of someone I loved.

That night my dreams were dark and haunted, with my shadow in front of me, instead of behind. Wherever it moved, I was forced to follow. And I wasn't alone: Everyone in the dream was being led around by their shadows, which, instead of following them, moved around a parched and barren landscape, almost dragging the person behind them. I struggled to break free, and saw Jeanette struggling to free herself.

As I got ready for work in the morning, I covered the dark circles under my eyes with makeup. With each day of professional assault, no matter how tough it made me, I couldn't help but wonder if I was becoming a shadow of myself.

There's a woman here asking for you. She says she's a friend—Jeanette Sebillot," Madeline's voice announced through my phone's intercom.

"Thanks, Madeline. Send her back here." Scooping up a stack of papers, I thought, how odd. I would have to tell her about last night's dream. Jeanette worked in New Jersey, so she wasn't dropping by for lunch. I checked my watch—I was due in a meeting with Hadus but I figured whatever it was, it wouldn't take long.

"Um, I think you might want to come out here." Madeline sounded a little worried.

Very odd.

Jeanette was sitting in a corner of the reception area, her face turned away from us.

"Hi!" I greeted her cheerfully. "What a nice surprise. I've got a meeting in about ten minutes but come on back . . ." She turned and I saw she was wearing sunglasses.

"I'm sorry to bother you at work . . . but you're a lawyer and I didn't know who else to talk to." I could hear her struggling to keep her voice calm. "I don't know what to do—" Her voice broke.

This was not going to be a five-minute visit.

"It's O.K. Come on, we can talk in my office." She got up slowly, as if every bone in her body ached. She was impeccably dressed in a vividly colored suit. With her elegantly styled hair and her shades she looked every inch an opera diva, and everyone looked up as I escorted her back to my office.

"Would you like a cup of coffee?"

She shook her head. We sat in silence. I glanced at my watch. Jeanette opened her purse and took out some tissues. She turned away and stared out the window. "Could you close the door?"

"Of course." I waited for her to say something. The tension was thick, filling the room with the deafening impact of an onrushing train. "I'm afraid I've got a meeting so I can't visit for long." I was careful not to sound impatient. "You said you need a lawyer?"

"I shouldn't have bothered you at work."

"No, it's really O.K. Just tell me what's wrong." I glanced at my watch—two minutes to go. "What happened? Were you at work?"

"Yes, but I left. Now they're going to fire me. . . . I can't afford to lose my job."

O.K., this I could deal with in the one minute remaining. "Do you have a union?"

"No, it's not that."

"Why would they fire you?" My phone line beeped and lit up. I watched it nervously. Madeline would take a message.

Jeanette was crying. The minute was up.

"I'm sure you can talk to them. Do you want me to?"

"I'm sorry. I shouldn't have come here." She lifted the glasses to wipe her eyes and I saw her right eye was swollen and purplish.

"Oh, hell! What happened?"

Jeanette's chest heaved gently as she struggled with the shadow surrounding her. "It's my ex-husband." Her voice was small and hard. She stared out the window and the sky darkened. There was a sharp knock on the door.

"Just a minute," I called.

"What about your ex-husband? Jeanette, talk to me. Did he do this to you?"

The door opened.

"He's going to kill me."

I turned to see Hadus standing in the doorway, glowering. I smiled, reassuringly, signaling that I would be right there.

"I'm sorry, what did you say?" Hadus curtly asked her.

"She said her previous lawyer's going to kill her if she dumps him. Jeanette's just been offered a very attractive contract." I was covering as best I could. "Jeanette . . . Dumas, a possible new client. John Hadus, my boss." I hoped Jeanette could hold it together until I could get rid of him. "I know we have a meeting. We'll be just a few more minutes." And then I found myself doing the outrageous—I took Hadus by the arm and escorted him out.

"Ten minutes, I promise." And I closed the door in his astonished face.

Jeanette was standing by the window, her back to me. "He *is* going to kill me. He got out of jail a couple of weeks ago. He's been calling but I wouldn't see him. Today he showed up where I work. I don't know how he found me. He was waiting in the parking lot when I left for lunch. He wanted me to give him money, it was terrible. My friend Mary helped me get away, and I came here. But he's going to find me."

"You can stay with me. I have to do this meeting, but we can leave together as soon as I'm finished. I'll call Jake and he can go with us to your place so you can get some things. Did you call the police?"

She shook her head.

"Were there any witnesses?"

"I don't know, it doesn't matter."

"Don't worry about that now. Your phone's listed, isn't it? You should change your phone number. We'll get you a restraining order." I was in my rational lawyer mode—no problem I couldn't solve. "Let me call my friend Rachel—I know her from my union work. She makes her living doing domestic and general practice stuff. She'll help you." I wrote down Rachel's number and handed it to her. "Here's her number. I'll tell Rachel to expect your call."

"It's not gong to do any good." She was as cold and still as stone. "I don't know what to do," a soft moan ancient as the first sorrow escaped her lips. I could hear her world collapsing around her.

Rachel was in court so I left her a message.

"It's going to be all right."

She nodded numbly.

When I got back from Hadus's office, she was gone. I called her apartment a dozen times over the next few days, but there was no answer and no one had heard from her. I was sick with worry, which lessened only a little when Rachel told me Jeanette had called her.

A thin sickle of waning moon hung in the sky as I hurried into circle, hoping Jeanette would be there. Stepping into the sweet air and the sound of women's laughter, I was entering a space of safety and peace. But Bellona's energy was troubled and urgent, and Maia was huddled in a corner that seemed abnormally dark. Gillian was sitting with her, talking to her softly, holding her hand.

"What's wrong?" I asked Naomi.

"I don't know," she replied, her usual merry expression replaced by a worried frown. I heard the front door open and saw Jeanette, still wearing her sunglasses.

"Thank the Goddess you're here." I wrapped her in a hurried hug. "I've been so worried about you. Where've you been?"

Gingerly she removed her shades. I could see the swelling of her eye had subsided and she'd covered the bruise with makeup. In the darkened room, unless you knew it was there, you might not even notice.

"I took a hotel room out of town for a few days."

"You could've stayed with me. Did you meet with Rachel?"

Before she could answer, Bellona anxiously urged us into circle. The temple was lit with black and white candles in pairs. Thick red clouds of an unfamiliar and redolent incense billowed from the altar. As Bellona cast with a gleaming sword raised up before her, she called the ancient names Nemesis, Sekmet, Morrigan, Hecate, Andrastea, Kali, dark goddesses all, forces of power, reckoning, and righteous anger. I had never seen her so grimly determined.

We stood in a circle, holding hands, waiting for Bellona's direction. Her head was bowed. Suddenly a cry ripped from her throat, a wail of primeval pain and rage. Bellona began to move counterclockwise around the darkened room. This was widdershins, the direction of banishings. Slowly we followed, pushing against some unseen resistance, as if our bodies were dragged down by an extraordinary gravity.

Bellona began to chant so quietly it sounded like muttering. Her voice gradually rose to a clear and forceful pitch, pronouncing a spell for banishing. We chanted with her, moving faster and faster until we were running and the chant became two words: *Be gone!*

The room was growing colder. As I moved from the west to the south, I found the temperature was icy cold by the locked entrance to the temple. The skin on the back of my neck crawled and that's when I saw it: a black, viscous cloud, over six feet tall, hovering by the door.

Sheer, irrational terror seized me. I was afraid to pass it, to turn my back on it, but I couldn't stop the circle. I moved closer, and at the moment I dreaded, directly in front it, I felt anger rising up in me so forcefully that there was no room for fear.

I will not let you, I raged. *Be gone!*

Twice more we circled past the diabolical manifestation. We came to a sudden stop on the third pass as a ceramic bowl on the altar shattered. I turned quickly to the temple's entrance—the shadow was gone.

There was no feasting tonight, no laughter or shared stories. Bellona remained in the temple, her arms wrapped protectively around an exhausted Maia. She instructed us not to touch the pieces of broken bowl, but we quickly cleared the rest of the altar and left the temple.

Jeanette was seated at Maia's reading table, tying the laces of her elegant Victorian boots.

"Is Rachel going to get you an order of protection?" I sat down beside her. In contrast to the way I felt after most circles, I was tired.

Jeanette nodded. "It's done. We went to court today. I'm going home tonight."

"Are you sure it's safe? You can stay with me."

"The truth is, if he wants to get me, no court order is going to stop him. No place is safe if I let him terrorize me. I won't be safe in my own skin. I've got to stand up to him. I did it before, I can do it again."

"Before?" We sat together in silence, as Jeanette struggled with her demons. Finally, she spoke, her face turned slightly aside.

"He used to beat me. I was young and foolish and beautiful and he was insanely jealous. I thought the sun rose and set on him—that he just needed to feel secure in my love. But after a while I was just terrified. He told me if I left him he'd kill me. And I knew he would."

"I'm so sorry. . . ." We sat together in the strange, silent aftermath of the magic that had just passed and the memories that remained. "What did you do?"

"I found the courage and I turned him in."

"You're amazing!" I took her hand as she finally turned to look at me. There were tears in her eyes, but her face was firmly set.

"No, I'm a survivor. But I paid a terrible price for my fear. I was pregnant, and I knew the baby would never survive unless I got away. I waited until he'd passed out. I'd packed a small bag and I had it hidden under the couch. It was bitter cold and I had only a spring coat. It was so pretty, a beautiful coral color with a little collar and big buttons." Her voice faded and her eyes saw something too distant for anyone else to recognize but too familiar for her to forget. "I was out the door but I was still three flights away from freedom. He woke up." She stopped as the shadow I now recognized passed over her face.

"They told me at the hospital that the baby was stillborn. It was too tiny to survive the fall."

"Oh, Jeanette . . ."

"A little girl. When the social worker came to see me I told her I would press charges."

And she laughed, low and sad. "The district attorney wasn't very enthusiastic about pursuing what he called a 'domestic' case. But while I was still in the hospital, Richard was arrested for dealing drugs. So I guess he got his karma. Or some of it, anyway. But now he's out."

"I guess you talked to Maia. Did the circle help?"

"No, I haven't told anyone but you. Please don't say anything, I don't want to worry them. I have to find out who told him where to find me. I'll deal with that, then I'll deal with him. And I discussed it with Rachel—tomorrow I'm filing charges with the police. I'm sure someone at work saw what happened." I could see her determination. "I'm not going to take it. Not ever again."

She hugged me, long and hard.

"Thanks. You were a big help."

"Me? I didn't do anything."

"You were there when I needed you. You were my sister. Now I need to get some rest."

"Call me tomorrow."

She nodded, and she walked out of the shop with a strength and beauty I'd never seen before.

Maia looked exhausted when I reentered the temple, and I hesitated to bother her, but after everyone had left, I told Maia and Bellona about the mysterious shadow I had seen during the banishing. They exchanged looks and I could feel but not hear their unspoken dialogue.

"It was by the door to the temple." I said.

Again they looked at each other.

"It was freezing, and terrifying. But I just got incredibly angry and that energy carried me past my fear. Was I just seeing things?"

"No," said Bellona quietly. "We saw it too."

I didn't know whether to feel relieved or more frightened. I had thought the banishing had been done for Jeanette, but there was another reason. I was stunned as Bellona explained that Maia had been sexually assaulted that afternoon. The circle's energy was being used to banish the effects of the attack and to bring retribution to the perpetrator.

The predatory energy had invaded the lives of at least three of us, with varying degrees of effect.

All the following week I woke, worked, and slept in the shadow of that banishing circle. I relived the harrowing night and realized that in order to banish something, you must first invoke it. It was one thing to summon a sylph or even an unpredictable animal spirit like a pookah. It was another matter entirely to invoke something loathsome and terrifying. Until now, our work had been . . . charming. It was serious, sometimes deeply emotional, but never so viscerally frightening. What had I stumbled into? I had trusted my priestesses implicitly, but by not warning us about what might happen during a banishing ritual, they created a crisis of trust for me. Though perhaps they didn't realize the negative energy we were banishing would manifest in such a frightening, physical way.

I began to see that my priestesses were not all-knowing, all-powerful. They were teachers—gifted, generous, and wise, but human, and thus imperfect. They could do no more than import the tools and techniques of this ancient system. They could guide and advise me, but ultimately, I was responsible for myself. By the time the moon had swollen to fullness, I knew that I trusted them to teach me what they knew. The rest of it I would work out for myself. After all, this was not a spirituality that insisted its followers obey religious leaders that claim infallibility. The question now was whether I trusted myself to continue on this path that had suddenly entered a realm where dark and unknown perils lay in wait.

I needed to find out what I'd encountered in that banishing circle. I needed to test myself. A few sleepless nights later, at the dark of the moon, I set up a scrying mirror. I propped the darkened looking-glass in front of me, and between it and myself, I placed a small candle. The flame blocked everything from view but my eyes. I knew this device could be used to see one's past incarnations, but tonight I was seeking something, or someone, else. I was protecting myself with the light shield at work, and while my efforts seemed to reduce the effect of Hadus's assaults, something far more disturbing seemed to be draining my energy. And it seemed to be getting worse ever since the banishing circle.

It had the texture of fear and self-doubt. I knew Nonna wasn't feeling well, and it had been weeks since she had been to circle. I missed her wisdom, but I spoke to Maia and she had given me a purification bath which cleansed much of it away. But it surfaced again, embracing me and twirling me in a macabre minuet whenever I least expected it. I doubted the wisdom of my choices; I questioned whether I wanted to continue my job; then I questioned being in circle. I doubted myself. I was filled with waves of uncertainty that threatened to drown me with each rising tide.

What was it? Where did it come from? And how was I to free myself? I stared into the mirror without looking away from myself. It was a hot, sweltering night with no relief from the day's hellish accumulation, but the temperature in the room began to drop. A chill seized me; and then it appeared. A black ghost robed in open wounds crept toward me, undulating visibly the way air does when scorched by the summer sun. The skin on the back of my neck crawled and a wave of nausea hit me, but I did not look away. The room was freezing. My heart was racing. I was terrified, afraid to look away, more afraid to turn around and confront it—for then my shadow would stand before me, as in my dream. I forced myself to turn, counterclockwise, feeling as if my body was made of lead, hoping that it was no more than an illusion of smoke and mirrors.

It was a Shadow. It hovered at the threshold of my front door, blocking my exit. I moved, slowly, as if underwater, to the left; it followed. I moved to the right; it followed. I felt as if I were suffocating. I was unprepared; I hadn't cast, nor had I invoked the aid of any goddess. I hadn't armed myself with a magical tool or even words of banishing. And then I remembered Nonna's words: The magic comes from within. As quickly as the bowl had broken in circle, my fear shattered and my body felt light, free. A rush of courage seized me and I took a step toward the shadow. It didn't move.

"What are you?" I demanded, remembering that knowing the name of a demon gives you power over it.

Nothing. And then I knew, I heard it, within. "I am the Guardian at the Gate, I am the Shadow. Push against me."

Touch it? I stood paralyzed and the Shadow moved toward me. I seized the candle, a tiny torch of fire, of will and passion, and thrust it into the approaching darkness. A shadow slid up my arm, but the light pierced the blackness. And it vanished.

I looked down, and my arm was glowing. My knees buckled and I was shaking. I sat on the floor, pulling my knees to my chest, hugging myself. What had I accomplished except scaring myself more thoroughly than I already had been? I pulled out the bundle of cleansing herbs and quickly sprinkled them in a circle around the room. I was still trembling. I drank water. I breathed slowly and waited for the confusion to pass. And as I became calmer, I began to understand.

Push against it—and you'll discover what you need to overcome the obstacles that stand in your path. Obstructions are opportunities. In overcoming them we give ourselves strength and character, insight and compassion. They are the means by which we take form. If we turn away from them, we remain stuck, unchanged. But by confronting them, we discover the measure and the meaning of our lives.

Any truly spiritual journey will, inevitably, lead you to the Guardian at the Gate. Until we confront it, and master the challenges this shadow presents, it will hold us back from the fullest experience of our true, divine selves. Once we understand the shadow is our teacher, in whatever shape it assumes—fear, doubt, hunger for power, shame, selfishness, or any self-destructive or harmful trait—we can wrest from it the keys to the realm of the Goddess.

When you look deep enough into a magic mirror, you will see the Shadow looking back at you. For everything casts a shadow—it is the companion of a body that dances in the light. Like the image in a mirror, it is a reflection of truth. But, also like the image in a mirror, it is reversed. By seeing our "dark side," we see not only the rest of ourselves, whatever is normally hidden from view, but also our shape, our movement. We can't run from our shadow, we can't turn our back on it. If we deny its existence, we succumb to our own weaknesses, or more dangerous still, we risk projecting them onto others, which can lead to the unspeakable brutality with which people have treated each other for far too long. Though it often comes to us in the shape of another human being, the Shadow is a part of ourselves. And no attempt to bury it within our unconscious, or to rationalize its dominance of our culture, will free us from the terrors of its presence.

How do we defeat it? In magical stories the hero is always given several aids to make his or her way: words of wisdom from a holy woman or man; a magical tool—a sword or cloak, amulet or book; and often a guide—an animal, spirit, or friend. The Guardian at the Gate challenges us to find those tools, those powers, within ourselves.

It began to dawn on me that the negative energies I was encountering at work were *not* separate and apart from my Wiccan spiritual pursuits. In fact, they were a reflection of that work. They expressed the very shadows that stood between myself and the sacred. The journey of our life, the people we encounter, the challenges of the world, are actually the daily expression of a profound spiritual journey to conquer fear, banish ignorance, and liberate our spirit. I was coming to understand that my confrontations with the Guardian at the Gate were a test, as were the events of my daily life.

Much of magical work is about the purification and transformation of these negative, destructive, confining energies into positive, life-affirming, creative impulses. I now knew that in order to banish something, you must first invoke it. And then be strong enough to push against it. I was learning to master the Guardian at the Gate. I knew I had begun to find ways to conquer shadows, but I still did not know if I could find the Goddess.

For thousands of years, priestesses, Goddess worshippers, women, and Witches have had the culture's shadow projected on them. They have been branded as evil. The fear of women's power and sexuality made them the culture's scapegoat, held them responsible for the existence of sin and the cause of man's expulsion from Eden. Witches were not evil, yet certainly evil existed—the terror of the Witchcraze had been a projection of this cultural shadow with ferocious consequences. As I struggled with the images of Maia's pain and Jeanette's bruised face, my own humiliation, and the countless nightmares presented by the media everyday, I had to wonder: Was a part of every human essentially, biologically, unalterably evil?

To find an answer I knew I should turn to nature as my spiritual teacher and, as if the universe had heard me, it answered my need with beauty and luxury—Gillian invited me to spend the weekend at her parents' twenty-four-room "cottage" in Southampton. As we drove past fields and pine barrens and I felt my spirits rise, I realized how easily our souls became lost in the concrete labyrinths of cities. We spent hours together, working in the little garden she'd tended since childhood, walking, meditating, and circling at the edge of the enormous ocean. We talked about Maia's attack and Gillian told me that she had been raped, years ago on a date with a young man from one of America's most prominent families. We immersed ourselves in the ocean and rejoiced as the powerful tides pulled the sorrows from our souls.

Reclining in the sand, the sun on my face, the water lapping at my legs, the answer was as clear as the fresh air. Evil does not exist in nature. If a tiger eats you for lunch, the tiger would not be evil, it would merely be a tiger. But clearly evil does exist in man. History, and my own life and the people who had filled it, were full of shining examples of the goodness of the human heart. From their examples, I knew evil was not innate, but how does it arise? Standing in the cleansing, empowering surf, I knew that evil is something that arises within human beings when they become disconnected from the natural world. It is the shadow of pain and madness filling the place left empty by a lost soul. In finding our connection to the earth, we can retrieve our lost connection to the sacred. We can heal the wound from which evil arose and find the spiritual sustenance which we are starving for.

I now knew you must be prepared to face your worst nightmare or you cannot free yourself from it. You must name your demon and you must confront him. This is the journey that gives you strength and compassion, wisdom and freedom, and reverence for life. This is the journey I was undertaking. And I was blessed to be taking it in the company of others, for we could sustain and encourage each other as we faced the shadows.

Saltwater baths—that's what Maia had recommended to cleanse away the cobwebs and confusion. And so we swam in the ocean. Though the days were filled with long sunlight, the water was still shockingly cold. But I gave myself to the pounding waves, to the incessant tugging of the tide, to the salt water in my ears and nose and mouth and eyes until I added my own salt to the sea's. And when the ocean had willingly received my tears, I thanked it, and struggled against the weight of her receding waters, collapsing, at peace and on shore again.

Bone weary, cleansed and consecrated in the womb of the first mother from whom we came so long ago, I sat on her glassy sand, shivering. As I stared out at the summer sun resting upon the shining waves, I remembered the Ace of Cups Tarot card with the chalice and its radiant, overflowing waters of life from which the sun rose, that I had envisioned and drawn so many months ago. I thought of Gillian's search for the Grail, and my first magical tool, the silver chalice. I thought also of the wounds of women and of men, how they are intertwined, and how their healing must proceed together. I began to understand one of the darker, little-known tales of the Holy Grail, and its profound meaning for today's world.

In the stories handed down to us since the 1200s, the Holy Grail was the cup used at the Last Supper and that held the blood of Christ. The Sacred Grail also held the waters of life, and to drink from this cup was to be reborn. All the knights of the Round Table searched for the lost Grail relentlessly, in a quest that every man and woman in our Western culture unconsciously continues to this day. It remains a symbol of spiritual pursuit, the search for a meaningful life. But for centuries the Grail has eluded us because we haven't known what we're looking for. No wonder we cannot find it, for it has been described to us as a symbol of redemption through sacrifice, suffering, and grief.

But the true Grail awaits our discovery, shrouded in the obscuring mists of time. Its essential shape and purpose still shine for those who can defeat the Guardian at the Gate—for the Holy Grail is an ancient symbol of the Goddess, of the divine feminine.

Long before the story was Christianized, and its original mythological meaning was altered, the Grail was an ancient pre-Christian symbol of the fertile, holy earth and the divine feminine spirit that animates the natural realm. In this tradition, the Grail was a stone platter that held all the bounty and blessings of the earth, the Goddess incarnate. The knight's quest was to find this Grail and discover his true masculinity by serving the divine feminine—within himself, in the land, and ultimately, in the form of his beloved. In the earliest stories, the Goddess was often called Sovereignty, and it was only through marriage to her, through the agency of her priestess, that a man became king. His role was to honor and protect the sacred land, the Goddess, and her people. But in one of the ancient stories, the Grail King, who is also called the Fisher King, came into his power, not by quest, but by inheritance. He had never been tested and so never mastered himself, nor learned the responsibilities of his sacred role. Indifferent and unaware, he raped a young priestess of the Grail. Failing in his hallowed trust, the king was challenged to a joust by a pagan knight whose lance wounded him in the groin and thus rendered him impotent. The world fell barren; it had become a wasteland.

Though the Grail, from which all blessings flow, remains within the king's reach, neither he, nor his people, can take sustenance from it. The landscape is made sterile by promises that have been violated, and that remain unfulfilled. The king sits fishing beside a lonely river, crippled in pain from the wound that will not heal. He is unable to walk, dance, make love, or care for the people withering around him. How is he to be healed, and how is the world to be healed, if the Grail cannot heal him?

Most men live in the shadow of this now ancient wasteland, unable to serve the Grail, already wounded and crippled by inheritance, and too often abusing, not only their inherited power, but the priestesses of the Grail. They suffer a wound that separates them from their feelings, thwarting their ability to give and receive love. But the king *required* the wounding in order to open his soul. The wound, and its location, is like the opening to a woman's body, and a woman's soul. The wound unites him with the injured feminine; it gives him empathy, compassion, the capacity to feel. But neither the Grail nor its priestesses can heal him. To restore life to the land, the king must heal himself—by touching the pagan spear to his wound. He must reclaim his masculine energy, which honors the Goddess, in order to heal the wound in his soul, his psyche, his sexuality. In the reclaiming and redirecting of this masculine *chi,* the king returns to the Grail as its guardian and servant. He returns to the Goddess, to her land and her people, as her protector, her lover, her champion. Then the Fisher King may partake of the Grail's healing blessings, for he will have rediscovered life's meaning and learned that sacred insight is always possible—one need only ask. When men once again honor the Divine Feminine, we will heal in the Wasteland.

Throughout time, women have shared this wound, passed on by their fathers or inflicted by the demands of the world in which they now work, though they are increasingly aware that the Grail resides within themselves. As a result, women have too often become victims, inhabiting the Wasteland the world has become in the absence of the feminine. We too must heal ourselves.

I sat in a circle drawn in the sand, thinking of an age-old wisdom that all faiths share—to complete the cycle of being. We must travel through the Wasteland, the time of barren winter, when the invisible seed of rebirth lies hidden within the earth. This is the time when we most need to connect to the divine, and it is from this connection that faith arises with the certainty that the unseen sacred will return: not in some far-off land, but in the Wasteland of our daily lives, in the bleak landscapes of our television sets, which each day deliver into our homes such images of desperate brutality it is a divine gift that we are still capable of wonder. But it is in the midst of darkness that we must discover a seed of light within, the Grail within ourselves and our world. And we have the ability to nurture that miracle into being and visibility—to find within ourselves, both mother and father, Goddess and God. It is our journey to find Eden within the Wasteland.

It was the magic hour, when light is the color of poured gold and the shadows are almost as long as they are at noon in winter. Blinded by the light, I turned away from the sun—and that was when I saw it. The silhouette of a young woman, her long hair, the curves of her body, her quick gestures. I faced the earth and saw my shadow and it no longer terrified me. In its shape, its exotic movements, I saw myself, filling space and time for as long as I was graced with form. I knew a shadow would always accompany me. How that shadow moved was a reflection of the woman to whom it was attached. Whether it danced or grieved, made love or murder, was entirely up to me.

CHAPTER 9

Drawing Down the Moon

The doorway of the Mysterious Feminine
Is the base from which Heaven and Earth sprang.
It is there within us all the while.
Draw upon it as you will, it never runs dry.

—LAO TZU, *Tao te Ching*

"Can I help you?" The saleslady's silver hair was pulled back in a neat chignon, her dusty pink suit copied the Chanel classic, and on her feet were low-heeled pumps.

"Yes, thanks—I need to look like you."

Her carefully tweezed and penciled eyebrows arched and her pink lips pursed a little more tightly.

"I beg your pardon?"

"You look so . . . nicely put together—tasteful, conservative, understated." *Asexual* was what I meant, but I wasn't going to say it. "I need some things for business."

"Ah," she nodded. "Designer or ready-to-wear?"

"Ready-to-wear will be fine."

She ushered me into a dressing room the size of my apartment. The Louis XVI chair was upholstered in gold striped silk, the lined drapes in gold moiré framed a breathtaking view of the park, and the cream-colored carpet was thick beneath my stockinged feet. In a huge gold-framed mirror I caught the reflection of a vulnerable young woman. I squared my shoulders and lifted my head, swiftly sweeping up my hair and securing it with clips. I had a strategy. If my workplace was going to be a battleground, I was going to don armor. After my encounter with Don Marshall, and with Hadus's intentions now clear, I needed not just a psychic shield, but a physical shield that would cover my body and my sexuality. Whatever it took, I was determined to survive and succeed.

Power dressing hadn't been invented yet, so dressing for success meant wearing female versions of men's suits, because that's what we were expected to be—female versions of men. High-performance work hadn't been enough; would changing my appearance make any difference in how I was perceived? If any hint of sexuality was removed from the picture, would I be treated with more respect?

The saleslady had commandeered assistants, a small army with whom I found myself confiding my recent tribulations. They clucked and commiserated, sharing stories of frustrated promotions, unfair paychecks, and sexual harassment that ranged from sly remarks to supply-room gropes to outright intimidation. With gales of laughter, they shared tales of victories and accomplishments. A sisterhood of sympathy assisted me as I reconstructed my image. I tried everything—boxy, tailored, long-skirted, figure-concealing. Navy, black, brown, and gray. Serious. Very serious.

They carried in armloads of blouses with loathsome Peter Pan collars and floppy bows that reminded me more of little girls than big business. These, and a discreet string of pearls, were the feminine substitutes for a man's necktie, a formal demarcation slicing head from heart and now the standard uniform for professional women. Next came boxes of sensible shoes.

I was going for Katharine Hepburn, but modern designers hadn't yet caught up to her stunning, elegant professionalism. I surveyed myself in the mirror. It would have to do. An iron mask covered my gentle soul.

"I'll take them." We congratulated ourselves on the transformation. Lunch hour was over. I had my armor—let the combat begin.

The shopping bags were bulky and heavier than I expected, but I was stopped dead in my tracks by a dress—spotlit, hanging in a sculpted niche, it was perfect, a feminine work of art. Long and flowing, it was silver moonlight captured and spun into a dress that would make a woman feel like Diana, or Aphrodite, no matter what her size, a dress that honored the female figure, its absolute power, and its beauty.

And, at least for a time, this designer was blessed by the Goddess's inspiration, as he honored her in his emblem of ancient female authority—the Gorgon head of Medusa, snakes curling in ringlets around her raging face. It was an evocation of dark femininity. Attached to his dresses, it is a badge of power, the dangerous sovereignty of seduction. We knew Medusa as grotesque, but I had already learned so much more of the truth that lay behind these distorted images of women.

Medusa was one of the ten Sibyls, the priestesses of prophecy. Her name, in ancient Libya, land of her origin, was also Lamia, which meant "snake," symbol of the great earth Goddess. This Libyan Sibyl was a priestess of Isis, presiding over the mysteries of the Underworld, of descent and return, death and rebirth. She was one of the five Sibyls painted by Michelangelo on the ceiling of the Sistine Chapel, ironically and deliberately immortalized in the sanctuary of the religious institution most responsible for the destruction and distortion of a priestess's value. *Sibyl,* the magical word that opened the world of meaning to me, was the title of prophetic priestesses, derived from the Greek *sios* or *theos,* meaning "divine," and *bola,* meaning "advice." A sibyl was a woman who spoke the poetics of the divine. How could I not marvel, when the first sibyl I encountered, the sibyl who pointed to where my path lay, was the same beautiful Libyan Sibyl? The world was full of magic.

My watch tugged at my sleeve—it was time to get back to the office. Where could I wear a dress like that? It was hardly the choice for the combat that awaited me. I struggled through the crowded aisles and then the swarming streets. In the lobby of my skyscraper, I played my little psychic guessing game and stood in front of elevator number three as the crowd gathered elsewhere.

Ding! The red "3" lit up, and the doors opened. I got on, followed by the rushing crowd.

"Well, that's a change!" Madeline greeted the new me with widened eyes.

"Whatever it takes." I listened as she read from a stack of pink message slips:

"Schwartz at ICM, Tony Pagano, Harper at CBS, and Nonna called and asked you to bring an apple tonight."

"An apple?"

"That's what she said."

I piled my gold-embossed bags in the corner of my office and tightened my bow, steeling myself for the afternoon's battles.

I knew when I took this glamorous position that the work wouldn't be about the pursuit of social causes, but would, to some measure, be about economic justice. I thought my role was to assure fairness in the marketplace, to assure that an artist received his due. But that goal was becoming increasingly obscured. I was seeing too many young artists, who had no leverage, forced to accept exploitive deals. And there were other powerful and treacherous currents running beneath our celebrity culture, dangers inherent in the adoration of masked idols who starred in the circus of modern media. Artists and performers were meant to fulfill the ecstatic role left vacant by slaughtered shamans and priestesses. And some, like Jim Morrison, had been brought down by the overwhelming Dionysian force they embodied. But in the absence of awareness of that sublime and dangerous responsibility, it was inevitable that art was reduced by commerce to being no more than a trivial distraction—junk food for the soul. And I was becoming one of its purveyors.

One of the ancient, magical skills was the creation of an illusion, what Nonna called a "glamour." It was part of the ancient shamanic ability to shape-shift, but like so many other remnants of the Old Ways, it too had fallen prey to distortion. When theater began in the sacred rites to Dionysus, god of ecstasy and revelation, actors created a glamour by wearing masks to portray the gods. In ancient shamanic rites, in carnivals and rituals all over the globe, the wearing of masks allowed the performer to embody and reveal the divine. But now masks had become a means to hide oneself. And so, like everyone else I met in this strange business, I would wear a mask. It felt like a mask made of shadow, as each morning the folds of dark fabric fell across my body.

Using my inner eye, I peered behind the masks of domination worn by Hadus and his cohorts and saw that they were terrified of powerlessness. Behind the masks of sexism lurked desire, impotence, and anger. And beneath all of these, fear curled around the pain of some deeper unhealed wound, a Fisher King's wound. Our partners, in work and in love, were wounded and it was out of this pain that oppression and violence sprang. This understanding gave me more compassion, and patience, and power. But I reminded myself that the Grail alone could not heal them unless they chose to heal themselves.

Even knowing this, in the face of what was required of me, I began to fear that I might be transformed into my disguise. I was becoming disoriented by the outer world. My inner compass whirled in confusion as I sought to guide my course using markers set by a culture that had lost its soul. Behind my veil of conformity and control I struggled with my growing self-doubt and insecurity. And something more poisonous—a loss of my sense of power. A quiet kind of helpless despair set in as I sat down at my desk and fastened on my mask. Immediately the phone started ringing and as I picked up the phone, an inner voice whispered, *What do we need an apple for?*

Nonna placed the apple on the copper pentacle in the center of the altar. Several weeks had passed since our banishing circle, and the women in circle, aware of Maia's suffering, had been mothering her, shouldering as much responsibility as the priestesses asked of us, and asking for more. Maia's maternal self-assurance was returning, while Bellona now struggled with her own anger and feelings of helplessness. Despite her obvious but unspoken health problems, Nonna had been running circle since the banishing, and I was happy she was back.

The temple was resplendent: Pink candles and voluptuous bouquets filled each quarter. There were more flowers, ripe fruit, sea shells, and shining crystals on the altar. Exotic incense perfumed the air in floating lavender drifts. The women had covered the pillows in silk brocades and hand-blocked Fortuny velvets the colors of a queen's jewels. Nonna, in her vivid red silk gown, looked as if she'd lost weight, and I noticed her hands still trembled as she picked up the willow wand. She rose slowly, and with difficulty, but a soft glow colored her cheeks and she seemed to grow stronger as she invoked the Goddess.

The Goddess was called from the misty realms beyond space and time, from the primordial expanse from which all life arose. She was stirred from the ashes of countless pyres on which women had been burned, summoned from our hearts, from our bodies, from our ancient memories. She was called to share her blessings, her wisdom, and her healing. I reached out for her with my longing but no image appeared, no gracious apparition, no irrefutable sign of acknowledgment. I waited in the invisible, enveloping void.

Nonna picked up the brazier, incense filling the room with the scent of spices, the sap of myrrh hardened after its harvest from the Goddess's sacred tree, lotuses opening in the floodwaters of the Nile when Sirius rises in the east, and figs sticky with thick pulp and seeds. She faced Gillian.

"With air and with fire I consecrate thee. Blessed be your breasts created in beauty and strength that they might sustain life with the milk of paradise. Blessed be your womb created in beauty and strength that it might create life."

She held the brazier before Gillian's right breast, moved it across to her left breast, then down to her womb and back up to her right breast, leaving a smoky triangle floating in the air. She returned the brazier to the altar and picked up the bowl of salt water.

"With water and with earth I consecrate thee." Nonna repeated the gesture, blessing her breasts and womb. When she was finished, she gently kissed her, and instructed her to repeat the ritual with Onatah, who was seated beside Gillian. In this manner, moving deosil around the circle, each woman received and bestowed consecration and blessing.

Tears of gratitude sprang from my heart as gruff Marcia enacted the ritual consecration with me. Her bearlike gestures bespoke the powerful grace of the warrior goddess Artemis, who was also the protector of women during childbirth. Intimacy and trust encircled us, and with that embrace came a feeling like the love of a mother of infinite expression. Peace, confidence, and grace flowed through me as I, in turn, shared the sacred moment with Jeanette. Words and gestures, air, fire, water, and earth, and a sublime quality of generous purpose wove us together. Sitting in that sanctified circle with the other women, my heart filled with joy. It did not occur to me to wonder where the Goddess was to be found.

Nonna held up the apple. "In the Bible, this is the fruit Eve ate, the fruit of knowledge. By eating it, she was said to have caused humanity's downfall."

She picked up her curfane and cut the apple in half, not as we usually halve an apple from stem to base, but along its equator, slicing not along but through its core. She held up the two halves. "There is a secret that those of us who honor the Goddess know: Within the apple there is a star, symbol of the Old Ways. It is a symbol of the Goddess and her gift of divine life." The circle murmured with delight to see five sliced seeds forming the shape of a star at the center of each apple half. Nonna smiled at our surprise and continued. "We are priestesses of the ancient Mother, of the Craft of the Wise, though some, in their fear and blindness, may call us the daughters of Eve. We honor knowledge; we do not fear it. As we take a bite from this apple, we accept the responsibility of knowledge, to use it wisely in the world, and to share it with others. We reclaim our power as women, our sacred wisdom as priestesses, and our knowledge of the gracious Goddess who resides in all things." She bit into the apple.

Nonna handed the apple to Gillian, who held it aloft, and spoke to us: "I remember when women were priestesses, when women were healers. I remember when women were honored, I remember Avalon, and I remember the Goddess in our hearts." And Gillian bit into the apple.

Tenderly, Onatah took the apple from Gillian. Solemnity overtook her usually laughing, beautiful visage. Her chin thrust forward and her eyes narrowed, as if she were spotting game. "Knowing the difference between right and wrong is part of learning to grow up. I am not a child, I am a woman." Onatah bit into the apple and a warrior spoke. "I deny the power of those who would call me evil, and I reclaim my power as a woman."

And so the fruit of knowledge traveled around the circle of wisdom. I removed my mask, for I recognized that it was a Gatekeeper that blocked my entrance into Avalon, secret and Fortunate Isle of the enchanted apple orchard. It was the Celtic Eden, presided over by the priestess Morgan le Fay. *Fay* meant fairy, a reference to the spirit realm of the Old Religion, and it was forbidden by the Church to speak her name. Like Eve, whose fruit of knowledge was also the apple, she was branded evil, and the truth of her gifts as a wise woman of the Goddess remained hidden within the shadows of history. Originally a goddess, perhaps the Morrigan, in the later medieval tales of King Arthur she is his half-sister. In keeping with the diminished status of women and the suppression of the Goddess, in these later accounts she is an ambiguous villainess. But her true character remains visible beneath the distortions—shape-shifter and healer, artist and scholar, speaker of prophecy and secret, beloved mate of Arthur. It is she who tests the worthiness of all those who would rule the sacred land and care for its people. And it is she who heals the land.

Even in the later Christianized versions, after the Round Table has been shattered and after the terrible battle of Camlan, the mortally wounded King Arthur is brought to the sacred isle of Avalon to be healed by Morgan le Fay. Like Osiris restored by the goddess Isis, like the Celtic goddess Cerridwen of the sacred cauldron, Morgan's healing powers could revive men who had lacerations so deep they were rent asunder. But her magic would take many years to work. By the power of her divine gift of rebirth, the inscription on King Arthur's tomb anticipates his reincarnation as "the once and future King."

Avalon was the invisible isle of the Goddess's mystical sisterhood, of the nine priestesses who preserved the rites of the Goddess Sovereignty, her land and her people. Here, in our sacred circle, and by her sacred rites, the isle was made visible, and we too were made visible. But would the Goddess appear to me as she had to the priestess Morgan?

When the apple came to me, I grasped it as the symbol of reempowerment. It smelled sweet and my fingers were wet with the juice that ran from its golden pulp. "I give thanks for the knowledge that Eden surrounds us, that we have never left Paradise. I give thanks for the wisdom that will help us honor and protect this sacred earth, and its people. I give thanks for the sisterhood who preserves the rites of the Goddess. I remember Morgan le Fay, and I tend her secret garden." And I bit into the apple. "I reclaim my power as a woman."

The serpent who urged Eve to eat from the Tree of Knowledge was also maligned as evil, but I had discovered that in the earth religions the snake was a symbol of the fertile goddess. She was Coatlicue, the five-fold serpent-skirted goddess of ancient Mexico. She was Benten, also called Benzaiten, a Japanese goddess of luck, wealth, art, and love whose form was also that of a dragon swimming the seas in the company of sacred white snakes. She was Vila, healing goddess of the woods and wild creatures of eastern Europe who shape-shifted from snake to bird, horse to wind, and whose mysteries were kept by a sisterhood of the full moon.

For the Hopi, she is the sacred snake of the waters of life descending from the heavens and through the mountains to make the blue corn grow. And it was from the valleys made fertile by her great serpent rivers Tigris-Euphrates, Nile, Indus, and Ganges (named for the goddess Ganga), sliding across the skin of the earth, that civilization was born. In India, she is known as the Dakini, the fish-bodied attendants to the goddess Kali in her death aspect, but Tibetan yogis know that beneath this frightening mask of purpose, Dakinis are the mothers who bestow the gifts of vision and magical powers to those who practice Kundalini yoga. And it is her snakes that symbolize the sacred powers that rise along the spine, granting ecstatic communion.

Snakes wrapped themselves around the arms of the Goddess's priestesses in Minoan Crete and it was her snakes that curled around the caduceus, still the symbol of the healing arts. The snake is the symbol of the Goddess's sacred powers of regeneration, undulating messengers of intuitive and scientific knowing, organic spiralers of symbolic meaning and life itself. Pythagoras discovered the mathematics of life and music, and the hidden structure of a sacred universe at her serpent-tended oracle at Delphi. Dr. James Watson followed her siren whisper when, walking down a spiral staircase at Oxford, he had an intuitive vision that DNA is composed of snakelike, interwoven spirals, which we now call the double helix.

In the Bible, after the serpent "tempted" Eve, it is said that God feared she and Adam, having eaten of the fruit of the Tree of Knowledge, would eat next from the Tree of Life, which bestowed immortality. Thus, he banished them from Paradise. In the Old Religion, the Tree of Life is also known as the Goddess. Like the apples of Avalon where the wounded are restored to life, the tree bestows the blessing of eternal life—through knowledge of the constancy of energy in the universe, which cyclically transforms from one manifestation into another, energy to matter, matter to energy, like the moon or the earth in changing seasons, or the snake which is reborn by the shedding of skin. The Tree of Life is the *axis mundi,* the pillar that connects heaven and earth, the spinal column of each human expression of infinite love and creativity. I sat up straight, feeling the energies of life spiraling up my spine as I handed the apple to Jeanette.

Cupping the rosy apple between her brown palms, Jeanette spoke: "I honor the nourishment and the strength the Goddess has given me— she sustains me with the fruits of life."

She returned the apple to Nonna, who held the apple core aloft. "One thing becomes another, in the Mother, in the Mother."

Maia and Bellona began singing quietly, their voices blending in loving harmony. I leaned in to hear them and quickly recognized the melody from our earliest gatherings.

"We all come from the Goddess
And to Her we shall return

Like a drop of rain
Flowing to the ocean"

Softly, supportively, we joined them. Spontaneous harmonies enriched our singing, and soon we were chanting a call and response while
Nonna kept the beat with steady clapping. We transformed the chant
into a whirling round and the power intensified as our voices soared
into a song of deep empowerment. The song, and its magical energy,
crested and ebbed. The power we had raised remained within us as we
sat in electrified silence. When I finally opened my eyes, I was astonished to behold the radiant beauty that surrounded me. Nonna seemed
stronger and healthier, and both Maia and Bellona looked more at
peace than they had in weeks.

As was our practice, after the consecration of wine and cakes, our
priestesses led us in discussions that, like our magic, stretched far beyond our expectations. We passed a silver basket filled with red apples,
and pitchers with chilled cider spiced with cinnamon.

"Witches have always experienced the Goddess's presence in the
world," Nonna explained. "We see her in the cycles of the seasons, the
beauty of the earth."

"For me, the most amazing spiritual mystery is the relationship between the moon, the Goddess, and women," Bellona added.

Nonna nodded, continuing, "The cycles of the moon—waxing, full,
and waning—correspond to the stages of our own lives: Maiden, Mother,
and Crone, premenstrual, childbearing, and menopausal. This is the
Threefold Goddess. Western culture dismisses a woman's worth once
she's passed the years of being either 'sexually desirable' or fertile, but in
the Old Religion, the crone is a respected elder. Her powers are known to
increase with age, not decrease, because she contains both the Maiden
and the Mother within herself, with their powers of independence and
sexuality. The Threefold Goddess was the first Holy Trinity of Western
religion, preceding the Christian masculine triad by at least six millennia.
In ancient Arabia, she was Al-Lat, Al-Uzza, and Menat."

"In Greece the Triple Goddess was Persephone, Demeter, and Hecate. She even survived Christianization as the Virgin Mary, her mother,
St. Anne, and her grandmother, St. Emerentia," Maia added.

"For the Celts, she was the Morrigan, a triple battle goddess," Bellona said. "And there are many others—Crones, Mothers, and
Maidens. . . ."

"Maiden goddesses—those were virgin goddesses, like Artemis, right?" Marcia asked.

Maia nodded. "And Athena and Hestia."

"But you find the concept all over the world," Bellona added. "Virgin actually meant a woman unto herself, not a woman who had never had sex. It meant a woman who was self-defined, not defined by her relationship to a man. Even Aphrodite, a goddess of love, was virginal—each year she bathed in the waters by her temple in Cyprus to cleanse herself of the influence of men and restore her autonomy."

Onatah laughed. "Honey, that sounds like a ritual I could use."

Nonna nodded. "If it speaks to you, use it. All of this ancient wisdom is meant not as dogma, but as inspiration for your own spiritual practices. Many of our rituals are traditional, but it's up to us to retrieve and re-create ancient rites and to create new rituals that are meaningful to modern women. And as we work, you're going to recover the spiritual wisdom of your bodies."

"What about the moon?" asked Gillian.

"The moon has long been a symbol of the Goddess, women's spirituality, and the spirituality of the unconscious. The phases of the moon are also important to the timing of our rituals. We do magic for manifestation, growth, and increase during the waxing or full moon," Nonna explained. "A full moon is the best time to draw down goddesses of fertility. A full moon circle is called an esbat. And magic for banishings is done during the waning moon. The dark of the moon is a good time for scrying."

"I bet you didn't know that all early calendars were based upon the twenty-eight day cycles of the moon, *and* of women. And the reason there are thirteen in a coven is because there are thirteen lunar months, and thirteen full moons, in a year. That's why the number thirteen is the number of the Goddess," Maia added to our delighted surprise.

What about Friday the thirteenth?" Mindy asked. "I turned thirteen and thirty on Friday the thirteenth, so I've always considered it a lucky day for me."

"And in the Old Religion. Friday is a day devoted to the Goddess—to Freya, which is where the name Friday came from. Friday was also the day of Venus in the Roman or Italian tradition. So, Friday the thirteenth was originally a day sacred to the Goddess. But, like so many other aspects of the Old Religion, it was turned around to be considered an unlucky day."

"Women's monthly menstrual cycles were, and still are, an integral part of women's spiritual mysteries. Menstrual blood is part of the divine, life-giving power of women, not a mark of sinfulness or uncleanliness as fearful patriarchal theologies have claimed. The forced isolation of women during their menstrual cycle was a repressive distortion of women's previously honored and sacred 'moontime,' when women withdrew from daily tasks in order to experience communion with the sacred. This is a time when women's bodies are profoundly harmonious with this numinous undertaking," Nonna explained to us in a way we all wished our mothers had.

"Orthodox traditions continue to treat menstruation as a taboo. Women are required to engage in 'purification' rituals after menstruating. I think it's their outdated attitudes that need purifying," Naomi added with her usual spark.

"My Native American grandmother described a Moon Lodge to me," Onatah offered quietly. "Everyone else in the community stepped in to take care of her daily chores and her children."

Annabelle's drawl interjected. "My momma called her periods the 'curse.' Maybe if she'd had a way of experiencing herself as powerful instead, things would have been different for her. Sure, she was respected for bein' a 'good' wife and mother, but not like my daddy was for his roles."

"If you're taught that your body is sinful, it makes sense that you wouldn't consider your menstrual cycle a sacred time," I added. "I've noticed I feel particularly psychic when I have my period. If I take something for the cramps, which I have to if I'm working, I notice it less. But if I'm not working, I try to just go with it—it's almost as if I'm in an altered state."

Nonna nodded. "You are."

After circle, as we straightened up, we continued to talk, discovering that our menstrual cycles had fallen into rhythm—half began at the dark of the moon and half at the full. We lingered for hours, reluctant to leave each other, but I had to get to work in the morning.

"May I take the remnants of the apple?" I asked.

Nonna wrapped them carefully in a napkin and hugged me. I walked out onto the city street, past billboards with air-brushed images of artificial perfection, and store windows filled with magazine covers featuring flawless fifteen-year-olds. Women have lived in a state of profound insecurity and alienation from their own bodies, their powers, their experience of the sacred. For millennia we have wandered in exile while all along, Eden lay within.

For women to regain their powers to create life and culture, they must have a description and an experience of the divine that includes those aspects of being we call feminine, and which Taoists call *yin*. Only in this way can women achieve wholeness. Only in this way can we emerge from the shadows to reclaim Eden.

Nonna's words deepened my appreciation of one of the most important aspects of Wiccan spirituality: the idea of personal ritual and revelation. Wicca was not a system of dogma, rules, or regulations. As a spiritual practice, each individual could master and make use of techniques to personally experience the divine. And because the divine was immanent as well as transcendent, feminine as well as masculine, yin and yang, anima and animus, it was immediately accessible to us as women. This was to become a wellspring of creative spiritual exploration and expression, not only for myself, but for the entire Goddess movement.

Together, as a community of spiritual women, we would draw upon the ancient ways of the Goddess and our modern experiences, to create rituals that celebrate the cycles of the earth, the phases of the moon, and those of a woman's life. Together, and alone, we would create sacred rites to bring a girl into the community of women when she begins to menstruate; rituals of commitment and marriage, regardless of gender; rituals that honor a woman's divine power to create life when she becomes pregnant, gives birth, or creates some body of work, art, or personal expression; rituals of responsibility and grieving when a woman chooses not to bring forth life by having an abortion, or when through force of circumstance, health, age, or miscarriage, she is unable to have a child; rituals that heal and enable a woman to move through the trials of life, illness, and loss; rituals to honor a woman's contribution to the community as she passes through menopause and becomes a wise crone; rituals that bring us together, that connect us to the sacredness of the moon and the earth, and open us to the divine within ourselves and each other. Together we would create rituals that restore our faith, not only in the Goddess, but in ourselves.

Here was the possibility of religious ritual that liberated one's mind, body, and spirit, rather than restraining it. And in the empowerment of personal ritual, here too was the possibility of ritual with profound meaning for women. I felt fiercely reinforced when I discovered that the word "ritual" comes from the ancient Sanskrit *rtu*, which meant "menstruation." And the ancient root of the words "menstruation," "moon," "mind," "meaning," and the name for prophetic priestesses, was all the same—*mense*.

Defying fear, sitting alone in the dangerous, late-night subway car on the way home, I softly intoned the many names of the Goddess. The subway hurtled like a mighty snake through the tunnels of the Underworld. A rhythmic thrumming sound filled my head as I flew up the stairs into the coolness of the night above. I stood at the entrance to the park beside the river, another rushing serpent that twisted, wove, and wound about the enchanted island of the Big Apple. But none of the city's secret or visible charms was as magical as the little piece of life I pulled from my pocket.

At night, the park became a denizen of danger where shadows waited with unnatural intent. It was not Eden that had been lost, but man's soul, his connection to the earth and the divine. I stood, wondering whether to enter. As swiftly as I wondered, something sacred attended me, a presence, a sense, a subtle certainty that I was safe. I entered, but no more than five feet, inhaling the sweet green air.

I visualized a circle of light surrounding me and dug five seeds from the apple core. Carefully, I wrapped two of the seeds in the napkin and returned them to my pocket. I struggled to dig a small hole in the hard, packed earth with my house key. The dirt was coarse and moist between my fingers as I buried three seeds. I left the remaining pieces of apple for the birds and squirrels and even the city's medieval vermin, and gave thanks for the knowledge that was changing my life.

The Goddess remained a mystery to me, but now I knew with certainty that there were times and places, people and cultures, who revered the feminine and for whom the Goddess was a reality. I knew that a woman's worth resided in such divinity. And that was more than I had ever dreamed of.

I was determined to hold onto the empowerment of last night's circle, and to put it to good use. I was determined to clear the air with Hadus and to establish my boundaries. As soon as I arrived at work the next morning, I headed straight for Hadus's office.

"I need a moment of your time." I closed the door behind me, ignoring Hadus's startled expression.

"I've always got time for you," he smiled as I sat down across from him. "New look, eh? A little conservative for this office, but . . . reminds me of the fantasies I used to have about my eighth grade English teacher."

"Funny you should mention fantasies—that's exactly what I wanted to talk to you about."

"Really?" He leaned forward smiling. "I can't wait."

"When I accepted this job we had an agreement—strictly business. Lately it seems that you expect something else."

Hadus cut me off. "How do you know what my expectations are? If you're not happy . . ." His eyes narrowed and he straightened up in his chair. I could sense a salvo coming and I tried to stay on my course.

"I've brought in a lot of work and I've put in a lot of time. And I think I've done an excellent job. If you're not satisfied . . ."

"Satisfied? You want me to be satisfied? Yeah, your work's been fine, but you think dressing like that is going to make any difference? It's just a tease."

I was startled by his reaction to my appearance. I was also suspicious. I knew he was projecting his own sexual preoccupation on to me. I pressed on. "No, it's just the opposite. How can I make myself any clearer? I knew our personal history might make this difficult, but I've been completely honest with you, and I've certainly never led you on. I just want you to treat me like any other associate."

He laughed, and I was completely thrown.

"You come in here thinking that you're just like Hanley, or any other guy in the locker room? Just how naive are you?" I could feel myself shrinking, my insides collapsing. I couldn't believe what he was saying, and he didn't stop. "You think I can send you in to deal with the big boys? They'd eat you alive." He smiled salaciously and leaned forward. "And there's nothing wrong with that—you're a nice piece of bait." I could feel myself blushing and my confidence disappearing. "You've been around long enough now to know what the score is."

"I don't agree. What about Dutton?"

He laughed again. "Sweetheart, she's the biggest bitch in the business. Is that what you want to be? Believe me, there are easier ways to success."

Rage replaced humiliation, but I was determined to keep my job. I struggled to keep control. "There are other choices. I'm as good as any male associate you've ever had. I've certainly brought in more business. I just want to be treated fairly."

Hadus leaned back in his chair and loosened his tie. "I've been more than fair. Were you fair with me when you walked out?"

"Is that what this has been all about?" I asked, stunned by his unexpected honesty. My voice softened as I asked him, "What kind of choice did you leave me?"

"As you just pointed out, there are all sorts of choices." As quickly as he'd opened the door to our past, he now closed it. His voice was flat and cold and his eyes were filled with anger. He picked up a file and handed it to me. "You think you're ready—prove it. Close the Taylor deal."

I took the heavy file, surprised at his response.

"You've got work to do. I suggest you get to it." He picked up his phone and turned his back.

I stared down at the brown folder. We both knew it was a test that couldn't be passed, a deal that couldn't be done. As I returned to my office, I couldn't help but wonder whether I could earn Hadus's respect, and put an end to his anger, if I could make it work. But with his sexual agenda now surfacing, I feared the trouble ahead.

The moon was gloriously full that night, filling the room with ethereal silver light spilling in through the skylight. A large white candle burned in the east, a red one in the south, a blue one in the west, and a green candle flickered in the north. In the name of the Great Goddess, the elements had been purified and consecrated, circle had been cast, and the ancient powers of the quarters had been summoned. The fragrance of lilies and oranges mixed with the exotic oils of patchouli and clove we had rubbed into our skin and onto the candles, and mingled with an offertory incense that curled moonward in a billowing spiral. We had grounded and centered ourselves. A chant of the ancient Goddess was now weaving our energies into a sacred circle:

"One thing becomes another, in the Mother, in the Mother."

The power of enchantment was palpable.

When the chant ended, Bellona and Maia stood facing each other in front of the altar. It was good to see Maia at the center of the circle again, and though she remained somewhat hidden by the shadow of her terrifying experience, tonight she was more serene and joyful than she'd been in weeks.

Maia slipped the rose-colored gown from her shoulders and it fell in a soft and shocking puddle at her feet. She was naked. Her breasts were small, her hips full, her stomach round. Her olive skin glowed in the candlelight and I noticed how tiny her hands were. She was completely composed, unaffected by our startled attention. I realized I was more self-conscious than she, and as I watched her calmly fold her arms across her heart and close her eyes, stillness radiated from her. I saw she felt neither shame nor pride. I marveled at her imperfect beauty and understood the perfection expressed in her nakedness. She embodied the simple, profound, spiritual power of truth.

Bellona bowed her head and crossed her arms over her heart. I noticed that their breathing had become synchronized. Bellona opened her eyes, uncrossed her arms, and raised the slender willow wand in her right hand, placing its tip in the center of Maia's forehead. Slowly, with visible, graceful concentration, she moved it down to Maia's right foot, then up to her left shoulder, across to her right shoulder, down to her left foot. Drawing a pentagram on Maia's body, she spoke:

> "By leaf and by stem I invoke thee
> By bud and by flower I invoke thee
> And call upon thee to descend, gracious Goddess
> Into this, the body of thy High Priestess Maia
> See with her eyes, kiss with her lips, speak with her voice
> That your children may receive your wisdom.
> Now listen to the words of the Great Mother,
> Who was of old also called Artemis, Astarte, Cerridwen, Diana, Arianrhod,
> Isis, and by many other names."

With these last words, Bellona brought the wand to rest at the point of its beginning. With its final touch in the center of Maia's forehead, a current of energy shot through her body. Maia's head tilted back, her lips parted. Slowly her arms opened, her elbows bent with the palms of her hands facing outward, a posture of priestesses I had seen depicted on ancient Egyptian murals, Greek vases, and Minoan carvings. The energy that filled her seemed to settle over the circle like a mantle of moonlight on a summer night.

Maia began to speak. Her voice was soft and distant, but it grew stronger as she continued.

"Whenever you have need of anything, once in the month, and better it be when the moon is full, then shall you assemble in some secret place, you who are fain to learn the mystery, yet have not won its deepest secrets; to you shall I teach things that are as yet unknown . . . and you shall dance, sing, feast, make music and love, all in my praise for mine is the ecstasy of the spirit and mine also is joy upon the earth, for my law is love unto all beings. . . .

"I am the gracious Goddess, who gives the gift of joy unto the heart of humanity. Nor do I demand aught in sacrifice, for behold, I am the Mother of all things and my love is poured out upon the earth. . . ."

I sat in awe. As Maia continued, her voice shifted in tone, texture, and cadence, as if someone else were speaking.

"I am the beauty of the green earth, and the white moon among the stars, and the mysteries of the waters and the desire of the heart of humanity. I call upon your soul: Arise and come unto me, for I am the soul of nature who gives life to the universe. From me all things proceed and unto me all things must return, and before my face, beloved of Gods and of humanity, let thine innermost divine self be enfolded in the rapture of the infinite.

"Let my worship be within the heart that rejoices, for behold—all acts of love and pleasure are my rituals. Therefore, let there be beauty and strength, power and compassion, honor and humility, mirth and reverence within you. And you who think to seek for Me, know that your seeking and yearning shall avail you not, unless you know the Mystery: For if that which you seek, you find not within yourself, you will never find it without. For behold, I have been with you from the beginning, and I am that which is attained at the end of desire."

Maia fell silent and I held my breath, longing for her to continue.

An electrified silence followed. Maia's arms closed and Bellona wrapped her quickly in the grounding warmth of an embrace. Carefully, Bellona helped her to sit. She gently brushed a lock of hair from Maia's cheek and kissed her palms. Silently we watched as Maia emerged from her trance and gradually returned to herself. When she was ready, Bellona took the silver bowl from the altar and placed it in Maia's outstretched hands. Bellona then picked up her athame. Again they faced each other, their eyes full of love. Bellona raised the knife as Maia spoke: "As the chalice is to the Goddess . . ."

". . . so the athame is to the God," Bellona replied, plunging the blade into the bowl.

"And conjoined, they bring blessedness," the two finished together, kissing over the symbolic union. This was the consecration of the wine.

Nonna beamed with evident satisfaction; I knew she was relieved to see Maia able to resume her work in circle. Bellona handed Maia a round loaf of bread. Using her athame, Bellona sprinkled the water and wine from the silver bowl onto the bread. "Bless this bread unto our bodies, bestowing upon us the gifts of health, wealth, and the eternal blessing which is love."

Maia broke off a piece and dropped it into the bowl. The next piece she fed to Bellona, who fed her in turn. The silver bowl was then passed around the circle for each of us to share a libation. This was done by pouring wine, water, or juice from our cups into the Goddess's goblet, offering words of prayer or inspiration, and then drinking from our own cups. It was said that this offering of libations was the origin of the social ritual of toasting, and some said it was also the origin of the Catholic Mass. Tonight we offered our libations in awed silence.

"You've gotta eat something, you need to ground," Bellona urged Maia after the chalice was returned to the center of the altar. Maia was radiant, and without memory of anything she'd said.

"Was it the Charge?" she asked. "I wanted to do the Charge tonight."

Bellona nodded.

"What is the Charge?" I asked quietly.

Maia seemed too dazed to speak, and Bellona was completely focused on her care. The two were wrapped lovingly in each other's arms.

Nonna answered: "The Charge of the Goddess, as it is practiced in our tradition, was first spoken by Doreen Valiente, a remarkable British high priestess. She drew language from many sources—material published by Charles Godfrey Leland, who lived with Italian Witches during the nineteenth century, elements of classical material, an ancient invocation of Isis, material from Aleister Crowley, and the Goddess herself—combined and interpreted first by Valiente's former high priest, Gerald Gardner, and then by Valiente's sublime poetic gift. The Charge is memorized by all high priestesses in our tradition, and used in Drawing Down the Moon."

"Drawing Down the Moon?" I asked, hungry to know more.

"It's the trance technique you witnessed tonight. It is used by high priestesses to experience communion with the Goddess. It's a mystical, altered state in which the priestess becomes a vessel for her. She may have visions, receive guidance or empowerment. And the Goddess may even speak through her, a skill that usually takes years to master."

I nodded at Nonna's explanation, wondering what it must feel like to be filled with the presence of such poetic power. And wondering also, was it the Goddess who spoke, or was it Maia?

Maia turned to me and replied as if my words had been spoken, rather than silently thought. Or perhaps, to her, my thoughts had not been silent. Her voice was like a mother's warm embrace, and light seemed to radiate from her as she spoke slowly.

"You'll draw down, and then you'll understand. I can't explain what happens, you have to experience it for yourself. If you prepare properly, if your heart's open, and you welcome her, she'll come to you. With practice, she'll speak through you. Sometimes I'm aware and I can hear myself speaking, as if from very far away, but the words I speak aren't mine—you don't think them, they come from her. And when she fills you . . . it's indescribable." She sighed happily, turning to the plate of food Bellona had prepared for her.

That was why metaphors had always been used to describe the Goddess. Later I would understand through personal experience how the speaking of the Charge facilitates the deepening of trance, and also the priestess's ability to speak while in an altered state. The Charge releases the flow of language when she draws down the moon, enabling her to give herself over to the Goddess as she fills the priestess and speaks through her.

But the Goddess was more than poetic metaphor. As I looked around the circle, I saw the astonishing beauty of the Goddess in the women around me. Most were now only partially dressed, disrobed by the confident example of our priestess, and by the energy that still radiated from her. Their breasts, waists, and thighs were every imaginable size and shape. Annabelle, with her long raven hair and the face of a fairy princess, had the undeveloped body of a young girl. Jeanette, who remained dressed, was "overweight" by society's standards but her full figure was gorgeous nonetheless. Gillian was tall and slim, with tiny breasts and no hips. Onatah had a voluptuous hourglass figure with heavy thighs and a tiny waist. Mindy was small and athletic, her muscles well toned. Naomi was round and plump, and Marcia was built like a body builder. Some had stretch marks, cellulite, rounded bellies. Each woman was unique, none conformed to the stereotype of the "perfect" face or figure, and each was astonishingly beautiful in her own, utterly individual way.

They joked and confided, touched and sat silently. Their gestures and their postures revealed an unmasked truth. They were confident in their physicality, perhaps some of them for the first time in their lives, liberated from the narrowness of the culture's standards, even Jeanette, who was so self-conscious about her weight. They were vibrant, still exultant from what they had witnessed. The magical words were already working their inner alchemy on each woman.

When circle ended, I was full of energy and reluctant to go home to my tiny apartment. Where could I go to sit beneath the whole and honeyed moon in this city? I would be far safer alone in the woods. Where was the Goddess's temple, crowning the highest hill, its columns wound with night-blooming jasmine, its floor covered with velvet moss, flooded with moonlight pouring in from above? Where was her sacred grove of oak and apple? Where could a woman, possessed by the Goddess, safely dance beneath the moon until the sun recaptured the sky? Where was the garden of earthly enchantments where a woman could await the embrace of her beloved? Would it always remain a million miles away, a lost Eden, a secret garden hidden by the shadows of a frightened world?

I opened the door to the roof of my building and crouched beneath the Goddess's silver mirror. What had happened tonight? Had I finally encountered the Goddess? The power in the room had been palpable, but was it no more than reflected light, like the moon made visible only by the sun? Were the words no more than a conscious expression of dramatic effect? But what else did I expect?

I expected proof. I expected a burning bush and granite tablets inscribed by lasers if not lightning. I expected physical manifestations of an eternal being. That's what I was raised to expect, even in an intellectual family.

Radios hammered the thick summer air with messages of confusion, sirens screamed through the streets, and huge dark clouds scudded across the darker sky, obscuring the shining moon. A sudden wave of ocean loneliness, pulled by the orb above, threatened to drown me. Where was the Goddess? I wondered desperately. I stood, a tiny, solitary figure in the midst of an alien metropolis. The heavens parted and rain began to fall like heavy tears pounding through my clothes, drenching my sadness with the Goddess's own. I washed my face in her waters, ran my fingers through my hair, bathing in the heavenly seas, the starry ablution. I felt the crust of encultured skepticism crumble, the uncertainty dissolve. I was renewed, restored, and released. I was a woman unto herself, and no longer alone.

Why are you standing there? Move! Dance like the sacred snakes that run down the mountains to make the blue corn grow. Dance like the white snakes that swim through the waters of life. Dance like the serpents of wonder that entwine within your spine, that spiral in your cells, that summon you across the infinite universe to dance the dance of boundless implication to the drumming of your heart and the singing of the stars. Dance!

I whirled around the rooftop, water flying from my body as the rain stopped and the silver moon reappeared.

I had struggled to find her, but it was she who had found me. I rushed downstairs, slamming the door behind me, and stripped off my soaking clothes. I stood naked in front of the mirror. Moonlight glistened across my wet skin. Slowly I turned, seeing myself as if I were a stranger. I turned, deosil, and turned again, remembering how radiant and beautiful the women in my circle had been tonight, illuminated by the energy our priestess had drawn down. I had experienced an extraordinary presence, a feminine force of transformative power. I *had* heard the Goddess, speaking through her priestess. I had seen her shining in my sisters' eyes.

The women stood beside me in the mirror: Marcia had the power and independence of Artemis, goddess of the wild things and the hunt; Gillian had the romantic poetry of Brigid, the muse of Celtic bards and goddess of the healing arts; Jeanette carried the power of Yemanja, from under whose skirts all the riches of the sea unfurled to the world. Maia was so much the generous earth mother; Bellona, the warrior maiden of the moon; and Nonna was the wise crone Hecate. They truly were the embodiment of the Goddess.

If the Goddess was inside them, perhaps she was within me as well. Suddenly I was dancing again, singing, and laughing. I remembered the rich pleasure of making love. I remembered the monthly pain of menstruation and the acute sensitivity that accompanied it. I remembered the love and astonishing awareness a dear friend had of her infant daughter—a connection so profound that it was genuinely psychic, a gift that had begun through their intimate months of absolute physical continuity—and the connection I had with my own mother. I began to sense the wisdom and the spirituality within my own body. I relived the dreams and intuitions that had guided me on my strange journey, the signs and omens that had directed me.

The longing in my heart which had seemed so much the yearning for a missing part of myself, that had lured and enticed me like the piping of Pan, had brought me to a sacred grove. I longed for that lost half, but until I had taken form, I would have no partner. Here, in the sacred grove where apple trees grew in fertile abundance, I was discovering the missing part of myself, the part of me that could, like our priestesses, open myself to the divine mystery. I was in the presence of an over-whelming power uniquely feminine in its energy.

Maia's words, the words of the Goddess, came back to me: "If that which you seek, you find not within yourself, you will never find it without. For behold, I have been with you from the beginning, and I am that which is attained at the end of desire."

My mask was gone, and as I danced before the mirror I felt an energy unlike anything I'd ever known rising up within me. From a cavern in my soul so deep it sprang from some measureless chasm of the universe, something stirred. And from the sheltering emptiness and inexhaustible possibility that surrounded me, from the Goddess's womb in which I lived, something came to me. The placental boundary be-tween inner and outer, call it consciousness or skin, was permeable. The Goddess I expected to manifest in the world that surrounded me was already within. And this unfamiliar epiphany would shape the ex-pression of my life. I hadn't lost my mind; I had found my heart, and it was the Goddess's temple.

These realizations felt enormous, and yet I knew I was only begin-ning to understand the mystery of the divine present in the world, and in myself. But there was one thing I knew with certainty, with the wisdom of my opened heart: The Goddess *was* reemerging from the Underworld into which she had been abducted thousands of years ago. The Goddess had returned.

CHAPTER 10

Cone
of Power

*Every step you take on earth should be a prayer. The power of a
pure and good soul is in every person's heart and will grow as a
seed as you walk in a sacred manner.*

—CHARMAINE WHITE FACE
OF THE OGLALA LAKOTA

I awoke from my night of dancing with the snake in the rain above
the rooftops of Manhattan, and stretched back into my brand-new
skin. Instead of the stifling summer air of the city, a soft breeze
blew in through the open window. The flowers I'd been coaxing on my
windowsill had blossomed and the view beyond sparkled in the morning
sun, scrubbed brilliantly clean during the night's downpour. I felt exqui-
sitely alive and longed for a day of sensuality rather than office warfare.

Just as I had stretched toward the moon the night before, I now
reached out for the sun, feeling the strength of my muscles, an awakened power surging through me. I breathed in the clarity of the new
day. I would look for the balance between combat and repose—the
satisfaction of accomplishment—and I would keep my focus there.

Music filled my studio as I stepped out of the shower—the overture
to the *Magic Flute,* the music that Mozart wrote, and later longed for as

he passed from this world of space and time into the immortal realms. It was an exquisite accompaniment to a mystical libretto of fairy tale and Freemasonry, love and liberation—and invocations of Isis.

I don't remember setting it to Auto. I wrapped myself in a towel and checked the radio. The dial was switched to Off. A little puddle gathered at my feet as I jiggled the switch. The music stopped. I turned away, and the music began again.

Someone was playing tricks on me. I spun the dial to my favorite rock and roll station. Three major chords and I was back to Mozart. I switched the band from FM to AM and heard the horrifying headline, "An eight-year-old girl was found strangled in her uncle's apartment today. It's not known—" I quickly switched it off.

I turned my back . . . Mozart. It couldn't be—or could it? Had last night's communion somehow caused this? Just last week Onatah had told me how all the electronic equipment in her apartment went crazy after she'd done a powerful working. Anthropologists had long complained that something would zap their cameras and tape recorders when they tried to record a shaman in an altered state. Maybe this was the same type of energy disruption.

It could also be a pookah.

"No, no, no! I don't have time for this today. I've got to get to work!" I protested to the empty apartment. "Harvey?" I called. It's not that I didn't love Mozart, but it was too early in the day for pookahs.

I quickly looked over my shoulder. You can't miss a six-foot-four-and-a-half-inch-tall white rabbit named Harvey. I looked under the bed. Of course, there's nothing specifically requiring a pookah to be over six feet tall, or white, or a rabbit named Harvey for that matter. I checked the closet. I'd loved Harvey ever since childhood. And Harvey loved show business; he was certainly the most famous pookah in America, rewarding Mary Chase with a Pulitzer Prize when she immortalized him on Broadway and in the movies. Maybe he needed a lawyer. I checked behind the curtains. The general parameters are that they are large, invisible animals, Scottish elementals to be precise, who were very powerful and frequently mischievous. And exactly the kind of critter to show up when I was about to return to the "real" world of entertainment law after a night of divine magic.

I quickly pulled open the front door and stuck my head into the hall. No rabbit.

My neighbor, Mrs. Morrison, gave me a startled and disapproving look.

"Morning!" I smiled, trying to act like it was perfectly normal for me to be sticking half naked out my front door. I waved.

Mrs. Morrison raised her eyebrows and headed for the elevator as I shrank back inside. *Hey, it's New York.* I padded back to the bathroom to put on my makeup. A faint phrase of music snaked into the tiled room, wrapping itself around my wrist. I ran back into the center of my apartment and stood surrounded by music that poured in through the windows, through the walls, the floor, and the ceiling. I laughed with the delight of a child watching a magician pull a white rabbit from a top hat. It *was* a magic flute. But whether a sprite had conjured the music, or the music had summoned a sprite, or whether something else entirely had beckoned them both, I couldn't say.

I finished with my makeup, put on a new yellow dress, packed up all my brand new, unworn suits, blouses, and sensible shoes, and dug out the receipts as the music played.

I put on my sunglasses and struggled up the slight hill from Riverside to Broadway. But even with the glasses, I could see a shimmering glow that surrounded everyone and everything. The sun was already high and unexpectedly hot. I was breathing hard as I pushed into the Hellenica, the corner coffee shop where I picked up breakfast every day, and dinner on too many nights.

"What a beautiful morning, huh? I took your advice," Elene, the owner of the Hellenica, gave me a radiant smile from behind the shiny Formica counter. "We went on a little second honeymoon this weekend. The Poconos. A heart-shaped bed, bad champagne, hot tub in the room. Ridiculous!" She lowered her voice conspiratorially and leaned her ample figure across the countertop. "It was wonderful. I used that love bath you gave me—it worked like a charm." She raised her black eyes heavenward and tilted her head from side to side in a gesture that managed to simultaneously channel Mae West and Anna Magnani. "On the house!" She handed me a brown bag. "I put in a nice cruller—you should have something sweet to start your day."

Elene's happy husband Joe had her locked in a passionate embrace, to the utter delight of their patrons. Sunlight filled the little coffee shop as I backed out the door with a peculiar feeling that I was being followed.

I struggled with my load, smiling at the strange reenchantment of the world around me. There's nothing enchanted about rush hour. I sighed as I stood in the street straining to spot a cab. Not one in sight. I resigned myself to the subway when a long, black limousine pulled up in front of me. The front window rolled down and the driver, an older man with snow-white skin, wavy white hair, and sunglasses, leaned forward. "Where ya goin'?"

"Fifty-seventh and Sixth, but I can't afford a limo." Limo drivers often made a quick extra buck by picking up short fares, usually businessmen or tourists at expensive hotels, but I'd never seen one at this time of day at Broadway and Eighty-sixth Street. It was the Upper West Side where schoolteachers, reporters, young executives, and intellectuals lived, not the limo set of the opposite side of town.

"Sure ya can. You'll never get a cab this time of day. It's my good deed—you can pay me what you'd pay a cab."

"Are you sure?"

He was already out and opening the door for me. He took my packages and put them on the front seat beside him.

"This is very kind of you."

"My pleasure. Mind if I play some music?" he asked as he turned into the luscious green of Central Park.

"Of course not."

He popped in a tape and began singing in the most extraordinary tenor. The music was familiar, but I couldn't place it. No matter. I settled back into the deep cushioned luxury of the ride, the car accelerating smoothly around green curves filled with sycamore and ash, weeping birch and willow, and hundreds of apple trees whose fragrant gowns of pink and white and red had now turned to rich green adorned with ripening fruit. As the driver serenaded the morning's perfection, we flew past mothers talking to each other as their children played, quicksilver messengers on speeding bicycles passing us on the downhill slopes, elderly men for whom time stopped while playing chess, and lovers of all ages, mysteriously free from the responsibilities of the workaday world, kissing beside the lake.

We cruised to the curb in front of my office building, and he stopped singing. I applauded till my hands stung.

"Thank you. I hope you didn't mind."

"Mind? You were fabulous. Do you sing professionally?"

"I used to—in the chorus of the Met."

"What were you singing?"

"*The Magic Flute.*"

I burst out laughing.

"What's so funny?" he asked, looking back through the open partition.

"I'm not laughing at you—you were magical. But that music's been following me around all morning." I reached for my wallet but he shook his head.

"It was my pleasure. You were a wonderful audience. Music needs a listener for its purpose to be fulfilled; otherwise, it's like love without lovers."

"A temple without worshipers."

"Precisely. Music is a sacred art. It heals, inspires, transports. Open yourself to it and it becomes a magic carpet ride to any place in this wide world, or any other world; and when it's done right, it can change the world. It'll take you to the center of the universe right there in the center of your heart. It's a holy communion and proof of our divinity. Well, that's my sermon for the day." He opened the door for me, and as I stepped out of the car, Hadus came to a dead stop on the sidewalk in front of me.

"It was magical," I said, extending my hand to the driver.

"It's a very magical opera," he said kissing my hand. He lowered his shades and as he winked at me I was startled to see his eyes were pink. "The music of the spheres."

"Pythagoras," I smiled, dazzled by the unexpected magic of my morning. He handed me my bags.

"Precisely. Have a great day."

I could have sworn I heard a duet as the car pulled away.

"Limousines at this time of day? Who'd you spend the night with?" Hadus asked archly.

"You wouldn't believe me if I told you. But you could say I woke up with . . . a Scottish movie star, a real animal." I smiled with satisfaction at his obvious confusion, pushed the door open, and held it for him. "It's going to be . . . elevator five," I said as I walked through the little crowd in the lobby. Hadus gave me a look of annoyed bewilderment. I stepped on as the doors of elevator five opened, looking back to see Hadus stuck in the lobby as a sea of rushing passengers surged past him. The doors closed on his aggravated face. I chuckled. Nothing could go wrong today. The world was a magical place. Instead of looking at their shoes the way they usually did, people were joking and laughing on the ride up.

During my lunch hour I returned all the new, unworn suits—

replacing them with a few perfect pieces by Donna Karan, one of the only women designers in the world. Her clothes were professional yet feminine, and I felt both empowered and beautiful in them. The pieces I wanted were more costly than everything I was returning, but it was worth it. And on the way out I stopped again to admire the Goddess's gown.

A couple of T-shirts, a sweatshirt, jeans, shorts, underwear, socks, bathing suit, poncho, towel, notebook, flashlight, matches, bug spray, sunscreen, and there was still room for cooking gear, groceries, and water. I carefully checked each item off my organizing list. The knapsack held more than I expected. I had borrowed it from Jake, along with a tent, sleeping bag, and mat. I'd never camped alone, so my first impulse had been to ask him to go with me, but alone was what I needed to be—to experience not being alone.

I had a couple of days off, and just in time. It was the beginning of the hottest days of the year, the Dog Days of summer, the time when, in Egypt, the star Sirius, the Dog Star, rose from the depths of the Underworld into the eastern sky. The star was a heavenly herald of the season when the Nile flooded, enriching the parched earth with life-restoring moisture. It marked the time when the mighty goddess Isis, by the power of immortal love, traveled to the realms beyond space and time to return life to the dismembered body of her beloved husband Osiris. It was the starry harbinger of mystery, the beacon of our beginning and our destiny. It was also very hot.

I headed for the Delaware Water Gap with half of New York at my heels. It took almost an hour just to leave Manhattan through the Lincoln Tunnel, congested by the weekly migration of those with the means to afford a soul's restoration. Though unaware of the full meaning of their recurrent quest to the seashore and countryside, they were going to perform healing magic with the earth, the sea, and the sky.

By the time I hit Route 80, I was traveling. I had the windows rolled down, Bruce Springsteen on the radio, and the tires spinning like roulette wheels full of wild promises. Pulling into the part of the Water Gap's federal reserve land was like driving into a time warp. I could feel the shift in energy as I drove past farmstands empty of people but filled with the earth's sweet riches of white corn, zucchini, and blueberries. Nailed to the stands were handwritten signs—"Corn $1.50 for a baker's dozen. Please leave money in the box."—comforting reminders that life is meant to be filled with hard work that is appreciated, and that trust should inspire honesty. I stopped, bought food, and paid reverence as well as cash. I drove past the high ridges, watching hawks soar on the evening updrafts, past cornfields planted in staggered rows where I would soon hear the green stalks growing as I danced with deer and raccoon beneath the waxing moon.

I pulled in at the campground office and parked the car in the lot. As I hiked to my site, I was immediately refreshed by the scent of towering cathedral pines. I stopped to watch a cloud of starlings weave and spiral against the setting sun, a thousand particles of flight, each with its own heartbeat, yet all summoned, spinning, diving, and rising as one, responding in intuitive accord to an invisible, inaudible invocation. Something sang to them from within, and I stood, listening. The feathered cumulus settled in the treetops overhead, filling them with the hallelujah of a holy choir.

I dropped my gear, and before doing anything else, I placed an elemental offering in each of the four quarters of my campsite—in the east, a blue feather I'd found while hiking; in the south, a small red candle in a glass jar; in the west, a scallop shell filled with water from the river; and in the north, an ear of corn from the farmstand. What did I have to place in the center? I wondered. This is where the altar would go, where the priestesses would place a repository of the sacred, whether a statue, a cauldron, an apple, or a pair of stag antlers. As I stood upon the sacred, I realized it required no symbol, only recognition—the center of the circle was all around me.

I knelt to touch the ground, rich with moss and moisture, with brown pine needles and leaves restoring to the earth the life it had once given them. A tiny garter snake slithered swiftly past. I fell backward, landing on my backside, a childhood fear seizing me. I froze, watching with astonishment as the little creature sped across the campsite, a wave of gracefully undulating earth. There's nothing to fear, I realized as laughter and the earth's perfume filled my lungs, my muscles, and my heart. I remembered that I too could be a vessel for the divine mystery I was seeking. I sat in the center of the circle, where the spirit dwells, and placed my notebook beside me. I grounded and centered myself, rooting myself to the earth, my companion and spiritual teacher.

A soft gray dusk gathered like mourning doves in the forest. I got up slowly and stretched. The light would soon be gone, and it was time to set up camp. I walked the site, finding a level area for my tent. I cleared it of twigs and rocks, and then wrestled with the tent poles, finally erecting my small nest with enough difficulty to appreciate my accomplishment. I gathered wood and built a fire, which also took more time and skill than I'd anticipated. When the flames had finally taken hold and I'd given thanks, I cooked, ate, and settled in as darkness settled in around me.

The night air was much cooler than in the city where steam pipes and the overheated exhaust of countless engines and air conditioners kept the temperature unnaturally warm. But it wasn't just the difference in temperature that struck me. It was the silence. There was none of the background noise of the city, no relentless sound of engines, nor the invisible noise of telephone lines, radio waves, television waves, and countless other technological usurpers of the ether.

As my mind quieted, relinquishing the cares of the week, I began to hear the woods, filled with its own pulsing music: the rhythmic humming of cicadas, leaves rustling, water lapping against the riverbank, and the percussive counterpoint of crickets, an owl, sticks snapping in the fire. Incessant sounds filled this gentle grove, but they were the utterances of nature, and they evoked a very different feeling than the urban cacophony. As I listened to the earth's orchestra, I remembered the passion for music that, so long ago, would bring me magic.

I sat in the organic tranquillity we strove for in our circle meditations. Thoughts of work, the frustrations and the victories, intruded upon my revery. But they floated past, like fallen leaves on the swiftly flowing river beside my campsite. The techniques we had learned in the city now served me well, for with only a moment of grounding, centering, and breathing, I was open to the perfection this place offered with such natural generosity. In this untouched realm where the noise stopped and the rhythm began, I recognized a pattern that sounded like a heartbeat. I lay back on the earth, resting and nurturing myself with its power, listening to its song.

The campsite was covered by a thick canopy of branches and I longed to see the stars. You can't see the stars in the city—there's too much man-made light blinding us to the beauty of the heavens—so I picked up my flashlight and carefully found my way to the unobstructed sky down by the river. I was stunned to find the night ablaze with light. I crouched beside the river, shivering with awe as the watered serpent slid through the darkness, countless mirrored stars shimmering on its back.

Enraptured by the immortal movement of stars and river, I lost track of time. I knew I could remain absolutely fixed on this spot, like a hermit on a mountaintop, and no matter how little I moved, nor how removed I was from the trials and tribulations of the unnatural world I had left behind, time would flow like a river right through me. It would carry me like the stars in its waters from twelve years to twenty-five to one hundred, all in the infinite duration and fleeting swiftness of a single moment. The nature of energy was to flow through space and through time, to move, and to change from one thing into another. To remain fixed, to refuse to move, or to resist change was to block the natural flow of life.

Here was the hidden mystery of tidal pulls, of spiraling movement within the eternal current, the river in which I would always travel. And here too, following the ancient ways of the sacred earth, was the magic carpet to carry one into realms of sacred dimension and delight. Like the river before me, and in me, energy moved in waves—it was rhythmic. And the relationship of these waves to each other was harmonic. This was part of what Pythagoras, priest of the Goddess at the oracle of Delphi, had discovered so long ago. This is what he called the music of the spheres.

Sound, music, drumming, incantations, the music of the creatures of the moon, all of these reached deep within the sphere of my mind. Each trance-working, each visitation, each epiphany seemed like a moment outside of time, a crossing of the river to the other side. But even in stillness, there was movement, and if one wished, it could also be a journey carrying one upstream as well as down, forward or backward in time.

What was I to do with the energy that was my life? I had let the river of life carry me to realms of unexpected beauty and power, and equally unanticipated domains of despair and powerlessness, but where was I going? Could I know? If the destination was preordained, should I just ride the currents, or was it up to me to choose a destination? Was there a destiny for me to fulfill? What was I to do: remain passive, open, and accepting? Or strive, struggle, and challenge?

A golden crescent moon sat low upon the horizon and I stretched out my arms to embrace her. All magic begins first with cleansing and purification. I stripped off my clothes and carefully stepped into the icy, star-filled waters. I felt every molecule in my body shocked to life. The water surged around me with more force than I expected and the rocks beneath my feet were dangerously slippery. I quickly grabbed onto a tree branch that hung low over the river to keep from being swept away, feeling the rough bark against my palms, the frigid current against my body, and I stared up at the moon as the percussive night-music carried me to a trance of communion.

Magic is the fulfillment of destiny. Three dimensions are space, the fourth is time, and the fifth is where the spirit dwells. And there are twice these when you look into the mirror of the Goddess. Which realm casts the shadow and which is the reflection remains for your discovery. This is where your destiny awaits you. Open yourself to the movement of the divine and its energy will carry you beyond all limitations. It is present with every breath that you take. It spirals, uniting past, present, and future, energy and matter, love and desire. It is the journey of the heart's ambition and the soul's awakening. It is present in the music of the spheres, the light of the stars, the flowing of the river, the growing of the willow, the yearning that draws lovers together from the ends of space and time. It flows through all, it unites all. Open yourself and feel its power; it will guide and sustain you as you create life.

The moon grew smaller and brighter, turning from gold to silver as it rose in the sky. It filled the river with radiance, a cup that cradled the strewn starlight into its brilliant arc. Carefully, I turned around three times, each time confronting and adoring my moonshadow as it stretched across the river, arising from its own center and spreading outward. God, or Goddess, or both, was a sphere whose center was everywhere and whose circumference stretched infinitely outward. The barrier between inner and outer had once again become invisible. The fire of words worked their alchemy and I stopped shivering, enraptured by the message that heated me from within. My body, my soul were one with the river, the moonlight, the echoing utterance.

Now the moon was high, a bright crescent implying the full orb that remained hidden in its own shadow. In that moment I understood how much potential our shadows conceal, sometimes abducting, other times protecting that fullest part of ourselves that will inevitably, cyclically shine in luminous completion.

In an instant I was aware of how cold the river was. Suddenly freezing, I scrambled ashore and quickly rubbed myself dry with my shirt. I was light-headed, ecstatic, exhilarated. I was clean. I threw on my dry clothes, grateful for the cocoon of warmth. I hugged myself, rubbing my arms and legs to get my blood flowing, feeling them tingle and burn and return to life. I turned back to the moon and the shimmering serpent.

"Thank you," I murmured. "I'll remember."

I struggled up the slippery riverbank, my muscles stiffened by the frigid bath, and looked for the little path. I wasn't sure if I was going the right way, but I headed toward the dark woods. I'd gone a short distance when I realized the reverberating drone of peepers was growing louder. My flashlight flickered, then faded and went out. I found myself stumbling into a little gully by the river's edge. I stopped dead in my tracks, stunned by the sight before me. It was as if the stars had fallen from heaven—the watery ravine was filled with throbbing light. I stood surrounded by thousands of dancing fireflies. I sank to the earth in the presence of mystery and revelation.

Time stopped as I watched, slowly understanding that their flashing lights were not random flickerings but beacons; this was how these tiny creatures found each other. I watched as countless couples throbbed with lustrous energy, communicating their presence, their recognition, their rhythmic harmony, guiding each other until they were united. They flew about me, many of them alighting on my shoulders, my arms, my hair, their tiny flames flickering in countless pulsations of yearning, desire, and fulfillment.

I thanked the Goddess, the God, the cosmos, the woods, the river, the fireflies, my parents who had somehow found each other and given life to me. I thanked every minute of the past that had brought me to this extraordinary moment. Nature *was* a sacred teacher. Magic, I knew, does not work against nature but with her, and the wisdom that one needs to make choices, to experience magic, to live, to be in the presence of the divine, is ever-present in the natural world. True magic is to remain connected to that sacred source. Everything will flow from that.

I found my way back to my campsite, the fire's glow guiding me through the dark woods. I wrote down everything I could remember in my notebook, and then crawled happily into my warm sleeping bag. I fell asleep to the lullaby of the woods and the river, earth, and water, form and feeling.

I had learned that whether oracles illuminated destiny or just possibilities, the choice of what road to take would always be mine, and something, or someone, was there to guide me in those choices.

. . .

Candles of blue, the color of healing and peace, were lit in the four quarters and on the altar, and in the center was the pentacle.

"You've learned to raise energy by grounding and centering yourselves, by chanting, and dancing. Tonight you're going to use these techniques to raise and direct energy in a conscious and magical way," Maia said as we gathered for circle. The drawing down had restored Maia to her loving, powerful self and she spoke with authority.

When the casting was concluded, Maia explained just what we would do tonight.

"Some of you may already know that the reason Nonna hasn't been coming to circles lately is that she isn't well. She's asked us to raise energy to help her heal, so tonight we're going to raise a cone of power and send her energy for strength and healing. Your job is to raise the energy, Bellona and I will direct it to Nonna. She's casting a circle to receive our energy at home."

"What's wrong?" I asked, determined to get an answer. A few weeks ago I had asked Nonna, who answered me by smiling and reassuring me that she was following her doctor's orders. I thought back to how I pressed her, and the strange answer she'd given me.

"By the time you're my age, you like to think you've had all your serious challenges," Nonna had said quietly. Then she chuckled. "And just when you'd like to sit back on the porch and rock, the universe knocks you out of your seat. And maybe that's exactly as it should be. If you're not sure about why you're living, you're not. It's time to see what I've really learned. This is my trial of rebirth—it's time for me to shed my old skin."

She hugged me, telling me not to worry, and she would say no more. And if they knew, though we had all asked, neither Maia nor Bellona would say. But tonight, if we were going to help her, we had to know.

"It's lymphoma."

Fear squeezed my heart, and the women exchanged anxious glances.

"The doctors recommended radiation and chemo and she's been following their advice. But she's also using alternative treatments—acupuncture, healing touch and massage, herbs, diet. And, of course, healing magic, so she also needs our love and energy to beat this. We're also going to charge this talisman with healing powers for her."

On the pentacle, Maia placed a silver star and a perfect quartz crystal, which hung from a silver chain. We stood in the flickering candlelight, holding hands. We grounded and centered ourselves, drawing the energy of the earth into our bodies and sending it around the circle. It was invigorating, and as I opened my eyes, I was overwhelmed by the splendor of the altar, and the vitality of the women in circle. All were surrounded with a soft glow, what Nonna called an aura—some golden, some violet, others pale blue or green—and the altar was the purest white surrounded by flashing blue fireflies. Silently, I sent my love to my teacher.

"As you circle tonight, visualize Nonna healthy, cured, alive, happy. See her as clearly as you can, particularly at the moment we release the energy."

Softly, almost inaudibly, Maia began singing. I strained to hear her words. Her eyes were closed, and her body swayed as she began to sing louder. Her voice was a rich alto, which made me think of deep, red Barolo wine. Strange syllables spilled from her lips, repeating over and over again. Bellona began to sing with her, a reedy, tough soprano:

"*Hi* Gee Ah *Hi* Gee Ah *Hi* Gee Ah."

Their voices rose with a great exhalation of breath on the first syllable, creating a rhythm of power and urgency. We picked up the chant. Our voices filled the room, echoing back to us from the rafters. *Hygieia!* I realized in a flash: the name of the ancient Greek goddess of health.

We began to move, slowly, unevenly, bumping into one another. I watched our priestesses' feet as they began to lead us in a dance as ancient as the Goddess's name they'd invoked. Round and round we went, moving with elegant grace, circling clockwise, right foot crossing over left foot, left foot taking a step to the left, right foot behind left foot, left foot stepping to the left. I looked at the beauty that surrounded me. Here were the priestesses of ancient Greece, dancing the sacred spiral of life, the dance of Dionysian ecstasy, of death and rebirth. And here also was the truth behind the age-old image of Witches dancing in fields or woods beneath the silvery moon. An exhilarating surge of energy raced through me.

Faster and faster we moved, the chant sustaining us and urging us on. A sudden burst of laughter punctuated the chant as we struggled for breath. And then there were no dance steps because we were moving too fast for the pattern, whirling around the room at a dizzying pace. Around and around we went, our voices dropping to breathless whispers, our hands pulling each other on in a chain of heart-driven purpose. We moved beyond exhaustion, breaking through to an entirely different level of energy. Our voices grew, renewed in strength and power.

"*Hygieia, Hygieia, Hygieia.*" We sang in harmony, astonishing ourselves and the Goddess who heard us.

We wove an ivy braid of footsteps into a circle of healing energy until again we were running, fortified by the unexpected strength we had found within ourselves. We were empty of thought, filled only with spiraling, throbbing vitality. It rose from the earth beneath our stamping feet, through our bodies, our arms, our hands. It spun above us, rising to a stunning peak.

"Now!" Maia called out and we stopped in our tracks, energy humming through and above us, our arms outstretched toward the sky. Light radiated from the palms of our hands.

My entire body felt electric. I was lightheaded and ecstatic. My breathing was deep and forceful as air, and life filled and then left me, and then filled me again. I drew the energy up from the earth, feeling its powerful current run through my body and pour outward from my hands.

Nonna, I thought, envisioning her standing before us, smiling, laughing, healthy.

The energy flowed through us into a cone of power, a cornucopia of light, spinning clockwise around the circle and spiraling upward, coming to a point far overhead, and disappearing into the sky above us. I watched, stunned.

"Nonna, we send our love to heal you, to nourish you, to make you strong, to give you life," Maia declared. The pentacle and the talisman on the altar glowed with light, as if the sun had been captured.

I looked down and saw my shining palms. I cupped my hands and the light gathered into a radiant orb. Slowly I brought it to my heart, inhaling deeply and feeling it enter me. My heart opened, and energy raced through my body. Tears of gratitude ran down my cheeks as again I felt the power of the rushing river that pounded through me during my magical camping trip.

"Down!" Maia commanded us.

We dropped to the ground, palms flat upon the floor, some of us with our foreheads touching the soft carpet.

"Let the energy drain from you. Let it return to the earth from which it came."

My tired muscles rested on the sustaining earth. Curled upon the mother's breast, I remembered how dogs, wolves, cats, and other animals lay upon the earth to heal. I felt the strength of my healthy body, and sent a magical message of wellness to Nonna. Each day, until she was well again, I would send her energy for healing.

Maia stood with her arms raised in the Goddess posture she had assumed during the drawing down and spoke: "In the names of Hygieia and Asclepius, bless this healing circle. Bless Nonna with health, strength, love, and life."

"So mote it be," declared Bellona.

"So mote it be," we repeated, a chord of certainty ringing from the centers of our souls.

Wine and cakes were consecrated and the circle was closed.

"Did you see that cone of energy?" I asked Gillian quietly, still in awe.

She shook her head. "But I felt all this incredible energy in the room and the pentacle was glowing. Did you see it?"

I nodded.

"I've never seen anything like it," Jeanette said softly. "It was a spinning white vortex with all these bands of glowing color shooting around in it."

"It was crackling and throwing off sparks, like sparklers on the Fourth of July," I said, still feeling the tingling aftereffects.

Onatah nodded enthusiastically. "That's it—like whirling sparklers! It was amazing! But all I saw was white light, no color."

So our sensory perceptions varied, but we also shared experiences, just as when we did trance work.

The art of magic is the ability to work with the natural flow of energy. We characterize energy as moving in waves, as light and sound do, but a wave is only a two-dimensional depiction of a multidimensional movement through, and beyond, space-time. Energy moves in spirals, the spirals of seasons and snakes, seashells and stars, DNA and dogs curling to lie before the fire. Here was the meaning of the Goddess's coiling serpent.

The spiraling movement of energy, or cycles, flows back and forth from peak to valley, from being to nonbeing, waxing to waning, summer to winter, masculine to feminine, yin to yang, birth to death, and back again. Opposites do not exist separately from each other, but instead are joined in the curving dynamic of the universal flow. Witches know that energy cannot remain forever at one end of the spectrum, for its nature is that of ceaseless, swirling movement. Night is followed by day, action by rest—a pattern adhered to by our own bodies as we inhale, exhale, then inhale again. Most mysterious is the beauty of the connection of opposites, their dynamic interaction from which new life and new forms emerge.

This was the nature of the cone of power—the ancient origin of the symbol of the Witch's pointy hat—the spiral of energy that we drew forth from the earth, and from ourselves as energy-bodies, to assist Nonna in healing. It worked through our conscious and loving connection to her and a deliberate investiture of our energy with healing and nurturing power. I was also discovering that, as with much of magic, it also worked with our extraordinary unconscious powers that were only just beginning to emerge, like mythic dragons from their caves of treasure.

Three weeks later, Nonna was at circle with a wonderful story for us. She had cast her circle and awaited the arrival of our energy. When it did not come by midnight, she finally went to bed. Around three in the morning, she awoke from an extraordinary dream, feeling better than she had for months. She dreamed she'd been hit by a beam of light that filled her with energy. And her body was healthy and she was full of life. The feeling continued after she awoke, and she felt so "charged" she couldn't get back to sleep that night.

Nonna continued to come to circle and we raised energy and sent it directly into her body, visualizing her healthy and happy.

Three months later, a visit to her doctor confirmed that there was no sign of the cancer, and nine months later, her illness was deemed to be in full remission. It never recurred.

Now, many years later, Nonna's healing is just as extraordinary but I've come to accept our magical contribution as more than mere coincidence. As I've struggled to restore the health of my own body, and as I've witnessed and assisted friends in their healing efforts, the medical profession has also, finally, begun to embrace "alternative" practices. People now take an active role in their healing with meditation, prayer, the use of herbs, healing touch, guided imagery, acupuncture, and a variety of energy techniques. When these are integrated with the traditional Western techniques of allopathic medicine, doctors find that patients heal more quickly and survive longer. And studies have now begun to support these observations. Therapeutic touch has been found to lower the blood pressure and heart rates of unconscious patients; premature babies who receive therapeutic touch massages gain weight faster and leave the hospital sooner than untouched babies; women with breast cancer who participate in support groups survive an average of eighteen months longer than those who do not participate; and patients with heart disease can reverse the deterioration through an integrated program of meditation, exercise, group support, and a healthy diet.

Scientists now understand that healing rituals, once thought of as primitive and superstitious, ignite remarkable healing powers that are inherent in each of us. But perhaps most astonishing of all are studies that have shown that when people prayed for patients, even though all were strangers and the patients weren't even told they were being prayed for, the patients healed more quickly and survived longer than patients in the control group who did not receive the gift of such "magical" energy. We are all connected in the web of life.

All of these "alternative" techniques, and more, were part of the repertoire of shamans and priestesses, Witches and wise ones who served as their communities' healers. This healing wisdom was handed down from generation to generation, and if you ask a shaman how her great, great, great-grandmother first learned of a plant's particular healing powers, she will tell you that long ago the plant spoke to her ancestor. She may also add that if you know how to listen, the plant will talk to you now. Much of that wisdom disappeared with the loss of those wise women and men, and many of our ancient medicines have disappeared with the destruction of the rainforests and our other precious natural environments. But the techniques by which our ancestors first gained this wisdom remain, and we can use them for healing.

In circle, we were learning ecstatic, shamanic practices that opened us to the presence of the divine. We began to experience the expanded realms of nonordinary reality, the hidden world which coexists with the world of our day-to-day lives. In the months I had been working with my priestesses, I was discovering many different styles of magical work— from the spontaneous to the highly ceremonial. Magical energy can be raised by breathing, chanting, dancing, running, drumming, building a fire, sitting in the hollow made by the roots of a fallen tree, ritualizing, and making love.

There are many ways people raise energy without realizing that they're reaping the benefits of cleansing, empowerment, ecstasy, and even communion. For instance, they raise energy at large events with crowds who share emotions and excitement—such as at rock concerts or sporting events. They also raise energy when they are alone or with just a few people; when they sing to themselves or shoot hoops with friends, when they ride a horse, drive a fast car, motorcycle, or airplane; when they dance with friends or a lover, or when they become absorbed in a movie, play, or book. And also when they are moved by nature's beauty. Because we are unaware of its sacred nature or benefits, often-times this tremendous energy goes undirected. Too often we have seen raised energy deliberately manipulated and misguided to serve un-healthy, destructive purposes. Just imagine how we could direct energy with awakened awareness, honed skills, and spiritual insight. We could heal and enlighten humanity, and preserve our precious planet and its exquisite inhabitants. We could consciously embody the divine, and co-create Paradise.

All magic requires tremendous focus, concentration, and the refine-ment and cultivation of mental faculties that have been suppressed and denied by Western culture. Many Witches talk about magic as "the changing of consciousness at will," but it was increasingly apparent to me that magic is not merely about the mind, or the projection of one's will. It is not just another school of transcendent spirituality nor is it mere mechanistic ritual. It's not enough to wear the right-colored clothes at the right astrological configuration, or use the perfect in-cense, or invoke the proper deities with the precise words and . . . abracadabra, you've got magic! If it were that simple, the entire human race would have seemingly superhuman powers.

Magic must be fueled by your passion, your body's power, your heart's deepest feelings. Focus, clarity, and concentration are all essen-tial as well, but without courage, compassion, and groundedness, magic will be no more than an imagined daydream. There is another ingredi-ent, however, without which magic cannot work. Some say the energy we work with is neither good nor bad, but simply neutral, and therefore, it can be used for either good or bad purposes, depending on the practi-tioner's will. And yet the encounters I had with raising energy, witness-ing a drawing down, working in trance, and experiencing visions and epiphanies all convinced me that the energy we worked with was love. Sometimes its quality was maternal, other times paternal. It often had the quality the Greeks referred to as *agape,* or divine love. At other times, it was profoundly erotic. From these encounters I learned that no amount of magic can actually manifest change in a lasting or meaningful manner without a loving connection to the sacred.

This was the secret of true, spiritual magic. Yes, timing is important, and tools can hold a charge, and potions and props add to energy and help to shift consciousness, and the focusing of one's mind, and the directing of one's will are essential, but ultimately, the truly magical ingredients are you and your connection to the divine. Magic requires a capacity for communion with the sacred, because the magical realm that one enters is the realm of the heart. Without the capacity for compassion and love, no magic will be truly spiritual in its texture, form, or results. Wicca is a spiritual practice concerned with the union of spirit and matter—spirit animating matter, and matter embodying spirit. The true and sacred nature of this communion is love.

As I used these Wiccan techniques, I was deeply impressed with the implications of our connection to the sacred well of the Goddess's power. This relationship demands reverence and respect. In the face of such astonishing empowerment most human concerns are so petty that to use magic to address them is like using an atom bomb to kill a mosquito. But through my visionary work I had come to realize there was a kind of built-in safety mechanism—our own limitations restrict the extent to which this power is available to us. If we are petty and selfish, our magic yields insignificant results. But, generosity returns as generosity, and love as love, for the energy of the universe is a mirror of our deepest longings, and our deepest fears.

In working to heal Nonna, I had begun to heal myself. The world took on a new, intoxicating vitality, as if I were falling in love with life. It responded to my joy, my hunger, my generosity. My heart opened, and my yearning grew. I kept hoping it would lead me to a lover, a soulmate, but where it was truly leading me was still hidden. Through it all, I remembered to give back to the universe in gratitude for the gifts I was being given, by donating money to charity, helping out my elderly neighbor, or contributing to my circle. I treated Hadus with patient and good-humored care, ignoring his anger and innuendo, hoping it would have a salutory effect.

I was beginning to see the Goddess everywhere. And I was coming to understand that when we are connected to the sacred, we will conduct ourselves in a sacred manner, with reverence and respect for all expressions of the divine. We will learn to share the power of Witches, seers and shamans, priestesses and singers of the sacred songs—those who have long protected humanity's ability to work with the unseen sacred forces that flow through life, binding and uniting all in sacred reality. We will be able to live magical lives, with the divine power to reenchant the world.

But magic works in unexpected ways—carrying one into the deepest caves on the journey toward the highest mountains, through blinding light into nurturing darkness, through struggle to release and back again. The Old Religion is a chthonic spirituality—one first descends into the Underworld before ascending to the heavens—but I didn't yet understand this pattern or its meaning. The shadow realm was about to teach me.

"Did you see *Variety* yet?" I handed my copy to Max.

He nodded. "More bloodbaths." He sighed. He'd seen more careenings in the record business than the roller coaster at Coney Island, but he'd survived them all. "Got a minute?"

"For you, always." I followed him into his office. The stereo was on and I knew what was playing—Mozart's *Magic Flute!* I smiled with pure joy as I sank onto the slippery green couch.

"If you have time today, I need a contract of sale for a co-op apartment." Despite my now hardened star cynicism, a silly thrill shot through me when Max mentioned the name of the client. He was a huge star who also had a reputation for being a really nice guy. "He'll be in later, you can get the particulars from him then. So, how's everything else going?"

I hesitated—I longed to confide in someone, but would he believe me? And even if he did, what could he do about it? Talk to Hadus? I didn't want to put Max in an awkward position, and besides he had no power over Hadus—each partner was autonomous. And even if Max did talk to him, it would probably only make things worse by antagonizing Hadus, or getting me fired. No, I'd made up my mind weeks ago that I would deal with whatever I had to. So I was . . . diplomatic. "Fine, I'm learning a lot."

Max gave me a knowing look. "You're surviving?"

I nodded.

"Good." He smiled and patted my shoulder. His secretary knocked with his appointment and I headed for the file room to pull some contracts of sale.

"I'm happy to see you've given up the librarian look."

I didn't need to look up from the file drawer to know it was Hadus. I tugged on my skirt, which had ridden high up on my thighs as I knelt to dig out files.

"Don't cover up on my account."

I stood up, a folder clasped in front of me. The file room was small, crowded with boxes and cabinets, and stifling without air-conditioning. I wished I hadn't removed my suit jacket as he took a casual, calculated step forward and leaned in to me, carefully bending the folder and its contents toward him. He looked down, at the file or at something else.

"Need any help?" His voice was low and I could smell his liquid lunch.

"No, thanks. I'm all set."

"You certainly are. Something about you is different lately." He inhaled and ran his finger along the inside of my arm. "You change your perfume?"

I jerked my arm back, dropping the file.

Just the act of stooping down to pick up the scattered paper felt humiliating. It seemed as if the earth was slipping out from under me. Where was all that exhilaration I'd been feeling, that joyous certainty that magic on the inside meant magic on the outside?

"It's the scent of money—did you read my memo to you about Taylor? If you noticed, they'll give you the money you asked for if you give them worldwide rights."

"That's not all I've noticed."

I shoved the spilled papers together, stood up, and quickly took a step backward, slamming my elbow into a metal cabinet. "Damn!" I flinched with pain.

"Shall I kiss it and make it better?"

That's what a leer looks like, I realized. I didn't know whether to laugh, or cry, or get angry. Between a rock and a hard place, I thought to myself, and I laughed.

Hadus recoiled like I'd slapped him. He took a step backward, and I slipped quickly past him.

Riding on the back of the Goddess's serpent, I was about to discover how difficult and transforming this journey would be. After the rewards of confronting the Guardian and encountering the Goddess, I was dropping through a long and dark tunnel to the center of the Underworld. It would be some time before I saw the light of day.

Enchantments

So you're scared and you're thinking
That maybe we ain't that young anymore.
Show a little faith, there's magic in the night
—BRUCE SPRINGSTEEN, *"Thunder Road"*

Where's the Taylor contract?" Hadus snapped at me as I stuck my head in his office.

"I finished it yesterday. Sharon's got it."

"I asked her for it. She says she doesn't have it." He signaled me into his office.

"That's impossible—I gave it to her yesterday, right before lunch." He swiveled in his chair, turning his back on me. "I specifically told her you needed it today," I protested to his bald spot.

"This is bullshit. Sharon!" he spun around, calling through the open door. No reply. "Where the hell is she? Madeline," he snarled into the phone, "have you seen Sharon?" He paused. "Tell her I want her yesterday." He slammed down the phone. "She spends more time in the bathroom than an eighty-year-old man with a blown prostate. When I tell you I want something done, it's your responsibility to see it gets done."

I could feel the adrenaline starting to pump as my entire body tightened. "Maybe you should explain that to Sharon. She seems to feel that if you don't tell her, she doesn't have to do it."

"I'll talk to Sharon. You just make sure the work gets done." As usual, he was shouting and the entire office could hear him.

I nodded. One point for me: He said he'd talk to her. "I've finished everything you asked for so unless there's something else you need me to take care, Max asked me to do some work. . . ."

Hadus nodded impatiently. "As long as it doesn't interfere with your work for me. Cheap bastard, he should hire his own associate instead of stealing mine."

Sharon walked in, blowing her nose.

"So, what's with the Taylor contract?" I asked.

Sharon feigned surprise. "I told you, I've been waiting for it." A tiny smile played at the corners of her lips.

My radar flashed warnings as I struggled to keep my annoyance in check. "I gave it to you yesterday."

"No, you didn't. I'm sure if you check your desk you'll find it."

My suspicions were confirmed.

"Let's just get this done. You!" Hadus barked, pointing at me, "Find the damn contract, and you," he roared at Sharon "type it up. Now!" Sharon held the door open for me, a smug little smile on her face.

I went to my office and, sure enough, hidden beneath my morning's caseload of finished files was the redlined Taylor contract, returned by Sharon during my lunch hour.

"The only person you're hurting with this behavior is you," I said dropping it onto her desk. "I don't know what your problem is, but I'm not your enemy, so don't make me one."

Sharon did not acknowledge my words, but called out to Hadus, "She found it on her desk."

The world was upside down again. Count to ten, I told myself. I was furious and a world away from the self who had danced on the rooftop in the rain. I counted to ten and walked away.

As soon as the day was over, I headed straight for the merry-go-round in the park. It was warm, still sunny, and the music immediately lifted my spirits. I handed the ticket-seller a five-dollar bill. This was a cleansing ritual I had established in recent months and I didn't have to ask—he knew what I wanted and handed me back five tickets and some change, accompanied by a big smile. I walked around to the side of his vividly painted little stall, he opened the door, and I handed him my purse and my briefcase—as well as a book I'd promised to lend him about magic.

I stood in line with the children, most of whom were shorter than my belt. And their parents. I no longer cared what they thought when they realized that the child I was taking for a ride was me. More than a few adults had been inspired to start riding, and it was always young lovers who were the first to scramble on board behind me.

I climbed onto a beautiful black steed with red roses in her mane. She reminded me of my favorite mount at the carousel my father took me to with devoted regularity when I was a little girl. I'd learned how to stand in my stirrups and lean into the musical wind to catch the brass ring. This horse was smaller, and not as wild—or maybe it was just that I was larger, and not as wild—but she was a fine horse and would carry me through as many circling rides as it took to wipe away the woe and weariness of the workday.

Calliope music filled the air, so loud it compressed my anger into something small and round that I could hold in the palm of my hand and hurl away as I whirled, widdershins, around and around and around. Soon all the sadness had been whipped away by the dancing winds while the horse and I spun in joyous banishing circles. When I finally dismounted, cleansed of all my cares, I was wearing the brass ring.

A full summer moon graced the city sky. This was the salmon moon, named after that fish of mystical fortitude which, for Native Americans and Celts, was a symbol of the soul's capacity for divine questing and transformation. And this was the moon when the salmon make their ancient upstream journey of death and rebirth.

I knew we were going to cast a spell tonight and I was anxious to be on time. I arrived early with a large bouquet of sunflowers. Incense hung in an unmoving cloud in the bookshop's thick air. A few customers browsed the shelves or chatted. They would soon be whisked out with the nightly cleansing. I strolled through the long aisles, remembering how peculiar the store had once seemed. The large mason jars, at first so bizarre, were now full of magic. The colored candles, the statues of dancing Pans and serene goddesses, and the magical tools all had meaning. And the books, once threatening because of my own fears, revealed a rich and rediscovered world of wonder.

Nonna greeted me warmly and handed me the *Formulary,* an old leatherbound book containing secret recipes for potions that would bring you love and money, health and happiness, and much more. The pages were yellowed, with dog-eared corners and transparent spots where oil had consecrated paper. Beside it was a plastic Rolodex with handwritten cards full of spells, and a small tin box with file cards the colors of a magical rainbow—blue cards contained recipes for peace, protection, healing; white cards had spells for cleansing, purification, inspiration; yellow had formulas for success and accomplishment; red cards were filled with recipes for love and some for power; green for money and creativity; lavender for spiritual growth and insight. In the back of the little box, bundled together with a rubber band, was a small stack of cards for hexes. I thought we didn't do that? Nonna interrupted my perusal.

"Tonight we're going to cast a spell for prosperity so we'll work with the elements of earth—plants and metals. Find a recipe we can use for an incense and a charm."

"How will I know which one to use?" I asked.

"Intuition," Nonna smiled. "Your inner voice knows everything—listen to it. Gather the herbs, the oils you'll need are all in the oil office, prepare the potion, and when you're ready, bring them into the temple."

My intuition knows everything. In the midst of a culture that scoffed, and rationalized, and generated so much noise it was virtually impossible to hear that inner voice, most people wouldn't believe Nonna's assurance. But I'd had enough experiences by now to know she was right even if my intuition didn't seem to work all the time. I closed my eyes, took a deep breath, and flipped through the little card box. Even after all the amazing experiences of the last few months, the skeptic suddenly reappeared. Wasn't spell casting just old folklore and superstition? After all, if I was learning anything, wasn't it that the power lay within, not scribbled on some little piece of paper? Our concerns were spiritual and serious—they were about the growth and development of the human soul, not about pulling rabbits from hats.

But who wouldn't like to believe in magical spells? I ran my fingers over the *Formulary's* leather cover. Sacred energy lies within and connects all living things. This is the truth at the heart of magic. The energies of herbs and plants, of weather, natural settings, elements, natural forms, colors, tools, words, and unseen spirits and guides add to one's own energy, as does the invocation of divinity. By now I understood that magical tools, including herbal potions and correspondences, trigger a shift in consciousness, and enhance and magnify the energy one puts into a spell.

Wortcunning, Nonna had called it—mastery of the secret powers of plants. It was an important part of a shaman's wisdom, for plants have the power to nourish and sustain life, to heal, to kill, to bestow divinatory insight, to alter our consciousness, to aid sleep or relaxation, to invigorate, to cleanse, to protect, even to arouse as an aphrodisiac. Herbs are also said to have magical properties that could attract true love, increase wealth, conjure dreams, awaken spirits of the dead, erase memories of lost love, break hexes, stimulate astral projection, make one invisible, enable one to fly, unlock the door to nonordinary reality, and even make the rain fall.

What if they can?

My rational mind, having fully exercised its powers, was ready to relax and allow my intuition to take over. I used a magical technique I had come to love: Placing the old book on its spine, I stepped back, and allowed it to simply fall open. I looked down at the parchment page—before me, written in elegant penmanship, was a recipe for wealth. I ran my finger slowly along the careful lettering, softly reciting the musical names: cedar, cinnamon, five-pointed cinquefoil leaves, laurel, storax, star of anise, borage, bay leaves, mint, and vetivert, which is said to break a streak of bad luck and to bring good luck if you carry it with you. One after another, I pulled the great glass jars from their shelves. Pungent fragrances wafted forth as I removed their lids. I mixed the herbs together in an old wooden bowl, my hands covered with aromatic dust.

I dropped a small handful into an old mortar and pestle and added a few drops of bayberry oil, a few of almond oil, and three drops of High John the Conqueror root, which is very poisonous if consumed internally but can be safely used in an incense or to consecrate. The oils helped settle the dusty powder and transformed the dried herbs into a moist and grainy pulp. The work of grinding the potion was glorious. I was careful not to overload the pestle, crushing and combining small amounts with oil, then saving the mixed potion in another wooden bowl.

As I moved the heavy mortar in clockwise circles, I practiced the visualization techniques I had been taught, seeing clearly in my mind's eye, not the means, but the desired end of our night's magic.

I visualized wealth, for it is more than just money. It is well-being, accomplishment, a healthy, full, and fulfilled life. I focused upon images of prosperity, and the spirit and actions of generosity and sharing that accompanies riches, or *should* accompany it, since so often in our culture wealth and greed are partners. I visualized a rich and fertile earth, free from pollution and abuse. I imagined a large table filled with food and I saw all the peoples of the earth sitting at peace around that table, feasting together and honoring the earth for her gifts. I visualized the women in my circle, prosperous, happy, and successful doing work they loved. An unexpected image of myself appeared, standing in a field of high corn. In one hand I held an open book, in the other a radiant orb of light, my arms outstretched to the full moon, a glowing pearl floating in a black velvet sky. I found myself quietly chanting the name of Demeter, the goddess of the grain.

The others in the circle had arrived while I was working. I heard their voices, their laughter in the temple, which I imaged into the grinding magic. They knew what I was doing and so they had left me to work in quiet. As I entered the candlelit temple carrying the magical potion, I was greeted with warm hugs and kisses. There were green candles burning in each of the four quarters and on the altar, which also held a vase with the sunflowers. I placed the wooden bowl on the pentacle in the center of the altar.

Circle was cast and the room filled with the rich fragrance of the incense I had mixed.

"This is an old charm my grandmother taught me. Each of you place three silver coins in the bowl of herbs," Nonna instructed us. After it passed full circle, she returned it to the copper pentacle. We stood in circle, holding hands, energy already coursing through us, binding us together with magical intent.

"This is the season of the earth's great fertility, the full moon of abundance before the harvest. We gather to cast a spell for prosperity, to ask the Mother's blessing to enjoy rich and fertile lives." Nonna's voice was clear and powerful as she began to sing a simple chant:

"Her blessings we'll sow
Then green shall she grow
And bless us at harvest
In field and in forest."

We quickly joined in, soon adding the name of Demeter as a rhythmic counterpoint. *Enchant* means "to sing over"—and chanting, or singing, is one of the most important techniques Witches use for altering consciousness, casting spells, and reconnecting to the web of life. Nonna sat in the circle's center, and we danced around her, laughing and singing, tugging each other, then swirling with grace, certainty, and enthusiasm. The energy grew, building to a spiral spinning through and above us. I looked up to see it swirling with green and golden light. The faster we moved, the faster the energy spun, elongating into a cone of power above our heads.

"Now!" Nonna cried and our hands flew upward, the cone shooting heavenward. "Into the potion!" Nonna commanded and we plunged our hands into the aromatic herbs at the center of the circle. Energy poured from us into the magical mixture that filled the bowl. The priestess reached up, grasping the point of the cone with her right hand, then thrust her left hand into the herbs and directed the cone's power downward into the potion. Our hands still buried in the bowl, we sank to the ground and finally, sitting together, with our eyes closed and our fingers stirring gentle circles in the sacred herbs, we conjured our images of abundance and fertility and charged the potion with the full measure of our desires.

Energy pulsed through my fingertips as I imagined an investment portfolio with enough money to never worry about paying bills, a home filled with friends, generous contributions made to worthy causes. I imagined myself free to discover work I loved—work that would serve the gracious earth and her people and be well received. I saw the earth, green and resplendent with abundance, and revered by her children. And, again, unexpectedly, I saw myself bathed in moonlight.

"The potion is charged. Mighty Mother of the sacred earth from whom all blessings flow, let our efforts be rewarded with a fertile harvest. Nourish your children that we might nourish the world with your wisdom. Let us give thanks for the blessings of the Great Mother, in whatever form they may take." With her athame Nonna drew a pentagram through the herbs, finally resting the point of her magical blade in the center of the bowl. "Blessed be all the children of the earth—plants, animals, humans, and the spirits dwelling with us. May they flourish in harmony and prosperity."

We passed the potion deosil around the circle, watching and following Nonna's example: each taking a small handful of the charged potion and three silver coins, then placing the herbs in a square of green cotton cloth. Holding the coins in my palm, I cupped my hand to catch the moonlight falling in through the window above. Then slowly, deliberately, I turned each coin over three times. This strengthened the charm by the power of three times three. I added the coins to the herbs in the green cloth, then tied the bundle tightly three times, knotting three threads of green, gold, and silver.

Holding it to my heart, I charged the charm a final time with all the energy left within me. And then I bound the spell by tying the three threads together in a single knot, and quietly repeating the incantation we had used to raise energy. How familiar this quaint charm filled with the power of earth and dreams now seemed, and how comfortable I felt doing something that only recently would have seemed nothing but silly superstition. Too much had happened for me to allow the voice of doubt to impinge upon my sweet sense of peace and unexpected optimism. We grounded the power and opened the circle.

"Don't talk about your magic with anyone, not even from circle, for at least twenty-four hours," Nonna instructed us as we were leaving. "You have to give the spell time to set itself before speaking of it in any way. Keep the charm with you, or you can put it on your altar, or in your wallet or your checkbook."

A spell must always be set or bound upon completion in order to release the energy so the spell will work. Along with the binding off of the money charm by knotting the three colored cords, Nonna's final instructions to us were important secrets of setting and releasing a spell. It must remain undisturbed by discussion, thought, doubt, or the energy of others for a full cycle of the sun, and sometimes longer. There are many ways to bind a spell—tying off, consecrating, sealing with wax, scattering, burying, or any number of other techniques depending on the nature of the magic. These are the finishing touches that complete and send a spell into the world to take effect.

Equally important to the lasting effect of a spell, one must always remember to give back to the universe in thanks for what has been received, regardless of whether it was exactly what you had hoped for. I realized the wisdom of working in a somewhat open-ended manner, because magic works. Be careful what you ask for, you just might get it. And so I was learning to trust the greater wisdom of the universe— particularly in spell casting—for our perspective is so shortsighted. This was why we visualize the ends rather than the means of a magical working. And even this is best done open-mindedly, visualizing what is needed, but not necessarily its specific form. Don't ask for that handsome guy next door to fall madly in love with you, because if you do your magic properly, he very well may, and you'll then discover he's an alcoholic ax murderer and you can't get rid of him. And you will have missed your opportunity to meet the great love of your life, who may be cleverly disguised as a short, bald accountant.

I placed the charm inside my purse, wedging it carefully into my wallet. Not thinking about the magic we had done was like James Dean's remark about not thinking about the pink elephant that was sitting on your coffee table. When it came into my mind, rather than push it anxiously away, I simply sent a pulse of positive energy in its direction—a simple thought form of "Success!" But as I headed for bed the next night, I wondered if the spell would work. With all I was learning, could magic get me what I wanted? Was I sure about what I wanted? And even though the priestesses had said we could work for our personal benefit, was it really all right?

Spell casting is an ancient and instinctual art that lingers in our hearts as the evocative childhood memory of our first magical tool—most often a stuffed bear, bunny, or elephant that seemed every bit as alive as we were. These were the first visible representations of an unseen but ever-present spirit guide—they kept us safe in the dark, held onto us as we entered the sometimes frightening cave of dreams, and accompanied us on our first great journeys away from home. As children, we guilelessly understood the wonderful skill of "charging" objects with an energy raised within the magical circle of loving arms.

Magical spellwork has always been used for practical purposes. The role of the priestess and shaman has always been to know, to heal, to feed, to protect, to counsel, and to share the ancient path and the techniques that connect us so swiftly with the sacred. These functions were particularly important for the survival and well-being of non-technological cultures. As I was learning, Witches continue to use spellwork for health, love, meaningful work, prosperity, inspiration, insight, peace, justice, protection. They use it for coping with loneliness, depression, or loss, to aid a soul's passing over at death, and even to deal with enemies.

Magical tools, wardrobe, herbs and aids—including potions, oils, candles, amulets, poppets, and talismans—are all used in the working of ritual and the casting of spells. Through skillful magical work, such objects can become like batteries, adding their energy to ours and storing the power we have raised from ourselves, the earth, and the divine. This phase of the work was particularly exciting for the women in my circle because it provided some of the first dramatic moments when we could see the sacred in the mundane—when the hidden power and meaning of something ordinary became palpable.

The timing of one's magic is an important factor in its success—right down to the time of day, week, month, or year, the phases of the moon and the phases of one's life, for all of these have to do with the nature of energy. Energy can be expanding or diminishing, moving inward or outward, coming closer or receding, growing, declining, or resting. This natural flow of energy relates to one's magical purpose—are you seeking to banish or diminish something or create or increase something? By working with the natural flow of energy, Witches greatly enhance the results of their magical efforts. They can open up blockages, clean out stagnant energy, bring good things to fruition, and rest in the cradle of time and space when energies wane.

A specific form of the Goddess or God, whose energies correspond to the purpose of one's magic, is also invoked to enhance one's efforts. Witches work with the strength of a particular deity, or aspect of the divine, whose energy most precisely corresponds to a magical goal, such as the Goddess Isis for spiritual guidance; Persephone is invoked for rebirth, Spider Woman for creative work, Brigid for poetic inspiration, Freya for prosperity, Hecate for dreams and transformation, Kali for justice, Osun for love, Amaterasu for power. We also invoke the Gods— Jupiter for success, Dionysus for ecstasy, Cernunnos to reconnect to the earth, Hephaestus for creativity, Obatala for justice, Osinyin for the healing magic of herbs, Odin for wisdom. Each of these divinities embody a quality of a greater divinity, an accessible portal to a vast, ineffable mystery. This is quite similar to the Catholic practice of praying to various saints for particular purposes, or the Jewish use of Kabbalistic energies, or the Christian invocation of angels.

Because magic works by the principle of interconnectedness, in doing spellwork, what we do to another we do to ourselves. We become one with the object of our magic. Thus, in seeking to make someone fall in love with us, we become bound by our own infatuation. In healing another, we heal ourselves. In seeking to find our path, we find others who travel with us.

Many people mistakenly believe that Witches cast spells to have control or dominion over nature or others. But this is alien to Wiccan cosmology. Witches do use the forces of nature by harnessing the energy of herbs, lunar cycles, elemental forces, seasonal rhythms. But our communion with the divine guides and keeps us from crossing the line between working in harmony with nature and seeking to have control over and exploiting it. In Wicca, the Craft of the Wise, the insight needed to make wise choices about performing magic does not come from a religious authority or expert, but from the divine within our own hearts and in the world around us.

I decided to use the tools of divination to seek guidance before engaging in magic, to trust my instincts in constructing a ritual, and to use the techniques and symbols I had been given to communicate with the unconscious and the divine. The Old Ways still seemed to be best suited as a means to wisdom, not as a way to seek worldly fortunes. But the Old Religion is nothing if not a fertility religion—a celebration of an immanent divinity that makes the world a garden of Eden. The spell the Goddess had cast upon me was my longing to return to that garden. In a circle of green candles set in velvet moss, I cast a spell and invoked the Goddess of the crossroads to guide me to that garden.

In the meantime, I wondered, what steps should I take to manifest my magic on the material plane? This was called "acting in accord"—doing everything in one's power on the material plane to bring one's goals to fruition.

I was determined to practice divination for guidance, work even harder at the office, and, as best I could since it was still an unfamiliar path, follow my heart. These were all appropriate and wise choices. But the next fork in the road led where I could neither imagine nor predict.

I pressed the black button beside apartment 11. The foyer was cramped and dark, painted tan twenty years ago and lit by a single, small light fixture. It was a classic Lower East Side, semi-renovated tenement building with high ceilings, narrow halls, and a floor of unexpectedly beautiful inlaid tile. The door buzzed and I pushed its heavy weight open. I smelled dinners and disinfectant as I slowly climbed the steep, narrow stairs.

It was a moonless Tuesday night—perfect for the magic Jeanette had planned. She'd asked me to work with her, and I immediately agreed. Although Jeanette was older than I, and her life experiences and background were very different from mine, we had been drawn to each other from the very beginning, and over the months our friendship had grown. I was honored that she trusted me and wanted to assist her in any way I could.

I didn't know exactly what she had in mind, only that it had to do with her ex-husband, Richard. Despite the temporary restraining order against him, he'd been calling her relentlessly. And she was sure she had spotted him following her—always at the stipulated distance. He'd "accidentally" crossed her path several times—appearing right behind her in a restaurant or in a supermarket line. He made a very public scene of acting surprised, apologizing, and getting away from her quickly, each time accomplishing exactly what he'd been after: Jeanette was left feeling terrified and vulnerable. She told me she'd also received deliveries at work and at home. First it was flowers without a card, last night it was a package with contents she refused to divulge.

Jeanette was being stalked. Though she called the police to let them know, they said there was nothing they could do until he violated the order. By then, of course, it would be too late for the police to do anything.

I knocked on her door and saw the peephole darken. I heard the turning of locks, several of them, and the door opened.

"Thank you." She hugged me as I entered.

"Don't thank me yet." I tried to get her to smile, but she looked more serious than I'd ever seen her. She quickly locked the door behind me, turning the deadbolt and sliding a chain-lock across the top.

She smiled at the red and purple anemones I'd brought her, and made happy scolding noises as she opened the white bakery bag full of brownies. But it was the little brown bag of red plums I had impulsively bought from the corner grocer that worked magic on her mood—her tension evaporated as she nodded with mysterious approval.

She handed me a cup of tea as we settled into her living room. I noticed there were bars on the windows—and, as in my own apartment, they made me feel more caged than safe. Because we had no alternative, in order to survive, we had all come to terms with the vulnerability of living in an urban jungle. And this subterranean sickness that preyed upon women in the cities had already spread beyond. Both of my best friends from high school had been raped, one in the small town everyone thought was so safe you could go to bed at night without locking your doors, the other during her first year in college. For several weeks my mother had served coffee and cookies at the kitchen table to a polite young man who'd been putting aluminum siding on her beautiful old house, a young man who never finished the job because he was arrested and convicted of raping and murdering a girl from the next town over. Gillian was raped at the country club, and Maia in an alley. It was a daily, deadly terror, so ever-present it was almost routine, incidentally occupying a small piece of our souls, not enough to keep us from going to work, or dating, or going out alone, or being polite, but more than enough to be a shadow that abducted our power and our freedom.

A slight shudder overtook me as thought of the relentless mixture of anger and sex, and its more subtle variations in the condescensions of male colleagues, that I confronted every day. I turned my attention to Jeanette's apartment. It was small, but serenely sophisticated, decorated in shades of off-white and butter cream, with gold and black accents. A bookcase was filled to capacity, a desk sat beneath the barricaded window to catch the cross-hatched light. There were paintings from her days as an art student, showing more than a measure of promising talent, several striking pieces of African sculpture, and photographs of friends, family, and moments of joy. It was straightforward and unpretentious, yet elegant and warm, just like Jeanette.

"I thought of going to a *santero,* or a *manbo.*" Jeanette seemed tense again. No wonder.

A *santero,* I knew, is a priest of Santeria. A *manbo* is a Vodou priestess. Like Witchcraft, both traditions are greatly misunderstood, partly because they are depicted in movies, television, and books as animal-sacrificing devil worship when in truth these religions conveyed a rich, vibrant spirituality culled from the soil of Africa. They are Western variations on the indigenous African religions, primarily Yoruban, arising out of the mixture of transplanted culture and slavery, and mixed or disguised with the Catholicism of conquerors. Though I knew that practitioners of these traditions did sacrifice animals in certain rituals, I also knew the animals were then prepared in a feast and eaten. And, historically, many religions, including Judaism, Christianity, and Islam still practiced sacrifice on the holiest days. Certainly the sacrifice of God's son, Jesus, was the central mystery in Christianity. It is one of the terrible mysteries that life feeds upon life. I respected the Native American practice (shared, I later learned, by the old European pagans) of honoring the spirit of the animal you killed and making use of all of its parts. Still, animal sacrifice was a practice that I couldn't imagine myself using, and I remembered the words from the Charge: *"Nor do I demand aught in sacrifice, for behold I am the Mother of all things and My love is poured out upon the earth."*

"What did Maia tell you?" I asked, worried about what might be expected of me.

"She suggested I do a binding, to stop him from harming me. So, I was wondering if you'd help me."

I nodded without hesitating. "Absolutely. The legal version of that was supposed to be the restraining order." I was glad to see her smile.

A binding is one of the few forms of magic performed to control someone without their knowledge or consent that was considered acceptable. As we had learned, you could also send back the dark, destructive, negative energies that were being sent to you, do a banishing, or perform a ritual for justice in which you sought redress for a harm or injury done to you. As far as I was concerned, a binding was only to be done in the most severe of circumstances when you were seeking to prevent the person being bound from doing harm. You didn't harm them or wish them ill in any way. You worked only to prevent them from doing injury. The trick was to do it in such a way that you didn't bind yourself to the person you were binding, or bind yourself in any other way. Jeanette had been bound by and to her ex-husband, unable to live without fear—so binding him was actually returning his own negative energy.

"I'm so glad you'll help me." She looked relieved. "I've been thinking about this for a while now but I wasn't sure what to do. Then the other night, my grandmother visited me in my dream. She told me what to do. There are *tricks,* that's what grandma called them, that she taught me." As she was talking, she rose and went to her desk, opened a drawer, and pulled out a photograph. She handed it to me. "That's Richard."

Standing with his arms around a young, slim, and pretty Jeanette, he was very handsome. I could see why Jeanette had fallen for him.

"I don't know why I kept it, but it will be useful now."

She picked up a pair of scissors, a piece of black cloth, a bowl of herbs, and a brown paper bag, and dropped them all into the center of the room. "I just need a few more things before we can get started," she said over her shoulder as she headed for her bedroom. "Would you get the candles? They're in the kitchen."

Thirteen candles, seven white and six black, sat on her kitchen table. Beside them was a jar of sea salt. There was also a large piece of aluminum foil. What's that for? I wondered. I carried it all into the living room. I knew the candles were meant to be burned in pairs of black and white, and I placed a set in each quarter.

"Are you going to set up an altar?"

"The whole nine yards," she replied, returning with a needle and thread and a handful of red and white ribbons. She had changed to a long caftan of maroon and a necklace of dark red beads hung around her neck. They looked particularly beautiful against her brown skin. "I use my coffee table."

We cleared it off together, moved it to the center of the room, and turned it so that it faced northeast, placing the various items we would use beneath it. Carefully, she unsheathed her athame. It delighted me that months ago we had both, independently of the other, selected identical athames from the infinite variety available. The knives had simple, dark brown wooden handles with long, double-edged black blades. She drew a banishing pentagram over the coffee table, then scattered sea salt around it widdershins. The table was now cleansed and ready for use as an altar.

We smiled at each other as we placed our identical athames side by side on the altar. Next we placed the remaining two pairs of black and white candles in the opposing upper corners of the altar. In a row from left to right across the center of the altar we placed the brazier, a silver candlestick with a white candle, a ceramic bowl filled with water, and a wooden bowl filled with sea salt. Jeanette lit a piece of charcoal, quickly placing it in the brazier before it burned across, and shook some incense from a small glass bottle onto the burning coal. A thick billow of powerfully scented prayer spiraled upward.

"Protection." Jeanette answered my unspoken question.

In the center of the altar, just below the line of elemental tools, Jeanette placed a copper pentacle. Above it she placed a statue of a figure I'd never seen before. The figure was clearly African. All of her features seemed elongated—an aquiline nose, large and upwardly slanting eyes, narrow ears, and hair rising straight up from her head like a crown of waves. Even her breasts were long and narrow. Her entire upper torso was covered with lines of white dots, her lower half was painted with white lines from her waist to her toes.

"That's *Oya*." Jeanette emphasized the second syllable of her name. "She's a very powerful *orisa* of Ifa, the Yoruban religion of my ancestors. Maybe one of the most powerful. She's the whirlwind, the tornado."

I marveled that Jeanette's grandmother, or rather, the spirit of Jeanette's grandmother, had instructed her to work with a female deity whose powers were those of the spiraling force of air, the elemental pattern I kept encountering.

"She's the power of focused concentration, the power of instantaneous change. She's the Niger River, beloved of Chango, *orisa* of lightning and thunder."

"Did you know scientists have discovered that a microsecond before lightning strikes, an energy particle precedes it to earth? The lightning strikes where the particle goes. That's Oya," said Jeanette confidently. "She'll direct the energy to keep Richard away from me. She loves truth and honesty and she won't tolerate injustice. She's a ferocious warrior and doesn't takes crap from any man. She carries a sword in each hand. And look—" she said, pointing to our athames, "you have the second of her swords."

A spark of wonderment at the Goddess's magic struck me. Oya's spark. Jeanette disappeared into the kitchen, returning with a basket full of red plums, deep purple eggplants, grapes, and a bottle of red wine.

"These are the traditional offerings to her. She's also an *orisa* of Witchcraft and magic. She works in very mysterious ways, not what you'd think to ask for." '

"It's already begun," I said.

Jeanette's face lit in a smile and I knew that tonight would go well. We arranged the offerings around the figure of Oya, pouring the wine into a dried, half coconut shell, which Jeanette also placed before the statue. We lit the candles and then sat side by side before the altar. Holding hands, we grounded and centered together.

"Oya is a great, powerful warrior and she is mother of everything," Jeanette said, beginning her invocation.

And, closing her eyes in concentration, she exclaimed loudly: "OYA!"

"Oya!" I echoed, astonished at the sudden rush of power passing through me as I exhaled.

Jeanette rose and gestured for me to join her. We took our athames from the altar and Jeanette invoked:

"She of the mighty winds, of the air we breathe, whirlwind of power and justice, she who is a mighty warrior, Oya, I call you." She took me by the hand, and together we walked deosil three times around the altar, our athames held aloft before us—mine in my right hand as I stood on Jeanette's right, Jeanette's in her left hand, toward the outer edge of the circle of radiant red and purple light. We returned to the altar and replaced our athames. Jeanette then picked up a gourd and three times circled with it, rattling as she walked. She made one last circumnavigation, this time stopping and rattling in each of the four directions.

"This is called an *igba* and shaking it summons Oya to our circle," she explained as she returned to the center of the circle.

We sat together and Jeanette rattled. After a little while, or perhaps it was hours, I began to notice that the sounds of the city were altering. They were no longer chaotic, but had settled into a connected rhythmic wave of sound—tires, sirens, engines, voices all rising and falling in a whooshing pulsation of sound that seemed more like the wind during a great storm. The rushing wind that tears down trees from the top.

"She's here," Jeanette said softly, handing me the gourd. "Would you rattle while I work?"

I nodded, quickly finding the steady rhythm that gathered the outside noises into rhythmic harmony. We sat together for a while, our eyes closed, listening to the waves of sound, approaching and retreating on the night air.

"I'm ready."

I opened my eyes to see that Jeanette had picked up the photograph and the scissors. Carefully she cut the picture in two, separating her image from that of Richard's, cutting away his hand that rested on her shoulder, cutting away his body that pressed against hers. She placed her emancipated image before the figure of Oya. His lay on the floor.

"I am no longer bound to you, Richard, in any way."

Next she took the black fabric, folded it in half and cut a figure, with head, arms, legs, and body. It was a little larger than the size of Richard's photo image. Jeanette threaded the needle and picked up the picture of Richard.

"So you will do no harm," Jeanette declared with the certainty of a warrior entering the battlefield.

She stitched the picture to the fabric, then stitched the two pieces of fabric together, leaving it open at the head. She picked up the brown paper bag and hesitated for just a moment. Something passed over her—a visible wave of energy changing her aura to a brilliant aubergine glow. She shook the bag and I could hear things rattling and scratching inside. She opened it, reached in, and quickly pulled out a handful of scraps—paper, fabric, did I see hair? She stuffed them quickly into the poppet she had just sewn, adding herbs from the bowl on the altar.

"Oya, grant me the *ase* of these sacred plants, lend their magic power to my aid and protection." She stitched up the figure's head, sealing whatever she had stuffed into its dark shape. Three times she knotted the red thread.

I kept rattling, although it had begun to feel as if the gourd was shaking itself.

She held the poppet over the altar, running it through the cloud of incense rising from the brazier and then through the flame of the white candle. Jeanette sprinkled it with water and with salt and, speaking firmly, declared:

"To the purpose of justice, and to prevent harm, I consecrate this image of Richard, filled with the stuff of Richard, to be more than an image of Richard, be this the essence of Richard, be this the intent of Richard, be this the fate of Richard. Richard, I bind you with your own intent."

Jeanette picked up the two ribbons and swiftly, tightly wrapped them around the little figure, binding his arms, his legs, even his head.

I kept rattling.

"Oya, I want this man to stop harming people, I want this man to stop harming me. Oya, come to my aid!

"Richard, I bind you now to stop you from harming me and all whose path you cross. Your power to do harm is gone. You will never hurt anyone ever again.

"Oya, may he be captured and tried and sentenced and jailed for the harm he has done. Let the suffering he has caused others return to him. Let him boil in the cauldron of the Goddess. Let his soul undergo the trial of transformation. Let him emerge a good man who harms no one.

"Oya, give me justice! Oya, bind Richard's power to harm anyone. Oya, protect me from harm!

> "By air and fire
> By water and earth
> By the power of Oya
> By the power of my ancestors
> By the power of women
> And the men who honor them

By the power of sun
By the power of moon
By the power of plants and animals
By the power of storm and wind
By the power of all that is sacred
By the power of spirits than none can see
By the power of three times three
I bind you now away from me!
Mare, mare, mare!"

Swiftly Jeanette knotted the two ribbons together nine times. She soaked the poppet in the water, laid it on the brightly reflecting side of the aluminum foil, and sprinkled it with salt and herbs from the altar.

"From this moment on, let all evil that you do befall only you."

Then she took her athame and drew a banishing pentagram over it. She swiftly wrapped the little figure in the foil, picked it up, carved a portal in the circle, and disappeared with it into the kitchen.

I kept rattling.

I thought I heard the refrigerator door open, and then shut. Jeanette returned moments later with a metal trash can which she placed before the altar, then she sealed the portal shut with a wave of her athame. She threw the paper bag, and whatever remained within it, into the can, lit a match from the white candle, and dropped it in. Flames shot up, faster and higher than we expected. I stopped rattling as we jumped back from the startling heat. A huge curl of black smoke spiraled upward and suddenly we were laughing.

"I hope that doesn't mark your ceiling."

"I can always paint it over. Good-bye to bad garbage. I haven't felt this good in I can't think how long. If nothing else, it was the best damned therapy I've ever had. I have this image in my head of Richard waking up in the morning unable to move, waddling around like a cross between a duck and Charlie Chaplin with his hands flapping at his sides."

We collapsed on the pillows consumed again by laughter.

"I know we're not supposed to talk about this for twenty-four hours, but, where'd you put the poppet?"

"In the freezer. Grandma's advice."

"What does *mare* mean? And what's *ase*?"

"*Mare* is a Vodou expression. Binding, being bound. What we did to Richard. *Ase* is the energy in all living things."

We knew the power of what we had just experienced, but we were still surprised when we discovered that the black candles were almost entirely burned out, while the white candles continued to fill the room with beautiful light.

"It's over. His power's gone. If he tries anything, it'll turn back on him," I said to Jeanette, absolutely certain that I was right. We hugged.

We offered a libation of dark red wine to Oya, and toasted each other as sisters. Then we stood, and together, with our athames lifted before us, banished the circle, and Richard. The last thing we did was take the incense and the water into which we had mixed the sea salt, and carry them all around the house, into every nook and cranny, to completely cleanse and seal it against intrusion.

"I'm glad you were here." Jeanette hugged me as I left.

"So am I."

I heard three locks seal behind me.

The wind whipped wildly about me as I stepped out into the night. My hair lifted weightless from my shoulder, garbage cans rolled past, plastic bags flew about like wild, white birds, and little trees thrashed furiously. The sky was an eerie cauldron of tumbling light and shadow as huge clouds, their underbellies lit with the garish-colored reflection of city signs, sped low across the tops of the buildings. *Oya*, I exhaled into the rushing wind, and she carried off my laughter as her offering.

We might have put an end to Jeanette's problems. Mine, however, were just beginning. It was late and my shoulders and neck ached as I sat hunched over the papers on my desk. I was alone in the office, trying to finish some work. I leaned back in the chair, stretching my sore muscles. I shook off a shiver of worry. I closed my tired eyes, and two hands came heavily to rest on my shoulders, pressing me into my seat. Terrified, I jerked around to free myself and to see who was touching me. My heart was pounding in my ears and it didn't stop when I saw Hadus staring down at me.

"Didn't mean to scare you."

"Really." I made no effort to disguise my annoyance. We'd been here before, his hands gripping too tightly in the pretense of a massage.

"You sure are tight. You've gotta learn to relax. Not that I don't appreciate all your hard work, but you could make me just as happy in other ways." His left hand continued to press firmly while his right hand slid toward my breast.

"Ways that are not part of my job description." I stood up and he lost his grip.

I turned around to face him. He stood between me and the door; the desk was blocking me from behind. I'm trapped, I thought, and the only way outta here is through him. I should have done some binding work of my own. I was scared.

"You're right about one thing—I do work too hard. It's definitely time to go home." I struggled to sound calm, firm, and businesslike.

"How 'bout a nightcap? Take the edge off."

"No thanks. I'm outta here." I pulled my jacket off the back of my chair, and my briefcase from my desk. I bent to pull my purse from the bottom desk drawer and as I leaned over, he came up behind me and pressed himself against me.

I straightened up into him—exactly what he had in mind. I'm in trouble. Anger rose in me like a serpent ready to strike. I pulled away, turning to face him just as he reached out for me. I recoiled. He moved toward me.

"Listen—" I was interrupted by a soft voice.

"Hello, dear, you're workin' late tonight, aren't you?" It was Evadne, the elderly black woman who cleaned our offices every night.

Hadus stepped back quickly as her gray-haired head poked in through my open office door.

"Oh, I'm sorry, I didn't know you were in conference."

"No, no. I was just leaving." I grabbed my purse and pushed past Hadus. "How's your daughter doing—did she pick her major yet?"

Evadne knew. Whether she heard, or saw, or simply knew from too many years cleaning up after a world of shadows, she knew.

"Why, yes, didn't I tell you? She's always been so good in science, she's majoring in biochemistry." Evadne pushed the cleaning cart along beside me as we walked, together, toward the front door. I could see from the corner of my eye that Hadus had stepped into his office. "All that math, but she says it's easy."

"She'll do great."

She nodded, smiling her sweet, sad smile. "Such a sweet child—still after me to quit but I keep tellin' her I'm too young to retire."

We stood in the reception area. "Retiring young is the American dream. And you deserve it."

"Lord knows that's true."

"Amen." We heard a door slam. A sigh escaped me. "Thank you, Evadne." I gave her a hug.

"You take care of yourself, you hear. Don't be workin' so late alone in these big offices." She patted my cheek. "Be safe goin' home."

"You too. Good night."

I showered as soon as I got home but even with a scrub of sea salt and lavender I couldn't free myself from the anxiety that shadowed me as I climbed into bed. I twisted in the sheets, unable to sleep. How much longer could this go on? I wasn't going to give in and it was clear he wasn't going to stop. But who could I go to for help? It was my word, that of a young associate, against that of a well-known attorney. I knew the EEOC had recently published official guidelines defining sexual harassment, but there had never been a lawsuit, so there was no precedent. And litigation would also end up with his word against mine. He'd bring up our past, just say he was flirting and what's wrong with that, or he'd deny it. And even if I won, litigation would ruin my career. It was hard enough for a woman lawyer, no one would hire me. I was on my own.

I finally fell asleep as the sky turned gray. There were no dreams. I'd stopped dreaming several months ago, and I felt as if parts of me were missing. I dreaded going to work, but I got dressed and set out to do battle. The minute I walked through those doors, which had once seemed like the gates to heaven and now seemed more like the gates to hell, I knew what I would do.

I began to mentally carve banishing pentagrams on the office door of Mr. John Hadus. I didn't use herbs, or candles, or poppets. I didn't do spells, or incantations, or rituals. I just drew a banishing pentagram. Over and over again, visualizing the movements, I drew emphatically and with clear intent. *He will leave me alone.* While I answered the phone, I visualized his door closed, and I carved a flaming star on it. While I redrafted contract language, I inscribed the banishing star on his door. When he walked into my office to talk to me about a client, I imagined it on his forehead and he stood, as if frozen, in the doorway.

After about a week of mentally emblazoning banishing pentagrams on his office door, Hadus walked in one morning, went into his office, and closed the door. Doors were never closed unless you were in conference, even if you were a partner. Hadus's door was closed and stayed closed for the remainder of the day. I continued to conjure banishing pentagrams and his door remained closed for the next two weeks. Everyone in the office was whispering about Hadus's closed door. It was weird. What was wrong with him? I was thrilled, relaxed, and working more productively than I had in months. But magic works in unexpected ways, particularly when there are strong emotions involved. And when destiny is at hand.

CHAPTER 12

As Above,
So Below

O chestnut tree, great-rooted blossomer,
Are you the leaf, the blossom, or the bole?
O body swayed to music, O brightening glance,
How can we know the dancer from the dance?
    —W. B. YEATS, *Among School Children*

I move with the infinite in Nature's power
I hold the fire of the Soul
I hold life and healing

    —RIG VEDA

The Mabon sabbat was coming, a Wiccan holy day celebrating the earth's miraculous generosity. And because it was autumn, it was also a time in the Wiccan calendar for stripping away the old to make way for the new. I had volunteered to find a place for our circle to perform the traditional harvest ritual and I immediately thought of the Delaware Water Gap. There was a farmer who, I had a feeling, just might give us permission to use his field. I'd met him while camping—he was interested in organic farming and conservation, and he seemed quite friendly. But how friendly would he be when I explained that we were a coven of Witches looking for a place to celebrate a sabbat?

I drove out on Sunday afternoon, inviting Jeanette to come with me. Since the binding, she'd had a few more phone calls, and then they had stopped. But the silence was its own kind of stress. A day in the country would nourish her.

The farmer was repairing his tractor when we arrived. Jeanette immediately excused herself, taking off through the cornfields toward the river, the sunlit dust kicking up behind her. After some casual conversation, I finally, and nervously, asked the farmer if some of my friends could use his field for a "harvest celebration," and pick some of his corn for him.

"I remember celebrating the harvest back in Ireland on my grandparents' farm," he replied. "Course that was earlier in the season—at Lughnassadh. People came from all around—there were horse races, dancing, and things children weren't supposed to know about." He winked. "Mabon came later—end of the harvest. Folks used to say it was a Witches' ritual, but that didn't stop anyone from celebrating."

I took a deep breath, ready to launch into an explanation. But he kept talking.

"They said Annie Murry was a Witch, she was the county midwife—brought me into the world. My grandma, and then my ma, always went to her for cures. You a Witch?"

I was taken aback by his easy acceptance, but still I wondered how to answer. I was a lawyer, a professional, a graduate of an Ivy League university. I recognized myself by all those labels—but was I ready to call myself a Witch?

I remembered my shock those many months ago when my friend Sophia called herself a Witch. Why would I want to label myself with a word that would only make people fearful? Or scornful, or even violent? I was afraid I wouldn't be seen for who I really was, that I would be misunderstood and mistreated. Which fear was more limiting—mine or someone else's? I'd learned by now that if I waited until fear was gone, I might never act—the secret of defeating fear was to push against it, to act in spite of it. That's what gives birth to courage. I knew the truth about Wicca would never be embraced until those who knew it had the courage to speak it, to challenge the lies, to retrieve the healing power for which that word was once honored. And now there was so much more that required healing. When a woman calls herself a Witch, she takes back her power. She defies our culture's misogyny, demanding that it confront its shadows. It was a word I knew I would someday learn to embrace without apology or fear. But was I ready now?

"I'm studying with them," I answered.

He nodded. That was all. "Will there be dancing?" he asked.

I nodded. "And singing."

"But no nudity—wouldn't want to make my neighbors jealous." He laughed at his joke, and, amazed, so did I. I had trusted my instincts and taken a small but important step out of the shadows. The freedom was exhilarating—and empowering. I thanked him, and began to make arrangements. We would harvest part of a cornfield for him and he would pay us in corn for our labor. He showed me a fallow field we could use for the ritual and another to harvest from. He showed me how to break the corn from its stalk, and then, as we sat beneath an old chestnut tree sharing a cold drink, he showed me how to make a dolly out of corn husks. Jeanette returned, carrying her shoes and wearing a necklace of field flowers. She was completely relaxed and not even mildly surprised that I was answering the farmer's questions about what we were celebrating and why.

We talked about Mabon, one of eight sabbats. These are the seasonal rituals and celebrations of the Wiccan calendar, which is called the Wheel of the Year. The sabbats, from the Greek *esbaton*, meaning "a sacred or holy day," include four solar events—the Spring and Fall Equinoxes and the Summer and Winter Solstices—and four points of shift in the Earth's energy, referred to in the Celtic tradition as Samhain, Imbolc, Beltaine, and Lughnassadh. It was these latter four he remembered from his childhood in Ireland.

In the sabbat rituals, the spiritual meaning of the world is made visible. We experience the divine in the cycle of the seasons, the changes of heaven and earth, and our sacred connection to them. Through seasonal celebrations, the community links itself to the great sacred patterns, the ebb and flow of the energies of the universe. Rituals attune both the individual psyche and the entire community to profound shifts in these energies. They enable us to experience the sacred wisdom revealed by the earth and the heavens at these moments of transformation and change. People enact and embody these universal rhythms, bringing the inner and outer, the human and cosmic into accord and illuminating the occult maxim "as above, so below." We discover how our own lives also undergo these changes, for the universe is a mirror of brilliant clarity, reflecting the rhythms of life and the seasons of the soul—birth, growth, maturity, decline, death, repose, and rebirth.

The sun sat just above the ridgetop, bathing us in the thick golden light of magic hour. The farmer handed me the corn dolly. "My grandma taught me how to make these. Harvest never seemed complete without her and now I know why." He paused for a moment. "Anyway, I'll see you and your friends on September twenty-first."

We shook hands and he held the car door open for Jeanette.

"Good harvest," I said, waving as we pulled away.

"It should be, with Witches blessing my crop." He winked again and waved.

You're still not dreaming?"

I shook my head and Jeanette shook hers.

"You tried mugwort tea?"

"Didn't help. I even took Maia's advice and scattered it between my pillowcase and pillow and slept on it. I've been using it for over a month now."

"Nothing?"

"Not a thing." We were sitting in a small restaurant in the West Village waiting for Jeanette's lawyer and my old friend, Rachel, to arrive. She'd called us both this morning, promising us a story that would make us very happy. That was all she'd say.

"I am worried about you. A Witch without dreams is like—"

"A world without a moon. I know." I sighed.

"It's a sign."

"I know."

"So what are you going to do?"

"What I've been doing."

"You've still got that bastard locked in his office?" Jeanette asked as she poured our wine—a glass for me, one for Rachel, and half a glass for herself. After the banishing, she'd begun dieting and exercising and already she looked healthier. As I lifted my glass, I thought of the three of cups in the Tarot deck—symbolizing the magic of friendship.

I nodded and we both laughed.

"I just want to keep him away from me."

"Well, it's a start." She shrugged, smiling. "And all you've been doing is banishing pentagrams? That's all?"

I nodded again.

She laughed heartily.

"What about Richard? Still nothing?" We spoke to each other at least once a day now—sometimes twice since I usually called her at bedtime just to make sure she was O.K. and I was anxious for her reply.

"He's still on ice in my freezer and so far, all's quiet. I'd like to say no news is good news, but . . ." Her face grew solemn.

"We've got the good news you're waiting for." It was Rachel and Jim, her boyfriend and a detective in Narcotics. Rachel was pretty, petite, and polished, and yet somehow she fit perfectly with the roughhewn Irish cop.

"Ladies," he said as he flashed a winning grin that could charm a snake. He ordered a beer and we got up and switched seats so the two of them could sit together. "You must be Jeanette. Good to meet you. How ya doin' with that dick boss of yours?" This was addressed to me.

"He's a dick."

Jim laughed. "Ain't they all."

"So what's the news?" Jeanette asked impatiently.

"You guys are gonna love this." Rachel grabbed a glass of wine. "Mmm. Yummy. First of all, a toast: To sisterhood."

We clinked our glasses, and bottle. "To sisterhood."

"And the men who love us."

We clinked again.

"I'm going to explode." Jeanette looked like she meant it.

"O.K. You guys know I talked to Jim about Jeanette's situation a couple of weeks ago, so he knows all about Richard."

"I checked his rap sheet, talked to my friends in the Ninth," Jim said. "There was nothing they could do, but they promised to keep an ear to the ground."

"Did you learn anything?" Jeanette asked.

"It's a whole lot better than that. I'll tell ya, the universe works in mysterious ways." Jeanette and I exchanged glances.

"But you two gotta understand, this involves a case under indictment." He leaned into the table and lowered his voice. "My dick boss'd have my shield if he knew I was talking to you, so this goes no further—agreed?"

We nodded eagerly.

"O.K. There's a major deal been in the pipeline a coupla months, stuff's comin' in from Colombia. So we get the word it's goin' down in Red Hook. The stakeout's set—we got more manpower than God. And we got Feds."

"FBI!" exclaimed Jeanette.

Jim nodded. "And more. So we're set, but our foreign friends ain't showin'; the locals are startin' to get nervous 'cause it's gettin' late. We're thinkin', maybe there's been a tipoff," he shrugged and swigged his beer, "when this limo cruises up. The protection gets out first, and they meet. Everything's cool, or so they think. So the big boys get outta their cars. I don't get how these rat bastards can get anythin' done wearin' shades at night." Jim laughed, enjoying the dangerous memory. "Anyway, they shake hands, a briefcase comes out of the local car, they open it. All we got so far is money and that's not enough for a bust.

"So we're all waitin', and suddenly a friggin' ice cream truck pulls up. I thought the little bastard was dead—but he wasn't deliverin' ice cream. Outta the back comes a little white baggie, the locals stick their heads in the freezer, they got their Good Humor, and NASA, we've got lift-off! We move in on 'em screamin' our fuckin' lungs out: 'Freeze, police, freeze, you motherfuckers!' "

Everyone at the neighboring tables turned as his voice rose, adrenaline pumping as he relived the moment. Jeanette and I looked at each other, incredulous smiles spreading across our faces.

"And that's exactly what they did—for about a half a second. But a coupla their cowboys draw on us, until this big fuckin' wind comes up and all kinds of shit is blowin' in their faces. Weird," he started to chuckle. "Anyway, to make a long story short, I had the pleasure of cuffing one Richard James." He leaned back, a huge grin on his face.

"Praise the Goddess!" Jeanette cried, leaping from her seat and grabbing Jim in a bear hug.

"He wasn't behind the deal, was he?" I asked.

Jim shook his head. "Just a hired gun."

"Magic sure works in mysterious ways." I whispered in Jeanette's ear as she hugged me. "Any chance of him plea bargaining?" I asked, shooting a worried glance at Rachel.

Jim shook his head again. "Don't need him. With his rap sheet, we've got enough to put your dick ex-husband on ice for the rest of his unnatural life."

Jeanette and I exploded with laughter.

Our circle stood in the midst of a fallow field, waiting to celebrate Mabon. The field had been planted with purple clover to restore nutrients to the soil, but the simple flower holds other magical powers as well: In Ireland they say the fourth leaf of a clover will bring one the best of luck and blessings and, most particularly, the ability to see the fairy-folk. The other wild flowers of the field were also full of magic: bright blue cornflower, the sacred ritual herb used in the Mabon sabbat and in spells to restore love from past lives; milkweed exploding with shiny black seeds in their white silk parachutes to carry your prayers with them; sharp-leaved thistle, which in Scotland was used as a magic wand to conjure spirits, heal the sick, break a hex, and protect one against sadness and the loss of soul; tall goldenrod, which, when held in the hand of intuition (the left, for right-handed, the right, for left-handed), leads you to buried treasure, to things that are lost or hidden from view, to an unknown lover, or unseen wealth. All these grew thickly beside the low clover. The bees knew that even a fallow field sustains life and they worked busily around us, pulling the last pollen for the final round of honey making. Soon they would enter winter's sleep, slumbering in frozen labyrinths of golden nectar to dream of flights among summer's flowers, but now their wings hummed a final ode to summer's fruition.

A green cornfield lay to the north of us, another lay to the south, the river bounded us on the west, and on the east was a bumpy dirt road that few but the farmer traveled. Overhead the blue sky was filled with clouds like the white mountains of heaven. On the far side of the road lay a forest that climbed to a high ridge where hawks nested. A few cool breezes warned of winter and I turned my face to the fading sun. The light was more precious, for it was shorter in its attendance, and its ever-present partnering shadows came sooner, stretched longer, and lay darker across the land. Summer was a short season here in the North-east, and I was always amazed at how quickly things emerged and grew to ripeness in the few months of heat we enjoyed.

The altar, an old wooden farm cart lent to us by our host, was ablaze with color and life, piled high with corn, pumpkins and squash, leaves and acorns and the flowers of the field—and a pair of deer antlers. There were men with us today—members of other covens, husbands, lovers, and friends, and they added to our festive mood. Mindy's family had come and even Jim had joined us, with Rachel by his side.

This was the sabbat at which the crone presided, and so Nonna spoke to us:

"This is the time of harvest, of thanksgiving and joy, of sacrifice and surrender. The day and the night are of equal measure. We gather to mark the moment of perfect balance between light and dark. We witness, as our ancestors did, the miracle and the mystery of sun and earth, energy and life, death and rebirth. Since the Summer Solstice we have watched the Sun King's journey into the realm of shadows. . . . Soon the earth will slumber, while the seeds of new life rest before their rebirth in the spring. But today we work. The corn is cut down to sustain us during the long winter months that lie ahead.

"Mabon is the ritual of rejoicing in the richness of the earth, without which we could not live. It is the ritual of giving thanks to the Great Mother Earth for her gifts. It is the ritual of reaping what we have sown. It is the time we rejoice in the bounty we have harvested for ourselves in our work, our relationships, our spiritual journeys. This is also the time we reflect upon those aspects of our lives that no longer serve our growth and happiness, when we offer up all that we must let go of so that we may continue to grow."

The crone stepped into the center of the circle, a sickle in her hand. Nonna seized a bundle of dried brown cornstalks. In a flashing arc, she raised the sickle high then brought it swiftly down, cutting away the old, the outgrown and worn-out, and freeing a stalk of green-wrapped golden corn. The dead stalks fell to the awaiting earth from which they had emerged only a few months ago. Her arms upraised, one hand holding the sickle, and the other the ear of corn, she prayed:

"Blessed are we by the fruits of the union of sun and earth. Here is the mystery and the richness of energy encased in seed. Though the form changes, the energy of life is eternal."

As she spoke, I was filled with gratitude that she was with us today, that her energy remained within her beautiful form. She now lived transformed by her journey into the realm of shadows, and a sense of peace and gratitude for each day of life on our beautiful planet enriched her every word, every gesture. Nonna was our midwife of change. With her knowledge of the seasons' cycles, she delivered the sacred seed into the hands of the community, declaring:

"We recognize the mystery of the transformation of energy into matter, and matter into energy. We gather at this sacred moment when the sun has gone into the seed."

A shout of joy arose from the circle.

We stood in a circle paired in loving couples, back to back, men and women, women and women, and men with men. Nonna stood with me, and Jeanette faced me, standing with Gillian. A pair of musicians—a man with a fiddle and a woman with a *bodhran,* a Celtic drum—began to play. We extended our right hand to the person facing us and began to move, stretching our left hand to the next person who moved toward us as we danced toward them. And so we danced, two opposing circles, the energies of growth and decline, interweaving. It was the grand *alaman* we had learned, however reluctantly, long ago in grade school, but it was now coming alive with ancient power and meaning. We danced, hand over hand, singing as we moved:

> *"Corn and grain, corn and grain,*
> *All that falls shall rise again.*
> *Hoof and horn, hoof and horn,*
> *All that dies shall be reborn."*

The men were a welcome addition, their energy greatly boosting our own. They chanted with deep and resonating voices and their strength was felt in the sustained pace of our dancing, in the grip of their hands as they whirled past us in circle. Their laughter was as robust as their chanting, and their love energized all of us. Lovers who had been separated by the dancing exchanged kisses as they passed each other, and smiles were shared by all as eyes and hands met in mounting joy. I was without a partner, wondering what it would be like to dance with the man I loved. But there was no room for loneliness as I was swept away in the fullness of the moment. A second chant began to interweave with the first:

> *"We all come from the Goddess*
> *And to Her we shall return*
> *Like a drop of rain*
> *Flowing to the ocean."*

The dance, and our hearts, quickened as a third chant began—the name of the Goddess of the grain, Demeter—repeated over and over as the other two chants rose and fell. The musicians pushed us on and led us back to the first chant, building to a rowdy climax. A huge cheer went up as we lifted a bountiful basket of corn high into the air, into the cone of green and golden power that swirled above us.

Nonna laid her hands upon the basket, speaking ancient wisdom: "Blessed be the Mother of all life. Blessed be the life that comes from her and returns to her. Blessed be the Father of all life. Blessed be the energy that comes from him and returns to him. Blessed be the Earth and Sun and blessed be their union which is the spirit's form. The Sun has gone into the seed."

"So mote it be," we responded.

The basket was passed deosil around the circle. As we each took a piece of corn, we gave thanks for what we had harvested—new jobs, new loves, professional successes, and newfound wisdom, gleaned from the teachings of our priestesses, the earth, and our lives. When the basket came to Nonna she said simply, "I give thanks for my health, and for my kindred whose love helped me to heal. I give thanks that I am here today to celebrate with you." Nonna's smile was a blessing as she surveyed the circle, and her gaze came to rest on me as she gave me the basket.

What should I give thanks for? Much of my gratitude had already been given expression by the others. What else? My heart beat faster as I felt all eyes upon me.

I reached into the deep basket and pulled out a fat stalk topped with a thick brown tassel. I held it to my heart, inhaling its sweetness. "I give thanks for the courage to cut away that which no longer serves." I drew a quick breath, suddenly sensing that with those words I had unleashed some force of nature, some force of spirit that struggled like a horse with wings to take flight, to manifest a magic I had not yet dreamed of. I waited, feeling a little lightheaded as energy suddenly swirled about me, hearing as if from far away the circle's utterances of support, blinking in the brightness of summer's last light. I caught my breath, and continued:

"I give thanks for the richness of life that awaits after the hard work of harvesting. I give thanks for our Mother's generosity, and for the journey that brings wisdom, freedom, and love as its harvest." I handed the basket to Jeanette, who stood beside me. She nodded as our eyes met, understanding.

"I give thanks for the courage to secure my freedom. And for friendship."

We smiled at each other, stripped the green from the ears, and laughed together as we bit into the juicy kernels. Together, a circle of men and women celebrated and honored the Earth for her sacred gifts of life and her divine magic of transforming energy into form and form back to energy, preserving the eternal cycle of life. We feasted, and watched the sunset, and we rejoiced in our sacred connection to this great mystery.

We had spent the first part of the day picking corn in the fields, walking between the tall green stalks, listening to them rustle and whisper as the wind moved over the land. Tearing the green corn from their stalks had been far easier than I had expected and we quickly filled the burlap sacks. I loved the heat of the sun on my back, the rough texture of the living plant in my hands, the smell of the soil, the sound of singing and laughter as we worked. Our labor ended too soon. Instead of bending with exhaustion, I ran the length of the long rows, filled with the energy of the Earth; I spun in wild circles, dancing the energy of life that flourished in voluptuous sun-summoned green all about me. I collapsed, breathless on her fragrant breast, overwhelmed by her natural generosity.

Our presence in paradise was a partnership and I was grateful that the Earth required our efforts to render up her gifts. Our toil was rewarded with life, and with the realization of our sacred alliance. Work had never felt so perfect. The exertion itself was a ritual of connection and vitality and the ancient celebration of the harvest that followed, long kept secret from the world it revered, was a revelation to me.

Through the symbolism of the corn harvested at Mabon, I discovered the truth behind another dark stereotype of sacrifice at a Witches' Sabbat. We learn from nature that before we can harvest the seeds of new life, we must be willing to cut away that which we have outgrown—this is the Wiccan form of sacrifice. The sacrifice is from and of ourselves—our life is our offering to the divine. But contrary to the common misconception, it is not meant to be relinquished on the altar of death, but realized and fulfilled on the altar of life.

As we prepared to return to the city, I wondered whether the harvest of my own life would be as easy as our day's work and as joyous as our celebration. What was I prepared to sacrifice? What had I outgrown? Where would the knife fall? And what fruit would rest in my hand?

The sun, and its warmth, had slipped behind the horizon and the unexpected cold jarred us from the day's sultry reverie. It was time to go. The waning moon had risen, a crone's sickle shining in the black sky, reminding us of time's daily harvest. We piled the cart high with the rewards of our day's hard work and happiness, everyone joining in to push and pull it back to the barn. I lingered alone in the field listening to the joking and singing recede into darkness, turning slowly, drawing in the last blessing of the earth which now prepared herself for winter's rest.

A wild thrashing in the high stalks froze me in mid-turn, and my heart began to race. An enormous buck with a full rack of seven tines suddenly appeared from the northern field. He was white as the moonlight that fell from above, and we stood for an immortal moment, facing each other. My heart exploded and he leapt forward, flying across the field like a vision from a dream, and disappearing into the woods.

I was sure it was a sign—but what did it mean? The world was reenchanted, and everything was changing. I, too, could feel the shifting of my shape but I could not see my form. We had harvested, majicking a stripping away of encasement, a shedding of old skins. I had learned so much and yet I knew nothing, for what did I know of stags of seven tines and the journeys of rebirth they foretold?

Feeling as if I were living in a coma, I slowly picked up a stray cocoon of divine mystery, of sun encased in seed, stripped it to its tender kernels, and took a bite of milky sweetness. I stooped down and dug a hole with a stick. I broke the corn in half, buried the portion I had eaten from, and left the other half for the harbinger of my future. I turned and raced from the field, a final burst of energy lending Hermes to my heels. Or was it Diana who watched me speed with the swiftness of her arrow and the freedom of her sacred quarry?

We left some of our harvested corn for the farmer to sell at his stand, and some for the deer, the raccoon, and the field mice whose work would be a little easier tonight. We filled the cars with burlap bags bulging with the miraculous benefaction of the earth, sitting with our knees up to accommodate all the corn. We sang and joked as we drove through the Jersey countryside, growing silent as the abysmal industrial skyline forewarned the impending metropolis.

The black sky glowed phosphorescent orange, flames shot heavenward, and chemical clouds as white as bleached bones belched from smokestacks. Barbed wire fences encircled huge factories that produced paints and processed petroleum. They were strung with necklaces of artificial light so that men could work throughout the night, laboring on the "dead man's shift" in defiance of nature's wisdom. We drove through the surreal netherworld, rolling up our windows in a futile effort to shut out the assaulting sulfurous fumes. We passed old row houses where families were born, and lived, and died beneath the shadow of the industrial plants that gave them life and simultaneously stole it away. There were diners and bars, cheap motels and churches, and huge billboards advertising new cars and TV game shows. And it all got denser and more congested as we approached the city.

On the other side of the river, back on the little island which was home to the very best and the very worst modern culture had to offer, all of it supported by the wasteland it denied, we pulled up to one of the food banks that fed the city's homeless. As we unloaded most of our day's efforts, the smiles greeting our gift were a richer reward than any paycheck. We had celebrated the turning of the Wheel of the Year, and it was good to share our harvest.

I said goodnight to my companions and hauled a large plastic bag filled with divinity disguised as corn up to my apartment, sensing but not yet fully understanding this wisdom. I opened the bag and filled a basket with the golden ears. It had been a prosperous year, but what else had I harvested besides a healthy bank account? I held a piece to my heart.

The beauty and abundance, the actions and poetry of the sabbat ritual, had deeply moved me. My intellectual reservations and sophisticated skepticism were finally overcome. I realized the rituals of these Wise Women were not archaic, meaningless theatrics, but enacted prayers, active meditations. The ritual was art, and prayer, a living mandala, an evocation of spirit and an expression of the spirit's presence in everything that was life. The symbols were not merely allegorical, they were also real forms of divine energy. The corn didn't just symbolize the presence of the spirit's eternity as it changes form from energy to life back to energy. It *was* spirit in life-sustaining form. The corn embodied the conjoining fertility of the Earth and power of the Sun. The corn itself was the body of the Goddess, sometimes that of her son or daughter. It represented the fecundity of an illuminated mind, a mind cognizant of divine presence.

The Hopi honor the corn goddesses who tend the growing plants and bring fertility to all the worlds. To the Indians of Mexico, the corn goddess is called Seven Snake and the people dance slowly, their arms around each others' waists in a long and sinuous line, until the sun sets. The movement of the snake and the mystery of the labyrinth are one and the same. And the journey through the labyrinth is the voyage of the sleeping, the unconscious, and the dead through the sacred mystery to their awakened rebirth. This is the symbolic and literal meaning of the corn, wheat, apple, or other sacred fruit of life.

All things that grow from the earth, that sustain life, and that return to the earth, are children of the Great Goddess and are the Goddess herself. In ancient Crete and in Greece, this Mother Goddess of the Grain was Demeter and the grain itself was her daughter Persephone; in Rome she was Ceres. They are depicted with sheaves of wheat and garlands of poppies. The name Ceres is associated with the Latin *gerere*, "to bear, bring forth, produce," and the Latin *creare*, "to produce, create." Like Demeter, Ceres is a goddess from the earliest times of Western culture, for it is she who is said to have taught humanity the sacred, life-giving arts of agriculture, the origin of Western culture.

Demeter's worship originated in Crete and was ultimately celebrated in Greece at the Goddess's temple in Eleusis. Hers was the preeminent religious experience for several thousand years, with people traveling from all over in order to be initiated into her mysteries of rebirth. The Autumn Equinox was the time of the sowing of the wheat, the celebration of the Eleusinian Mysteries, when a stalk of grain was held aloft for all to behold at the moment of revelation and blessing with the words: "In silence is the seed of wisdom gained." The Goddess is the divine power of growth and that which grows. I recalled how the Buddha, when asked about the meaning of life, silently held aloft a single flower; how Jesus, in the Gnostic Gospels, said, "Cleave the wood and I am there"; and how the Taoists advise, when in the pursuit of the divine, to "chop wood and carry water."

The Old Religion is frequently referred to as spiritual environmentalism. Wiccan reverence for the earth reflects a deep ecological concern that is far more than pragmatic. As an embodiment of the divine, the earth is not treated as a utilitarian object to be exploited, polluted, and destroyed for man's short-term greed. Rather, it is inherently sacred in its value. Practitioners of the Old Religion know that to live in harmony with nature is to live in accord with the divine. This reverence has drawn many people to the practice of Wicca, and, as with other indigenous religions, it may be one of its greatest contributions to a world imperiled by ecological crisis. Its techniques had moved me at the center of my being, affecting me far more deeply than any scientific, intellectual warning about the environmental disaster which the dominant culture has wrought. During the sabbat I had an epiphany—I *was* the earth—and what was done to her was done to me; the waste poured into her rivers was in the blood coursing in my veins; the toxins poured into her air filled my lungs; the poisons buried in her soil poisoned my body. What we do to her, we do to ourselves, and to all of her children. But far more than self-interest is at stake, for that which we damage is divine, and to engage in reckless disregard of the earth is to engage in sacrilege.

The finest scientific minds have warned us that we stand on the brink of extinction, the result of our uncontrolled overpopulation, pollution, and depletion of resources. But species evolve when their survival depends upon it. Religious forms change when the old metaphors and explanations no longer reflect people's reality and understanding of the world. A transcendent God from whom man is eternally separated, having been born in sin and in flesh; a God who is only male and can be reached only by male priests, or rabbis, or mullahs; a God who is vengeful and who condemns women and requires their submission; a God for whom the earth is a mere storehouse and source of spiritual downfall; a God for whom all manner of war and violence is even now being justified, is not God. We live in a culture of cynicism and despair and these sides of God are merely a tragic image projected from man's lost and haunted soul.

Too much of our humanity has been separated from the divine. And yet the sacred remains all around us, within us, filling us and sustaining us, nurturing and enlightening us with every breath that we take, every morsel we eat, every soul with whom we have contact. All we need to do is open our eyes to see that we have never left the Garden; it is all around us. A divinity present in the world that I live in, a divinity that imbues all with sacred energy—this was a divinity that I could celebrate and honor with all my heart. This was the meaning of the Grail quest.

But how could I live in a Garden that was invisible to the world? How could the veil covering humanity's eyes be lifted? And most important, could the veil be lifted in time, before we annihilate ourselves and the earth with our destructive behavior?

I had come to understand, through experience, that our myths are not mere stories but mirrors of the great cosmic drama of seemingly impersonal forces. Myths and metaphors enable us to see our own personal stories reflected in their archetypal patterns. Here was the meaning of the ancient emerald tablet of Hermes and its mysterious language: "As above, so below." On earth as it is in heaven. Here too was a metaphysical description joining the laws that govern the macro reality of space, time, gravity, and the universe to those that govern reality at its most infinitesimal level of subatomic particles. Pythagoras has been proven right: Physicists now understand the universe as a harmony of interacting energies or "strings." Everything is connected in the Goddess's cauldron, the shaman's web of life, the physicist's quantum reality.

Myths are the dreams of an entire culture. And mythological symbols, just like those of our dreams, unlock the door to the greater dimensions of the divine. They are the metaphors that describe the great patterns of the universe. Rituals, particularly sabbat rites, help us to experience this truth, and so do our dreams and our divinations. They are the portents of our lives, the encoded symbols of our story. They are a mirror held up so we may see how, throughout our lives, we embody these great stories, and the divine.

Staring out the window at the city's starless sky, no heavenly patterns visible to my longing eyes, I could not help but wonder, what is the hidden pattern, the story of my life? What have I learned from this turn of the Wheel? What have I harvested? What do I have to let go of?

Months had passed since I had dreamed. I awoke each morning with nothing to remember, nothing to write down in the little notebook on my nightstand, no dream-envisioned evening star to guide the course of my days. I awoke tired, and sought my fulfillment at work. I had become invisible and so I struggled each day to fill the emptiness of lost dreams with the rewards promised by men with lost souls. Could I discover my story, the meaning of my life, without dreams? I pulled down the shade, pulled up the covers, and shut my eyes, longing for the revelation that remained hidden within the shadows.

Huge dark clouds gathered outside the plate-glass windows of the offices of Rosen, Meiser, Dutton and Hadus. It was the middle of the day and as black as midnight. A spear of lightning ripped from the clouds and thunder rolled behind it. Throughout the city, people shrank back from their windows, waiting for rain to soften the electricity that crackled through the air. But the rain didn't come.

"Hadus is looking for you," Madeline warned me.

I headed down the hall, bracing myself. The door to Hadus's office flew open, crashing into the wall as he exploded out. Everyone in the typing pool turned to see what had happened.

"Where were you?" Hadus shouted at me.

"Didn't Sharon tell you? Max asked me to go to court for him. He's sick and his client had to appear, so he asked me to cover for him." Suddenly I had the curious sensation of time slowing down, of details coming sharply into hyper-focus the way they do during an accident. I noticed the tiny speck of green between his front teeth, the smell of Sharon's Halston perfume, the sound of Dutton on the phone in her office.

"You had no business going without my knowledge."

"I didn't think it would be a problem. There were no appointments, no clients coming in. And I'd finished all the work we'd discussed before I left."

"I don't care. You shouldn't have left the office without my O.K." His eyes were bulging and huge. He was shouting, oblivious to the audience gathering in office doorways. I could feel my skin crawl as prickly heat spread across my body like brush fire. A flush of embarrassment reddened my cheeks. I was momentarily paralyzed. And then enraged.

I stood my ground, and struggled to keep my temper as he took a step toward me. I was burning up and then, as if a switch had been thrown inside me, I became very calm and centered; my body temperature cooled. I felt as if someone, or something, had wrapped a cloak of protective energy around me.

"I'm sorry if you feel I made the wrong decision, but you weren't here, it was an emergency, and I couldn't imagine that under these circumstances you'd say no to the senior partner." I spoke quietly, deliberately, keeping my tone steady.

"You couldn't imagine . . . I don't pay you to imagine! I pay you to work for me. FOR ME!" he bellowed.

I felt all the anger of the last year rising in me like a phoenix reborn from the ashes of my humiliation.

"You pay me to work, which I do. You do not pay me to put up with this or the rest of your abuse." I replied loudly, no longer caring who heard me. In fact, I wanted them to hear me.

"I don't pay you period. You're fired!" he roared.

"You can't fire me—I quit!" I turned my back on him and walked away, enjoying the stunned silence. I did not have to look back to know he stood alone, humiliated and abandoned on his battlefield. It was his worst nightmare come true.

I closed the door to my office, leaning back against it and listening to the sound of my heart pounding in my ears. I breathed deeply until time resumed its normal pace, then quickly began to pack my things—including the files of my clients. I heard a gentle tap and looked up to see Madeline standing in the doorway.

"I heard what happened. Are you O.K.?" She looked worried.

"The grapevine sure works fast around here."

"Grapevine—I mean I *heard* what happened. We all did, and we all think you were great. He's so crazy, it's amazing you stood it for this long. His last two associates were gone in half your time. What are you going to do? Do you have another job?"

I shook my head. "I have no idea."

"Max asked me to tell you to stop by." We hugged. "I'm going to miss you."

I took a last look around my office and closed the door. I walked down the hall toward Max's office, expecting to feel as if I were running a gauntlet. Would people be embarrassed for me, would they look away? Oddly, it was only Sharon who wouldn't look at me. The secretaries whispered "All right!" and "Good for you," discreetly flashing thumbs up. By the time I got to Max's office, I felt downright heroic.

Max looked worried as I sat down. "I heard what happened."

I laughed. I was feeling light, free, at peace. Or maybe I was just out of my mind. But the truth was, I couldn't stand it anymore. For the first time I wasn't listening to the voice in my head that warned and worried and told me what I should or shouldn't do. That was the voice I'd been raised with, the voice we'd all been raised with, the one that said work hard, do what you're told, be a good girl. I wasn't listening anymore. It was old, played out, and all about submission, not fulfillment. I was listening to my heart, the place where dreams were born and nurtured.

"Max, *everyone* heard what happened." We laughed together and I felt something stir and flutter, emerging through the crack that now ran down the center of my blue-shelled soul.

"I'm so sorry this happened. I'll talk to him. He knows I'll pay for your time. I'll pay him at the partners' rate."

"Thanks. I appreciate your offer. But he didn't fire me. I quit. I can't work for that bastard one more minute."

"You don't want to do anything rash. It's not your fault—how can an associate say no to the request of a senior partner? I'll help you work it out."

I shook my head.

"Are you sure?"

I nodded.

He leaned back in his chair and sighed. "I understand, but you don't know how tough it is out there."

"Maybe it's rash, I don't know. I'm just beginning to understand myself."

"I just wouldn't want you to wake up tomorrow morning with regrets."

"It's all the mornings for the last few months that I regret. You see, I've stopped dreaming."

Max's eyebrows went up but he didn't say a word.

"I need my dreams back." I rose from his luxurious green couch, realizing that I'd never liked the way the back of my legs had stuck to the leather. I felt calm and certain of my decision and as I shook his hand I felt power flowing through me the way I had only felt in circles. I smiled.

"If I can help you in any way, please don't hesitate to ask me."

"Well, actually, it would be very helpful if I could use this as a mailing address for a little while. And if you could give me a letter of reference."

"Better still, there's a little office in the back you can use until you get settled—rent free. And I do need help every once in a while."

"That will be wonderful. Thanks."

"It's the least I can do. Good luck."

The day was over, the office almost entirely empty. Hadus's door was open—but he was gone, as was Sharon. The space that had been filled with such tumultuous energy now seemed hollow. I called the building super and he helped me carry my files out. I stood on the street corner looking up at the huge glass tower and the enormous black clouds that rolled through the sky. There were no shadows anywhere. I was free.

Or so I thought. My dreams had returned, but so had my nightmares in which I relived Hadus exploding out of his office countless times. The measure of his rage made me realize the degree of angry, frustrated energy building up behind that closed door. It was an inevitable detonation. I had been furious when I'd inscribed those banishing pentagrams on his door. That was one reason the spell had worked so quickly and so well—there was a lot more rage feeding my magic than I had been aware of. But it was righteous anger, an emotion that women had been told all their lives they shouldn't feel. Good girls don't get angry. Well, I was good and angry and if I was reaping what my anger had sown, so be it, I thought defiantly.

No amount of money, no fancy apartment nor car nor designer dress, could fill the abyss that was left when my dreams had departed. Nonna was right: I'd taken what I'd needed from this experience—my self-respect and my values. When I quit, I took back my power. But the initial freedom and energy I had felt was fleeting. I knew the price of my paycheck had been my soul, my self-esteem, and, most important, my dreams. Now I was afraid the price I had paid for my freedom was more than I could afford. How would I live? The record industry was in a serious recession and jobs were impossible to come by. You can't pay bills with dreams. A wave of uncertainty and despair hit me, and I curled up into a tight little ball.

Was magic a lie? I remembered with conflicting emotions the prosperity and harvest rituals. But instead of getting a raise, or a promotion, I was out of work. Had I sacrificed my career and destroyed all my years of rational, hard work only to be left with fanciful dreams of spiritual fulfillment?

Finally, after months of holding it in, I wept, riding a wave of energy unlike any I'd ever known. I felt as if I were drowning in fear and self-doubt. As I stood alone before the mirror, assessing my smeared mascara and tear-streaked faced, I realized that I had been an image, a reflection of cultural expectations. I had donned first the clothes, and then the masks, and then the postures that society mandated. And in the process I had become a shadow of my true self. Without inner substance, these external raimants were merely Emperor's clothing. The universe had stripped those invisible garments from me. Patiently, the universe was teaching me to find the kernel of truth, my own personal harvest, not in my exterior surroundings, nor in the demands of society—however sumptuous, enticing, or intimidating—but *within*.

I stood between two worlds, refusing definition by the outside world, and uncertain of what dwelled inside. I stood on the threshold, unwilling to turn back to the carnival house of distorted, man-made mirrors. I knew that it was the mirrors of the universe—the stars that shone in the heavens above, the star-filled river that had rushed over and through me, the field of ripe corn, the birds that sang in the morning mist—those were the true mirrors.

But as I thought of the energy and strength that had resonated

through my body at the harvest celebration, and remembered the powerful slice of the sickle as it cut the corn from its husks, I realized I was
not afraid of the power of the blade. The truth, the mystery was in
letting go of what I had outgrown. Indeed, the inner strength I had felt
upon quitting my job was proof enough that I had made the right decision. I was glad to be rid of my husks. But what seed had I harvested,
what lay within? Would it, would I, wither and die upon cold, dry
ground, or would I flourish and thrive more richly and abundantly than
I had ever dared to dream? The truth was to be discovered in the journey that now remained. The sickle had fallen and the seed was tumbling
toward the awaiting earth.

CHAPTER 13

Crossing Over

We are gods in the body of god, truth and love our destinies. Go then and make of the world something beautiful, set up a light in the darkness.

"Hymn to Hathor," from Awakening Osiris, The Egyptian Book of the Dead, translated by Normandi Ellis

Whispering had begun about initiation. Our circle had worked together for close to a year and a day, the traditional time for apprenticeship before one underwent the mysterious rites. What purpose did initiation serve, and what would it demand of us? The priestesses would not answer my questions, not even Nonna. Although the text of initiations had been published, our priestesses advised us not to read them because they would not impart the experience accurately and could actually damage our quest.

The complete details of initiation were hidden, though the rite was said to be modeled on that of the venerable Mystery School of Eleusis, a secret kept for thousands of years. I knew it was the ultimate ritual of confrontation with the shadow, a transformatory experience of death and rebirth, and that surviving initiation led to becoming a priestess, or priest, of the Old Religion. And I knew Socrates had called it the most profound event of his life. But I did not know what any of that meant. My priestesses said I knew everything I needed to know.

"You have to ask to be initiated," Maia told us. "No one else, not even your priestesses, will tell you when it's time."

And Nonna warned, "Only you know. Once you have crossed the threshold, there is no turning back, so you must be absolutely sure."

My sisters knew this was what they wanted. But how sure was I? How could I undertake such a drastic ritual when both my personal and professional lives were in such disorder? I had, in a whirl of wild devotion to things as amorphous as a soul and its dreams, turned my back on the security and status of a coveted job. How could I devote myself to something that had made my world so chaotic? And yet I sensed that at the farthest edges of chaos, a pattern of meaning waited in radiant spirals of mystery.

I had prepared for this moment all year. But what if the price was too high? What if the challenge of confrontation and transfiguration destroyed rather than recreated? Maybe I should turn back before it was too late, before I lost the life I had worked so hard to create for myself. How could I abide two such different worlds at the same time, when one was ruled by the cycles of earth and moon, the other by the time clock and paycheck? I yearned for a world of the heart, while I lived in one ruled by the head. Hadn't I just learned that the two were incompatible? And how could I survive in a world where bills had to be paid, if I lived by the rhythm of the mother's drum and listened to the wisdom of my soul?

A few weeks had passed since I'd quit. Hadus had taken off for vacation, which made visiting my borrowed office easier, and safer. I stood in the empty reception area staring at myself in the black mirrors—I'd come full circle, but I was a very different person from the young woman who had arrived the year before. I didn't know where I was headed, but for the first time in what felt like a very long time, I smiled at my traveling companion, and she smiled back. The door opened behind me.

"Well, all right—a smile! I've got something else that'll cheer you up," said Madeline. "You know, Hadus took off right after you quit. You really rattled his cage when you walked out. He told everyone he was taking his summer vacation, and at first he called in every couple of days . . ."

She looked down the hall to see if anyone was listening, then chuckled with sly pleasure. "Well, we didn't hear anything for over a week. I guess he was trying to assert his lost manhood, but it completely backfired—he was trying to learn to play polo and he ended up in the hospital!"

"He had an accident?" I asked, worried. He'd treated me terribly, but I knew his behavior was an expression of his pain and insecurity. And then I reminded myself: Compassion, mixed with my own insecurity and caretaking patterns, had kept me tied to Hadus, and to an impossible situation. I'd repeated the pattern in our personal relationship, mistakenly thinking that I could help him, or at least, by my own hard work and good energy, change the working situation between us. In the process, because it terrified him, and he had terrified me, I had given up my power. It was only after I'd quit that I began to realize you can't change other people. You can hold out a hand, but it's up to them to determine the course of their own lives. You can only change yourself. Working for Hadus had been changing me in ways I couldn't live with. It had disempowered me. Sometimes, letting go and walking away is the bravest thing you can do.

Madeline shook her head. "He's got some sort of major bladder problems and he had to have prostate surgery. Can you imagine?"

I shook my head, a grin slowly spreading as her words sunk in. "Actually, I can." I was amazed at how quickly, and appropriately, the karma post office delivered.

"Anyway, that's why he's been gone for so long. Not only that, but Sharon told me he's losing a lot of clients. Speaking of which, these messages are for you." She smiled mischievously and handed me a bundle of pink slips that included several messages from Hadus's clients, all asking me to call them.

I leaned back in my borrowed chair, staring out at a neighboring office tower. Its shining silver windows reflected back a fractured image of the building in which I sat. Magic works, though not necessarily the way you'd expect it to. And its rippling side effects were not necessarily what one had in mind.

It was never my intention to cause Hadus any harm—I only wanted to be left alone; but I was hurt and angry, and those emotions had colored my magic. The living universe, or my perhaps own unconscious energy, had a sense of proportion and a sense of humor. In both protective banishings, mine and Jeanette's, fitting justice had been meted out.

A fine line existed between vengeance and justice. Silently, I vowed to be cautious about working magic when I was angry, even righteously so. I closed my eyes, inhaling deeply, noticing how the sounds of the office receded and with it the anger and fear I had carried for so many months.

I tore the message slips from Hadus's clients in half and dropped them into the wastebasket.

The past was disappearing before my eyes. When the future began, what would I be left with?

I awoke worried and cold. The heat had gone off during the night and a filigree of frost covered my windows. I wrapped the blanket around me and stared out at the barren landscape below. My prospects seemed just as bleak. I was tired of being afraid, tired of feeling sorry for myself. I turned back into the icy room.

The answers, I had come to know, lay within. But I asked, once again, how was I to get there? A loud thud startled me and I turned to see something huge and black shudder against my rattling window. I stepped back, frightened. The strident caw of a crow reverberated through my room.

A bird at your window portends a death. I stood frozen. It cried out again, turning and facing me. Slowly, ever so slowly, it lifted and flew off into the morning light. I opened the window and leaned out, watching the silver mist of my breath disappear with the bird into the realm of spirit.

"I never saw a wild thing sorry for itself. A small bird will drop frozen dead from a bough without ever having felt sorry for itself." I remembered D. H. Lawrence's lines about self-pity. In the Craft of the Wise, the mysticism of life, every death is followed by a rebirth. Passion, like fire, burns and then subsides, and courage gives way to doubts more terrifying and consuming than the fearsome winged monsters painted on the edge of ancient mariners' maps. But I knew who those creatures were, and I knew the Goddess of the Abyss, and the truth in Chaos.

The universe was right: It was time for a change, it was time for my new life. It was time for magic. I created a ritual of cleansing and self-blessing for myself. In a room filled with scores of burning white candles, I bathed in tears and salt water, and found myself astride sea dragons whose scales shimmered like wet emeralds and who taught me to ride the waves with joy. And when my fears had washed away on a tide of release and a waning moon, I used the tools of divination to understand the magical meaning of my losses. Wisdom rekindles the torch of courage and actions give it strength to burn.

I used my tools to light the narrow passage through the earthen maze of my uncertain days and I used my inner sight to see what had been hidden. I pulled the devil card from my Tarot deck. It no longer frightened me, for there was no devil in Wicca. He was a symbol of the Shadow, the Guardian at the Gate. The image on the card depicted a man and a woman, enclosed in a dark cave, each grasping the jewels of a rich treasure chest chained within the cave. With their free hands they reach desperately toward freedom, which glows from a distant opening. Their faces are filled with desperation, their bodies with the tension of futile struggle, for they won't let go of the treasure chest. It was called the Monkey Trap; they yearn for freedom but are trapped by their own refusal to let go of the very thing that imprisons them. What did it mean?

I grounded and centered myself, staring at the image on the card, allowing it to evoke the hidden meaning from my subconscious. And then I saw clearly: The world that offered riches had robbed me of things more precious than gold. It offered a path to security and power, but they were mere shadows of what I longed for. The world of riches, of glamour and power was actually the Underworld, and I had been abducted by its Lord, the God in his challenging, shadow aspect. The Shadow's very name, *Pluto* in Latin, means riches; and he is the master of a world of shades and shadows devoted to the accumulation of money. His nether-realm is the world we all occupy each day, the waste-land of illusory, hollow materialism devoid of spiritual vitality.

I was beginning to understand the meaning of Nonna's cryptic warning those many months ago. My dream job had been the opposite of what I'd expected. But it had taught me a great deal about myself, and about where my truth path was to be found. There was nothing wrong with wealth. The Old Religion was, after all, a fertility religion. Prosperity and comfort were joys everyone should have. But the pursuit of money for its own sake, at the expense of our self-respect, creativity, and compassionate humanity, was the worship of a false idol. Hadus was my shadow, challenging me to look deeper within myself, to the quest for the only treasure of real value: my soul.

I drew again from my Tarot deck. Three times I drew the tower card, another frightening image: a crown, representing worldly achievements, was set atop a tall tower being struck by lightning and bursting into flame. Figures were falling from the tower to a raging sea below.

I copied its divinatory meanings in my diary: "Unexpected challenges, abrupt changes, divine intervention." Again the image guided me to insight: The lightning, though terrifying and disruptive, was a blessing in disguise. It struck the phallic tower where so many princesses have long been confined, freeing them, albeit drastically, returning them to earth, via water—the element of feeling and fertility. Destruction is sometimes necessary to free oneself from entrapment. At last, I was liberated from a world where my mind had long ago been cut off from my body, a life where the privileged lived in protective towers, isolated from the struggles of the world. Lightning struck, and I had toppled from my fictitious safety. It was time to let go, to move on, and if I could not, then the divine universe would shake me free. And so it had.

Life's reason and meaning are not to be found in a distant heaven, but discovered all along the earthly journey, where the blessing and reward of wisdom and divinity are ever-present. I now knew that magic doesn't make one immune to life's hardships. As a path of spiritual quest, it may actually lead us into demands and dangers far greater than a life led safely at home. But the "magical" tools and techniques bless the journeyer with extraordinary powers, enabling her to transform challenges and hardships into wisdom, power, compassion, creativity, and communion. They guide us in the healing of the wasteland and the return to the bountiful Garden.

My spontaneous decision to quit my job was a crossroad in this journey. It didn't make sense, but it didn't have to, not in the old, rational style of assurance and justification. I remembered my rune journey, and I remembered TriVia and Hecate, the goddesses who stood at the crossroads of life. I had not come this far to turn back now, for it was true the heart has reasons that reason knows not of. Several years of struggle awaited me, but so too did the opportunity to work with an old friend from my labor days, a respected and successful real estate attorney. And as it turned out, I would work with him for several years, and then take over his lucrative practice when he retired. At his kitchen table, he taught me how to practice law in a field where all parties could emerge from a transaction happy, where everyone could win without someone having to lose. The years that would follow my initiation were to be marked by bountiful magic, blessed by the Goddess who guided my rite of passage.

You must have a magical name in order to be initiated. It's the most important clue to your story. The name is not who you are; rather, it is a beacon on the path to who you are becoming.

"How do I find the right name?" I asked Nonna.

"In any number of ways," she replied. "In a dream, or a book, by chance, or by following your instincts. By visualization, by journey, by vision. But when you find it, you will know."

I waited for a dream, and clues came, but not a name. I dreamed of caves and snakes that coiled in spirals and songs of wine and wheat and pomegranates that issued from their darting red tongues.

I walked slowly, seeking signs, almost in trance, through the Egyptian halls of the Metropolitan Museum of Art. I stood in the temple of Dendur, calling out to the mother Hathor, yearning for the strength of the glorious Sekmets who guarded the temple's entrance, sensing the soft wings of Isis about my head and shoulders, finally sitting before my Libyan Sibyl, rereading Coleridge's *Kubla Khan*, my poetic road map.

I did not know how close I was, for though it was right in front of me, I wasn't seeing the one clue that revealed all. So once again I searched books looking for goddesses and heroines of Abyssinian descent—maybe I was meant to take the name of the Abyssinian maid?

Softly, I uttered Abyssinian names—Myrine, Omphale, Sambatu, and Melanippe—all Amazon queens, and their names rang with incantatory music, vibrating in the air all around me. But still my name eluded me. Through the year I had been given many signs, but I could not figure them out, and so my search continued.

While I was poring through books, seeking my magic name, Gillian found hers. She was first in our circle to bravely ask for initiation.

"What's your name?" I asked as we stood together in the oil office. She was mixing an incense to open the third eye.

"Morgain," she replied, her eyes glowing with inner light. "Another name for Morgan le Fay. I've been searching for the Grail my entire life—and I've finally found it."

And then it was Annabelle's turn, our lovelorn fairy princess who astonished us all by cutting her hair short and taking the name of the mighty Celtic warrior goddess Macha. Marcia and Naomi, who had fallen in love, were initiated together, taking the names of Egyptian sister goddesses. Onatah kept her given name, for it was that of a goddess, the daughter of Nokomis, the Algonquin earth Goddess.

And then Jeanette decided it was time. She took the name Tara, goddess of the stars. Tara is a divinity of compassion and enlightenment, mysticism and self-mastery, honored by Hindus, Buddhists, Jains, and the Tibetan Lamas. She is a symbol of relentless hunger as the force that propels life—and it was this force that Jeanette had finally harnessed.

"Are you nervous?" I asked. We'd met at the shop to prepare a purification potion for her to use before her initiation.

"A little. But mostly I can't wait," Jeanette smiled as we gathered the ingredients.

"How can you be sure when you don't know what it is?"

"I can't be sure—maybe it's just a test of faith." She waved a little brown oil bottle under my nose. "Inspiration," she read from the label.

"Faith. Whenever tragedy strikes we turn to faith because we can't imagine how a truly all-knowing and compassionate God could let such terrible things happen." I perched on the stool behind her.

"I guess that's because when you need comfort, believing in a mystery is sometimes all the comfort you're going to get."

"But it's not enough," I insisted. "Using faith like that is a soporific to the irrational. Faith is trust in a sacred reality. But trust has to be earned, you don't just give it blindly. One of the main reasons I've been able to stay this strange course is its ability to prove itself to me. When I reach out, there's something to grab hold of—to see, to touch, to feel. There's a reply to my questions."

"And your prayers. We don't use that word very often either, but that's what they are. I certainly prayed to the Goddess for help with Richard." Jeanette's grinding released an invigorating fragrance.

"That's what magic is, to some extent anyway, isn't it?" I asked, and then, as I had learned to do this year, I answered myself. "Participatory praying. Not just relying on an external divinity, but on our own sacred power as well. People substitute faith for an understanding that God didn't do it, or let it happen. *We* do it. *We* let bad things happen. We are the divine's self-awareness, its embodiment and expression. It's by discovering the sacred within ourselves, in each other, that we can stop things like war and murder from happening. By treating each other and the world as embodied divinity. Relying on God to do things for you is like remaining an infant, expecting your parent to take care of you. It's up to us to take responsibility, to act out of our sense of shared divinity." I shook my head. "It's one thing to know it intellectually; it's another thing altogether to really live it."

Jeanette nodded. "What's the old expression—God helps those who help themselves? I guess that's what initiation is about, at least for me. It's my acknowledgment of in-dwelling divinity."

"And a commitment to the responsibility that it implies."

Jeanette nodded. "Heavy, huh?"

We laughed.

"Well, I'm ready to step off the cliff" Jeanette said softly. "This year taught me about faith. I think it is the certainty that when you step off, you're either going to discover you have wings, or the drop won't be so far that it will kill you."

"Or maybe it's that, metaphorically anyway, when you step off, even if the fall kills you, we have the power to give birth to ourselves again." I thought of the Tower Tarot card. "I think the rebirth comes when you understand the purpose of the fall. The magical power resides in the epiphany, the insight, the wisdom that comes. There's a certain freedom from fear when you realize everything is cyclical—spring always follows winter."

Maia joined us. "How's your search going?"

"My father's family was Norwegian, so I was thinking of *Freya*," I said, mustering enthusiasm. It was an intellectual choice, well reasoned, but without true inspiration.

"*Freya* . . . Do you really think so?" was all Maia said, for we both knew it wasn't my magical name. But she was not supposed to prompt or urge or even counsel, so she said no more.

I was waiting for a revelation, and though the signs and clues had already come through poetry and books and the events of my life, my search seemed fruitless. I decided to put the books away. I wanted to find the name of my true self by magical intuition. I wanted the universe to speak to me.

I decided to go in pursuit of it in the world, to travel to an old cave I knew in the little hills of the Delaware Water Gap. I would enter the belly of the mother, just as the ancestors had, to seek a vision. I left New York, crossing the dark flowing river to a little piece of my promised land. The woods were gorgeous but dangerous, for it was hunting season, and even in my father's heavy wool, red-checked Melton shirt, I trembled, chilled by each gunshot echoing in the distance.

I made my way through the golden woods to the entrance of the cave. It was filled with graffiti and rusted beer cans, left behind by teenage boys who had gotten drunk in unconscious memory, longing for an initiation of their own. I pulled out my flashlight and pressed beyond these modern tatters of ancient Dionysian rites, which gradually gave way to the richness of the dark, embracing, primeval Mother.

It was much colder than I expected. Daylight disappeared behind me and my way was lit only by the narrow beam of my flashlight. I reassured myself with flippant images of Alice headed down the rabbit hole, but a chill of thin fear and unexpected claustrophobia encircled me, smothering my courage. I ran my hand along the cavern wall, to steady my nerves as much as my descent, but it was deathly damp and cold. I moved slowly, cautiously, wondering what I pursued in this cavern of unseen confrontation. The ground was slippery and wet, and suddenly my right foot slid drastically out from under me. I crashed into the unforgiving stone, plunging into absolute darkness. The flashlight rolled away from my fingers and I lay unconscious, in darkness within darkness.

My head was pounding when I finally came to, and a terrible fear and confusion gripped me. *Where was I?* I felt nauseated as I struggled to my hands and knees, feeling my heartbeat pounding in my temples as the blood roared through my head. I crouched in the absolute blackness, panic strangling me. *I'm blind,* I thought in terror. *And deaf,* for there wasn't a sound. *Oh Goddess, maybe I'm dead.* And then it came to me . . . *Proserpina, Proserpina, Proserpina* . . . called three times by an odd, faraway voice. Was I dreaming? I felt trapped, ill with fear, my breathing fast and jagged. My foot kicked something, and I cringed, terrified, then relieved—the flashlight. I groped in the darkness, immeasurably grateful for my precious torch, and the tiny yellow light it provided.

I struggled to my feet, unsure which way to go, then sensing the ground had a subtle incline that I prayed would lead me out. It felt as though I was moving in slow motion. Gradually, mercifully, blackness gave way to gray, and gray to the details of my surroundings, until light shone through the cave's gaping entrance. A subtle cherished glow growing golden and piercing as I emerged to see the dawn. A streak of blood red, the color of life, separated night from day in one of the most exquisite sights I'd ever seen.

I pulled a bottle of water from my knapsack and quickly gulped it down. I washed my dirty face and sat, shivering, warming slowly as the sun rose. I leaned against a sweet-smelling pine, breathing slowly, laughing as I exhaled. *I'm alive.*

At home hours later, I could hardly move. It hurt to breathe; it hurt just to be in my body. I pulled the shades against the day and fell into bed. Proserpina—after my unnerving night I had reservations about the name. Despite my foreboding, a few nights later I told my priestesses I was ready.

It was Samhain, the Celtic sabbat when the veil between the worlds of mortals and spirits is the thinnest, the night when we, and they, could travel most easily between our realms. It was the night when we honored our ancestors, and when, if they wished, they could visit with us. It was the night when we were able to remember the lives we had lived before. It was the night on which the Celtic New Year began, the night when the Goddess entered the Underworld to confront the God in his aspect of Lord of the Underworld, of Death and Rebirth. It is a holy night of wild and unexpected energies, of unpredictable events and visitations, of keenest mortality and darkest death. It is a night of deepest mystery and revelations.

It was the night upon which I was to be initiated.

I stood outside the temple, waiting. Bellona graciously received me with a kiss and thanked me for the flowers, wine, fruit, and cakes I had brought.

"Maia's already in the temple. Nervous?" she asked with a wicked smile.

I nodded. What about Nonna? I wondered, but did not ask.

"Good, you should be."

"Thanks, that's very reassuring."

"I'm not trying to reassure you. It's up to you to be absolutely sure— if you have any doubts whatsoever, tell me before we start. Your life depends upon it."

A chill ran through me. Was she serious? She looked it. The women in circle had told each other terrible stories, which they had heard from employees of the bookstore who claimed to have been told by the owner himself. Stories of unworthy neophytes run through with swords, their throats slit, their heads cut off. Accidents or murders? Or sacrifices?

I told myself these were like ghost stories children tell for the peculiar fun of scaring themselves. I thought of my sisters who had preceded me through the portal of initiation, and the beauty and assurance with which they had emerged, the laughter that came so quickly to their lips, the light that danced in their eyes. I thought of the great distance I had traveled during the last year. I nodded.

"I'm ready. Is there anything I can do to help?"

"Not yet." She patted my cheek and disappeared behind the hidden door. I walked up and down between the long bookshelves, attempted some simple hatha yoga and breathing to calm myself.

The lights of the little shop had been lowered. I sat, yawned and closed my eyes, letting my mind drift. Calmer now, I thought about the misgivings I still felt regarding the name that had come to me. I was uncomfortable calling myself by the name of a goddess; it felt immodest. But I had searched no further after my night of dark descent. I knew it was the marker of my journey's path; I knew the aspect of divinity called by this name would be my guide. She was the ultimate clue.

Finally, because I accepted the process by which the name had come, I accepted the name. I had resisted the temptation to read about Proserpina, trusting that just as her name had been revealed to me, the universe would also reveal her meaning.

The waiting seemed interminable and I prowled the shop, propelled by a current of excitement. I opened bottles of oil, breathing in their magical perfumes—inspiration, peace, Isis. I drifted up the aisles, wondering when we would start, trying to be patient, trying not to worry. A book suddenly fell from the top shelf of the bookcase, landing at my feet. It didn't topple. It moved straight out, as if lifted by an unseen hand, then fell to the floor. I stood frozen in my tracks, then gingerly, I knelt and picked it up. I held it warily, then let the library angel guide my hand. I opened it at random.

A jolt of energy shot through me as I looked at the page and began to read about Aradia, an Italian priestess of Proserpina's mysteries. She was someone who may have actually lived during the 1300s, a kind of female Robin Hood. As a priestess of the people, she taught the ways and wisdom of the Old Religion, leading peasants and runaway slaves in rebellion against the brutal nobility and their allies, the Catholic Church. They gathered by Lake Nemi, where a temple to Diana once stood, in the Alban hills that surround Rome, and there they were attacked by their enemies. They struggled fiercely for their freedom, and terrible battles were fought, until those who survived were driven off, some hiding in Florence, others granted refuge by the king of Naples. It was said that Aradia herself was captured and imprisoned, and her teachings, which had been preserved on thirteen scrolls, were taken to the Pope who resided in Avignon, France. She was mythologized as the daughter of Diana, who willingly entered the Underworld to confront and challenge Death.

Chills rushed through me. The book store disappeared down a long tunnel in which I stood, sensing that if I took one step forward, I would find myself standing, not in Manhattan, but on a hillside overlooking a lake beside which the remnants of a temple to Diana stood. I blinked and the tunnel disappeared. I closed the book and returned it to the shelf. *This* was my Craft name.

Bellona emerged from the temple, dressed in a gown of purple silk. "What name will you take?"

"Aradia," I replied without hesitation.

Bellona smiled broadly. "We've been waiting for you."

She responded to me with the same strange words with which Nonna had first greeted me so many months ago!

"Please remove your clothes and remain seated here." Bellona pointed to the table where I had first met Maia. "When I return, it will be time to begin. There are certain words you must remember, or you will not pass the test." She leaned in, and softly whispered them in my ear. Then she hugged me and again disappeared behind the hidden door.

I pulled off my shoes and socks, my jeans and sweater, and my underwear. I sat in the darkened shop, my arms wrapped around me, shivering and colder than I expected to be. Time dragged. I practiced breathing and grounding, but I found myself growing cold, bored, and restless. Suddenly the door opened and Bellona reappeared. A quick jolt of adrenaline shot through me.

"Stand up, please." She came around behind me and swiftly tied a heavy scarf around my eyes.

"Can you see?" she asked.

I shook my head, smiling. This is not so bad, I thought, sort of like a sorority spoof. Her hands gripped my wrists tightly, pulling them behind my back. My amused confidence evaporated and was replaced by a powerful surge of resistance as I felt her bind my hands behind my back, then tug them upward. I felt a cord slip round my neck and felt her fingers quickly knotting it at my throat. Another cord was tied tightly around my legs and ankles. I felt her hands rub an unfamiliar oil on my seven chakrahs and my pulse points—beneath my arms, the inside of my elbows, my wrists, behind my ears, my knees, at my ankles.

Then I heard the door open and close again.

I could have complained, told her to stop. But I had stood silent and now I stood alone, outside the temple door. My legs began to feel like rubber. The bonds that restricted me seemed to disappear, but I was unable to move my arms and legs. I became very drowsy and wanted to curl into sleep. Time disappeared and I felt as if I were suddenly floating upward. The blindfold slipped away, and I could see the little shop below me. As if underwater, I could hear voices that were familiar, yet suddenly seemed full of menace. They were in the temple. Maia was within, as were Nonna and other elders of our tradition; but where was the laughter I had come to expect at all of our gatherings? Suddenly, I was no longer floating. I stood shivering, immobilized, and alone, outside the temple door.

As if a great tsunami were crashing down upon the shores of my secure island of certainty, I found myself overwhelmed with panic: *Maybe these people really are Satanists. Maybe it's all just an elaborate plot to secure victims for some hideous sacrifice. How long have I really known these women, anyway?* A terrifying shadow of fear confronted me at the threshold into an unknown underworld.

In the face of terror, I began the ritual of initiation.

Standing in Her likeness at the entrance to the temple, I was bound and blindfolded. Without sight of the world that surrounded me, I turned inward to the silence, to the cave within. There, emerging from the shadows of time, I beheld the multitude who had preceded me over centuries of persecution, isolation, and resistance—children, men, and so many, many women. I saw priestesses murdered in the Goddess's temples, peasants fall before the sword of church and nobility, old women drowned tied to dunking stools, and the smoke of countless pyres fueled by human flesh and torched by fear curling toward an empty heaven. I saw Giordano Bruno at the stake and Galileo in prison. I saw Native Americans, young and old, men and women, fall before a wave of blue-coated, gray-bulleted brutality, and Aborigines forced from the land. I saw a young Irish girl with bright red hair and eyes too large die of starvation. I saw Tibetan monks murdered in the snow-capped mountains and Jews mercilessly slaughtered at the Inquisition and in the gas chambers. A woman in Algeria bled on the streets, shot as she walked without a *chador,* another woman beheaded in Saudi Arabia for trying to escape her country. I saw children sold into slavery weaving carpets in Pakistan and girls enslaved in the sex trades of Thailand. I saw a young black woman, screaming in terror and pain, blood pouring forth from the inhuman incision that mutilated her genitals and stole her life on the ancient soil of Africa. I saw a black man hanging from a cottonwood tree and a black teenager fall before a bullet a block from where I lived. I saw Jesus taken from the cross, lying in the grieving lap of his divine mother Mary. I saw rifles exploding fire and death into a crowd of striking workers, and I saw a man killing himself with alcohol, unemployment, and despair, seated at a kitchen table in some small town somewhere. I saw a small child stepping on a land mine and one young Chinese man confronting a long line of crushing tanks. I saw high platforms from which small men looked down upon others, asking, "Are you now or have you ever been . . . ?" I saw tribunals passing judgment of torture and death and I saw those who refused to bow down before idols of cruelty.

Was I unwittingly offering myself as another scapegoat to the slaughter? Or was I deepening my commitment to the current of challenge and change that had always sprung from the deepest well of our humanity, where the sacred surfaced?

I heard the door open and strong hands gripped me, leading me as I shuffled toward the unknown within. I stood, as if at the edge of some high precipice, a black abyss waiting below me.

My heart was pounding. I felt the sharp point of a heavy sword come to my throat. It lifted, and I exhaled in relief only to feel it settle over my heart. A cavernous chill suffused me. It crept from my hollow chest to my weakening arms and legs. Isolated, blind, fettered, and scared, I fell away into an underworld. A transfiguration occurred as the fidelity of life and liberation flowed through me. I knew the answer to my question. The divine dwells within, in ever-changing outward form, its inner presence eternal. The journey is its discovery.

I was awakened by the challenge of my priestess's rising voice. With the veneration of the countless who stood with me, I replied, and suddenly understood the meaning of my declaration.

I heard the sword's exaltation as it responded, slashing the air between my spirit and my mind. Now, resting on my crown, the sword had severed the fear from my faith. Beyond the keening winds of doubt, I heard the ancient songs of wonder and, surrounded by darkness, recognized the womb of the Great Mother. Confronted with death, I embraced time and conceived radiance. Lost in the wasteland, I found the sacred wellspring. My heart knew the unity and beauty, the joy and promise of life. My soul, now joined to all that was, that is, and will be, had come home. I heard the words echoing forth across the cavern of space and time, across the abyss of darkness and fear: *If that which you seek you find not within you, you will never find it without. For behold, I have been with you since the beginning, and I am that which is attained at the end of desire.*

With gratitude and certainty, I entered the circle of rebirth.

Acting in perfect love and perfect trust, I overcame my soul-crippling fears in that moment of initiation. I became the Goddess in her ancient journey to the hidden world. There I confronted death and discovered the eternal, mysterious capacity to return with miraculous gifts of spirit and life, gifts I had received throughout the year and a day which had been the rite of passage to my new life.

I knelt before the altar and undertook my sacred oath, a remnant of the days when the practice of the Old Ways meant certain and hideous death. Those who learned and practiced and worshiped together held each others' lives in their hands and so each was sworn to secrecy. The commitment to this hidden community required extraordinary trust, and courage, and though we no longer faced death, I took it as an oath to those who came before me. And to those who would follow.

I was taught the use of magical tools, of sword and wand, cup and pentacle, and more. I was given the secret names of the Goddess and the God. And I was given my copy of our tradition's Book of Shadows. Cradling the book against my chest, I felt as if a child rested in my arms, a child whose life was a miracle of infinite promise. Purpose coursed through me—to protect and nurture its blessings to maturity, to bring its wisdom forth from the netherworld of shadows into the bright light of day. It was the promise of new life, of transformed consciousness, of healed heart and renewed divinity which might someday help restore vitality to the dying earth.

Finally, unbound and unveiled, I was presented to my community and to the Goddesses and Gods as Aradia, in whose name I emerged from my initiation consecrated as a priestess of the Goddess.

I now know my consciousness and my life had been forever changed.

I found the Goddess, and, with her, the key to the secret of my story . . . on the other side of the threshold, one life had ended, and yet another was born.

I slept through most of the next day, and when I awoke, I opened my *Book of Shadows*. I pored through it quickly, finding, not philosophy, theology, or explanations, but rituals, spells, secret alphabets, and poetry. The understanding would have to come, as it had all year, through the practice. No one would interpret for me. But now I had more treasured tools to work with. I'd gone to bed early and was surprised at how exhilaration and exhaustion mixed in my dreams. I awoke certain that there remained a last unsolved clue. I had undergone an astonishing transformation—the veil had been raised, but the mystery had just begun.

The next day, possessed by a sudden impulse, I flagged a cab and headed for Bergdorf's. My heart fell as I passed the spotlit niche, now featuring a warm coat for the impending cold months. I went to the designers' section and quickly perused the gowns. Not there.

"Hello! How've you been? I haven't seen you for months." It was one of my old helpers.

"I'm fine. I left my job."

Her eyebrows went up.

"It was definitely the right decision."

"As long as you're happy," she said kindly. "Are you looking for an interviewing suit?"

"No. It's probably long gone, but—the evening dress that was in the foyer this summer?"

She smiled. "Beautiful dress, wasn't it? So feminine, but so powerful. I'm afraid we've finished sales on the summer line."

It was a mad idea, I tried to console myself.

"Can I show you something else? We have some beautiful gowns. . . ."

"No, thank you—there was something about that dress."

She looked at my crestfallen face. "Can you wait one second? I want to check." She disappeared into the back. I stood staring out the windows to the autumnal park below, wrestling with my disappointment. The salesclerk reappeared, her face lit with delight. She was holding up the gown.

"We took it off the floor after it was damaged," she explained, showing me a torn seam and a small hole near the hem in the back. "It was supposed to be reduced during the end of the season sale, but somehow it never made it onto the floor." She smiled again. "I think it's one size too large for you, but we can easily fix that, and these little tears. Try it on."

I turned slowly in the mirror, seeing myself as I never had before. My hands slid down my body, which looked both graceful and powerfully muscular under the silver dress.

"You look beautiful—like a goddess," she beamed. I blushed. She looked at the price tag. "And with the markdowns, at this point . . ." She pulled a purple pen from her neat chignon, crossed out the original breathtaking sum and and wrote a figure on the tag. She showed it to me and I couldn't believe my eyes—less than a suit off the rack.

"I'll take it!" I exclaimed.

"Of course you will—it was meant for you. I'll call the dressmaker. We should have it for you in two weeks."

"Thank you." I hugged her.

As she rang up the dress, I stood staring out the window, almost afraid to look in the mirror. I was afraid I would still be invisible, even in this evocation of divine feminity. I turned slowly. There was a light in my eyes, and I recognized someone I'd never known before. It was as if I had finally arrived in my body.

I decided it was time to finally share the story of my quest with my mother. During the past year I'd hinted at my unusual feminist interests, and as a feminist my mother had listened with open-mindedness and sympathy. But she was an intellectual who'd long ago distanced herself from the superstition and oppression of religion. How would she react to a daughter who had discovered the Goddess? I was no longer nervous about her reaction. Some of my journey was explainable, some remained mysterious. I would do the best I could, and that was all my mother had ever expected of me. Today I was going to come out of the musty old broom closet.

My mother was waiting for me at an elegant Upper East Side restaurant where we often met before spending afternoons at the Metropolitan. Surrounded by the ladies who lunch, we talked for hours, and my mother, a very practical, sensible Eleanor Roosevelt feminist, found it all historically and intellectually fascinating. But it was the undeniable power of our connection which was the bridge to her acceptance. As she took in my radiant expression, she understood, in her heart, the truth and value of my experiences.

A few days later, there arrived in the mail a large, leather bound book which I recognized immediately—*Bullfinch's Mythology*. I read the note Mom had enclosed: "Found this and thought you'd like to have it. It brought back so many lovely memories of reading to you at bedtime, and it's filled with Goddesses."

Delight filled me as I ran my finger through the dust of my childhood and opened the book of ancient stories. Slowly, I turned the pages, with recognition and renewed affection. I remembered and reread passages with new appreciation. I could feel one tale calling to me through the dense pages, but I postponed turning to it—sensing in my lingering anticipation a new certainty that I would find meaning like treasure buried in a cave of shadows. And finally succumbing, I turned to the story of Proserpina, whom the Greeks called Persephone.

Long ago, before men cut down the forests and filled the land with noise, the world rejoiced in endless springtime. In a fertile grotto on the isle of Sicily, the maiden goddess Persephone, intoxicated by the perfume of a crimson hyacinth, plucked the flower from the ground. A chasm suddenly opened in the side of volcanic Mount Aetna and out rode the terrifying Lord of the Underworld, Hades, in a chariot pulled by six black stallions. He seized Persephone, abducting her into his netherworld, where he made her his queen.

Hearing her daughter's frightened cries, Demeter, goddess of the fertile earth, took the form of a bird and swiftly flew forth to find her daughter. Seeing nothing, she disguised herself as an old woman, asking all she met if they had seen her daughter. No one had seen her fair Persephone, but people were kind to the grieving goddess, and in thanks for their generosity, she gave them gifts of wheat and corn, and taught them the mysteries of agriculture. And a temple was built in her honor at Eleusis.

But grief and despair consumed Demeter, and she mourned her lost daughter until a gentle voice stirred her from her pain. It was a bubbling fountain which had seen Persephone seated on the throne of the Underworld, Tararatus, speaking the poetics of mysteries and giving solace to the dead.

Demeter demanded that Zeus order her daughter's return. But Hades was his brother and Zeus refused. Enraged, Demeter placed a curse upon the land so nothing would grow and the earth became a dying wasteland. The gods, frightened they would no longer be worshiped, consented to Persephone's release. Hades agreed to let her go, but persuaded Persephone to eat three pomegranate seeds, hoping that by this trick she would be forced to stay with him.

The swift chariot of Hermes carried Persephone from the Underworld, and mother and daughter wept with joy when they were reunited. But when Demeter learned that Persephone had eaten the three seeds, she refused to remove her curse from the land. And so a bargain was struck—three months of every year the earth would lie barren in winter and Persephone would return to Hades as queen of the Underworld. During this time, seeds and souls slumber in the womb of dreams while the Goddess works her rites and magic of renewal. In springtime, borne forth in the cradle of her arms, new life emerges with the Goddess and the earth grows green beneath Persephone's dancing feet.

But there was more, for after the story was a poem with familiar words faceted like gems in the burial mound of a queen—treasure and map all at once—the mysterious words of *Kubla Khan*. The message that had accompanied and directed me since the beginning of my journey, was finally explained:

Where Alph, the sacred river, ran
Through caverns measureless to man
Down to a sunless sea.

In the discourse that followed the story of Persephone, I discovered Coleridge's poetic Alph was the river Alpheus which began in Greece, disappeared beneath the Mediterranean, and surfaced in Sicily as the fountain Arethusa. It was this serpentine water that, in its subterrenean journey, witnessed Persephone's abduction. I had been right all along. Within the poem lay a tale of immortal resonance, the story of Persephone, her secrets of the inner world. Hidden, she had appeared to me in synchronicities and dreams, signaling from the dark potentiality of my unconscious an impending awakening. Persephone's symbol is the torch and she is the guide on every journey of discovery, the interpreter of meaning, revealer of the hidden pattern of our lives. And with her return from the Underworld, she restores the gift of new life, the wisdom and ways of the heart, to the barren land. In time, I would discover how the mysteries of Demeter and Persephone, and their priestess Aradia, had grown out of those of Isis, and her priestess the Libyan Sibyl, as the

Goddess's mysteries spread from Egypt and Abyssinia to Crete, Greece, Sicily, and Italy. I would also discover how much these had in common with the Grail mysteries.

I carefully closed the book, my mind racing with images and realizations. Here in this ancient myth of Persephone and her descent into the Underworld was the final and first mirror of my soul's journey—the meaning of my own quest, the pattern of my destiny. I saw myself in Persephone's invisibility. I too had been abducted by a male power of wealth and domination, death and disembodiment. I had tried to please, unable to find my voice, turning into a thin whisper of appeasement and despair. I was a shadow, insubstantial and vulnerable in my youth and inexperience, lost in a hostile netherworld.

Air ignited around me in a thousand sparks of fire as I realized this ancient myth was more than just my story: It was a story that spoke to the truth of all women. And it could speak to men as well, for without the balance of the feminine, they remained wounded and impotent kings in a dying land. It spoke with profound insight to our culture, for it was the story of our era. We have all been abducted, and in the absence of that part of ourselves which is divinely feminine, the world has become a wasteland, an underworld where all of its children now face a winter of extinction.

Though we were separated from the Mother Goddess, from the divine within ourselves, from our powers to create culture as well as life, women have refined skills of astonishing spiritual purity: We nurture life in the face of death, understand the wisdom of dreams, and tend the ever-burning flame that is the power of the compassionate heart. We employ the Goddess's gift of sight, what some call "women's intuition." We shape-shift, surviving among the temple ruins, even forgetting our own true names, but always remembering the promise of love.

For most of recorded history, governments ruled, men went to war, economies flourished and died, journalists wrote about it, and artists reacted to it, and through it all, women have been locked within shuttered towers, hidden behind black veils, victimized by religion and endless social prohibitions, refused the right to vote, work, travel freely, own property, preach in churches, speak the wisdom of their hearts. Until the recent past, women's dreams have gone largely unrecorded and unpublished. Yet even disembodied and disempowered, like Persephone, they have mastered the mysteries of the soul's rebirth. And like Persephone, they are once again rising, not as singularly remarkable exceptions, but as a global community, to their rightful, equal, and vital places as creators of culture.

For countless years, the archetypal story of heroic descent into the realm of shadows, confrontation with fear, death and devastation, and rebirth through the divine use of our inner resources and sacred, healing tools, has been told in terms of the lives of men—Moses, Buddha, Jesus, Mohammed, and others. In these versions of the story, the conclusion for women is always the same: Men are to journey forth to meet the divine, and women are to remain at home, or at best, to follow their leaders. But its earliest expression, which preceded all of these male reinterpretations, was the tale of the Goddess's descent into the Underworld. And in these early versions, the Goddess is not abducted but goes willingly to confront and transform the mystery of death into rebirth.

The Goddess has reached out her hand, dragon-winged messengers arrive in the nether realms, and with her summoning, we remember who we are and why we are here. At this moment of greatest crisis, at the end of a millennium, at the end of the great patriarchal epochs, a quantum shift is occurring. This is the moment of rebirth, the moment of return from the Underworld. It is no longer enough to believe in the journey of another, or to listen to the interpretation of that journey by hierarchs and psychopomps. Their stories cannot substitute for our own quest. Instead, they must inspire it, for there will be no lasting change until people have changed themselves, until they have awakened to their divine inheritance. In the mirror of this ancient tale, I realized the greatest magic of all: That we are all a part of the self-aware consciousness of a divine, living universe seeking to understand itself. Together, on this miraculous quest, we will restore to the world the gracious gifts of love, compassion, and reverence for life in all of its sacred forms. Then the wasteland will blossom forth as paradise. It is a journey being taken by women, and men must accompany them, for only together can we embody the mystery of rebirth. And this was a part of the journey that waited ahead for me.

I looked into the ancient mirror of the Goddess, and there I saw not only the past, but the radiant future. I saw my sisters and myself, beloved of gods and men, stepping forth from a realm of shadows, and we cradled the future life of this sacred, beloved planet in our arms.

. . .

Moonlight filters in through the city skylight. The air is fragrant with the scent of flowers and the smoke of burning incense. Candles flicker and glow, bathing our bodies in golden light. . . . I inhale slowly, feeling the energy rushing through me. I have never felt so alive. I look around the circle of women who stand with me—their eyes full of fire, skin flushed and glowing, their hair dancing about their radiant faces.

"Thou art Goddess," the woman next to me says. "Thou art Goddess," I reply and turn to send the blessing around our circle.

Our magic has just begun.

Appendix

TABLE OF CORRESPONDENCES
SPELLS, CHARMS, AND MAGICAL POTIONS
WHEEL OF THE YEAR
RESOURCES
BOOKS OF INTEREST

TABLE OF CORRESPONDENCES

	EAST	SOUTH	WEST	NORTH
Elements:	Air	Fire	Water	Earth
Nature:	Wind	Sun	Oceans, Rivers, Rain	Mountains, Fields
Aspects:	Mind	Will/Energy	Emotions	Body
Qualities:	Imagination Wonder Music	Passion Courage Determination	Love Compassion Dreams	Creativity Fertility Strength
Goddesses:	Nike Arianrod Isis	Amaterasu Brigid Pele	Aphrodite Yemanja Tiamat	Demeter Parvati Freya
Gods:	Hermes Thoth Quetzalcoatl	Horus Surya Lugh	Poseidon Njord Agwe	Dionysus Cernunnos Osiris
Animals:	Wing: Birds, Butterfly	Claw: Lions, Dragons	Fin: Porpoises, Whales	Paw & Hoof: Bear, Wolf, Bison, Horse
Time:	Dawn	Midday	Sunset	Night
Colors:	White Lavender	Red Orange	Blue Sea-Green	Green Brown
Tools:	Sword	Wand	Cup	Pentacle
Zodiacal Sign:	Aquarius Gemini Libra	Leo Aries Sagittarius	Scorpio Pisces Cancer	Taurus Virgo Capricorn
Plants/Herbs:	Lavender Bodhi Tree	Myrrh Olive Tree	St. John's Wort Willow	Patchouli Oak
Spirit Form:	Sylph	Salamander	Undine	Gnome

SPELLS, CHARMS, AND MAGICAL POTIONS

Cleansing and Purification Spell

This can be done whenever needed, but it will be particularly effective during the waning or dark phases of the moon.

Quick Formula: ½ cup of sea salt and 1 cup of epsom salts added to a hot bath. Light a white candle, get in the tub, and RELAX!

Prepare a potion by combining the following herbs in a pot with five cups of water:

> ⅛ *cup Valerian*
> ⅛ *cup Lavender*
> ⅛ *cup Angelica*
> ⅛ *cup Calendula*
> ¼ *cup Comfrey*
> ¼ *cup Hyssop*

Bring to a rolling boil, lower the flame, and simmer for twenty minutes, stirring clockwise every five minutes. Strain the herbs from the liquid and pour the liquid potion into a tub of warm water. Add 3 drops of carnation oil, 5 white carnations, 2 drops of eucalyptus oil, and 1 cup of epsom salts to the bath water. Place the strained herbs around the base of a white candle and light the candle. State what you wish to cleanse yourself of, such as loneliness, grief, self-doubt, stress, ill health, confusion, or any other negative emotion or situation. Ask for the purifying aid of the water and earth, and the divine power that resides within and around you. You may also invoke the blessing of a particular divinity such as Hygieia, Aphrodite, Cerridwen, Morgan le Fay, or Yemanja.

Get into the tub. Close your eyes and breathe deeply, feeling your muscles and your mind relax. Visualize your cares, problems, and negative emotions leaving you; see them drawn from your body by the potion. When you feel yourself rested and renewed, and before the bath water grows cold, get out of the tub, and visualize your cares disappearing down the drain with the water. Place the candle in a sink or other location where it may safely burn out. Thank the elements and the divine, which are always present. You may finish the purification with a soothing cup of chamomile tea. Dress in white for 24 hours. Dispose of the herbs in a compost heap or other spot where they can be recycled by the earth. Repeat as needed.

Self-Blessing Spell

This ritual should be conducted after the spell of cleansing and purification. For menstruating women, the rite is best performed on the first night of your menstruation. Post-menopausal women may wish to perform the rite during the dark of the moon, which is said to be the Crone's Moon, or the Moon of Hecate. Or anyone, including men (making the appropriate changes in the spell as necessary), may perform the rite during a waxing or full moon.

Prepare an incense from the following herbs using equal parts of each, approximately 2 tablespoons. In a mortar and pestle grind together:

Sandalwood
Orris
Mastic
Rosemary
Rose
Cinnamon

For this, you will need the kind of charcoal used to burn incense (not charcoal briquettes). Handle the charcoal carefully; it gets very hot. Prepare an anointing oil with:

Patchouli
Verbena
Cinnamon—use conservatively
Almond
Rose

Create an altar using white, pink, blue, or lavender. It should contain a symbol of the Goddess—whether statue, picture, goblet, bowl, fruit, flower, shell, or other natural object of beauty. Men may wish to add an image or symbol of the God—a statue, pair of deer antlers, ear of corn. You may also wish to place on the altar for charging any jewelry that you wear regularly or which expresses your spirituality.

Place the oil, incense, and bowls of water and wine or fruit juice on the altar. Place an offering you have created, such as a poem, song, work of art, on the altar.

Take your purification bath.

Emerge from the bath as the Goddess, or God, renewed. As you dry yourself, admire the beauty and strength of your body and give thanks for the many gifts it bestows every day. Do not dress.

Light the four point candles. (Turn off any electric lights.) Stand before your altar and consecrate the candle with the anointing oil. Light the candle.

Light the charcoal and burn the incense.

Ground, center, and breathe.

Cast a simple circle.
Invoke the Great Goddess.

Great Goddess,
Mother of all creation
Your child stands before you—
Inspire me to rejoice each day
In peace and beauty, wisdom and power.
Bless me and the life that I lead.

You may also invoke the God:

Ever present God,
Consort and son of the Great Goddess
Etc.

In the name of the Great Goddess, and the God if you have invoked him, you will bless yourself three times—first with water, then with wine or juice, and finally with the anointing oil.
Begin with your hands, consecrating your palms and saying:

Great Goddess, bless my hands that they may work with creativity, heal
with power, and connect me to you with their touch

Consecrate the soles of each foot, saying:

Bless my feet that they may walk your path with lightness and strength

Consecrate the base of your spine, visualizing the radiant light of the root chakra and saying:

Bless my body which is of and always connected to the sacred earth,
Bless this gift of embodied divinity
Bless me and consecrate me, fill me with your presence, enliven me
with your wisdom, your beauty, strength, courage and love
Bless your child who is one with you, whose body is your temple, whose
mind your self-awareness, whose love your perfect communion

Consecrate your genitals (womb or penis), visualizing the radiant orange light of this chakra, saying:

Bless my vagina (penis), that it may show me the joys of ecstasy and the
wonder of union,
Bless my womb, vessel of mystery and life (bless my penis from which
comes the seed of life)

Consecrate your stomach at your navel, visualizing the brilliant yellow light of the navel chakra, saying:

Bless my stomach, furnace of life, generator of energy and power,
cauldron of change

Consecrate your heart, visualizing the radiant green of the heart chakra, saying:

Bless my heart, let it open to your presence in my life, let it be filled
with love and compassion for all

Consecrate your breasts, saying:

Bless my breasts, miracles that sustain life with the milk of paradise

Consecrate your throat, visualizing the vivid blue of the throat chakra, saying:

Bless my voice that I may speak with your wisdom and compassion,
your humor and inspiration

Consecrate your third eye, in the center of your forehead, visualizing the shining indigo of the third eye chakra, saying:

Bless my mind's eye, that I may see you clearly in the infinite forms
through which you express your beauty and power

Consecrate your eyes, ears, nose, and lips, saying:

Bless my eyes, that I might see your wonders that are the world
Bless my ears, that I might hear your words, your songs, and your
laughter
Bless my nose that I might smell your fragrance in fruit, flower, and
beloved
Bless my lips that I might taste you in honey, grain, and the kisses of all
I love, and that I might speak your wisdom with poetry
Bless all my senses that they might show me your wonders which fill my
life with joy

Consecrate the crown chakra at the top and back of your head, visualizing
radiant lavender light and a rainbow of exploding color, saying:

Bless my soul which is of and always connected to the sacred heavens,
Bless this gift of divine energy,
Bless me and consecrate me, fill me with your presence, enliven me
with your wisdom, your beauty, strength, courage, and love
Bless your child who is one with you, whose body is your temple, whose
mind your self-awareness, whose love your perfect communion
Bless me, Great Goddess

Meditate upon the blessing you have received, and given. You may also bless and consecrate your offering and your jewelry. When you feel the presence of the Goddess flowing through you, give thanks, blow out the candle, saying:

Thank you Great Goddess, from whom all blessing flow.

Ground any excess energy you may feel and open your circle.

Spell for Inspiration and Sacred Sight Incense

Prepare an altar with an object symbolic of your goal: a book, CD, video, image of the Goddess, etc. Work with the colors pink or lavender for an altar cloth, candles, flowers, and clothing. There are many Goddesses, such as Inanna, Athena, Brigid, Lakshmi, Oya, Amaterasu, and Spider Woman, who may be invoked as muses.

In a mortar and pestle, grind together the following herbs:

1/8 cup Mugwort
1/16 cup Deer's Tongue
1/16 cup Sage
1/8 cup Solomon's Seal
1/16 cup Sandalwood
3–5 drops Heliotrope Oil (more if mixture is too powdery)
3–5 drops Sandalwood Oil (more if the mixture is too powdery)

Cast a simple circle. Sit in the center, facing east. Call upon the blessings of air and of your chosen Goddess for inspiration. Carefully light an incense charcoal and place it quickly in a brazier, or a small cast-iron cauldron with a tile beneath it, or a heavy ashtray filled with sand. Spoon the incense onto the charcoal, close your eyes, relax, use the deep breathing, grounding, and centering meditation techniques and allow yourself to experience visions of inspiration. You may wish to write them down when you are finished. Give thanks, close your circle, and act in accord.

Love Spell

See the text for how to do a love spell. Water is the element for love; it is also Aphrodite's special element, so here is a formula for a love bath. It may be taken alone or with someone you love. If you take it alone, it is wise to ask the Goddesses of love, such as Aphrodite, Lakshmi, or Oshun, for the love that will make you happiest and most fulfilled in the receiving and the giving.

Use one part each of the following herbs for the love spell bath:

Patchouli
Lemon Verbena
Cinnamon

Vetiver

Rose

Once the potion has been prepared and added to the bath water, add:

3 *drops of Musk Oil*

4 *drops of Frangipani (Almond) Oil*

3 *drops of Vanilla*

Amulet of Protection and Empowerment: Artemis's Shield

When you need to shield yourself from negative energies and to fill yourself with strength and confidence, make this amulet and carry it with you.

In a mortar and pestle, grind together:

1 *tablespoon Bay leaves*

1 *tablespoon High John (or Joan) the Conqueror*

1 *tablespoon Nettle*

1 *tablespoon Rue*

2 *tablespoon Vervain*

1 *tablespoon Rosemary*

1 *pinch Dragon's Blood powder*

Cut a four-inch square of indigo or blue cotton or silk cloth. Draw or stitch on it your name, initials, or personal symbol. Place the ground herbs in the center of the cloth, visualizing yourself safe, secure, and empowered. Tie up with blue thread or cord, knotting eight times and say:

> *I call upon the powers of the mighty Goddess Artemis, Lady of the Wild Things. Charge and bless this amulet of protection and empowerment. Shield me from harm. Strengthen and empower me. So mote it be.*

Hold the amulet to your heart as you visualize and feel yourself strengthened and protected by the divine power of the Goddess Artemis. When the need for protection has passed, empty the amulet to the four winds, and give thanks by helping someone in need.

Success Candle Spell

Mark an orange or yellow seven-day candle with the your name, the word *Success,* and a word for your goal such as *work, song, book, etc.* Also inscribe the candle with a picture of the sun (just as you would draw it as a child). Inscribe a star on the bottom of the candle.

Prepare a Success Oil made from equal measures of the following oils:

High John the Conqueror

Orris

Patchouli
Myrrh
Sandalwood

Consecrate the candle with the Success Oil, visualizing your success as you rub the oil in a clockwise direction around the entire candle. Light the candle, place it in a safe space, and allow it to burn continuously for seven days. Every day, preferably at the same time, focus on the burning candle as you visualize your success.

Potion for Psychic Dreams

This is best done on a weekend, as you may awaken feeling as if you haven't slept. Before going to bed, drink a cup of mugwort tea. Make the tea by pouring a cup of boiling water over two tablespoons of mugwort. Let steep for at least six minutes. Strain off the herbs and drink.

Prepare a dream-gathering powder using one part each of the following ingredients:

Cardamon
Coriander
Licorice
Cinnamon
Mugwort
Sandalwood
Deer's Tongue
Musk

Scatter the dream potion around and under your bed, on your sheets, and between your pillowcase and pillow. Also, burn the dream-gathering powder as an incense in your bedroom before going to bed. (Be sure the incense charcoal is placed in something fireproof because they get VERY hot.)

Place a pen and notebook beside your bed to record any dreams you may have. Write them down *immediately* upon waking.

Before going to bed, recite the following charm:

Spirits of the west,
Guides in the realm of dreams,
Swim with me,
And guide my soul to visions.

WHEEL OF THE YEAR

The names of the sabbats and their explanations that follow are from the Celtic tradition. There are numerous parallels to the Greek and Italian traditions, though they vary according to the differences in planting cycles.

SAMHAIN (pronounced Sowen)–October 31, New Year's Eve in the Celtic and contemporary Wiccan calendar. It is the night when the veil between the worlds is thinnest, when the spirits of our ancestors are honored as they visit with us. It is also the night when the Goddess enters the Underworld, and we enter the dreamtime. Appropriated by the Christian calendar as All Saints Day, November 1, and All Souls Day on November 2, the day honoring the dead. Popularly celebrated as Halloween.

YULE–December 21, Yule is the winter solstice, the longest night of the year. It is celebrated as the Festival of Light, when the Great Goddess conceives, or in some traditions gives birth to, her son, the Sun God. It is the sabbat for rejoicing in the discovery of light, and new life, within the womb of darkness, as each day now grows brighter. Appropriated in the sixth century C.E. by the Christian calendar when the official birthday of Christ was moved to December 25.

IMBOLC–February 2, *Imbolc* means "in the belly" in Gaelic and is the holiday that celebrates the first evidence of the return of life. It is also the holy day of the Celtic Goddess Brigid, goddess of fire, healing, smithcraft, and muse to the poets. The community gathers to honor her and the stirring life with candlelight and firelight, and the light of our laughter, poetry, music, art, and storytelling. Appropriated by the Christian calendar as St. Brigid's Day, or Candlemas, the Feast of the Purification of the Virgin Mary, the day on which the Church candles are blessed for the year.

OESTARA–March 21, Spring or Vernal Equinox, the holy day when light and dark are in balance. It is the day when life is born from the Great Mother, reappearing on earth in all its joy. It is said to be the day of the Goddess's return from her sojourn in the Underworld, and the rebirth of the God. Oestara is the Germanic goddess of the fertile earth, and her symbols are the ubiquitous eggs, rabbits, and flowers that survive to remind us of the Goddess's blessings. Appropriated by the Catholic Church as Annunciation Day, or Lady Day, when the angel Gabriel came to Mary to ask her to bear the Christ child. Also used by the Church as the date by which Christ's resurrection was determined, i.e., the first Sunday after the first full moon after the Spring Equinox, called Easter from the Goddess Oestara.

BELTAINE–May 1, Beltaine is also known as May Eve when celebrated the evening before, and May Day when celebrated on the first. It is the holiday in which the young Goddess and God first encounter and fall in love with each other. It is a celebration of the ecstasy of love as it fills the earth with blossoming life. Women wear crowns of flowers, and traditional dances around the Maypole celebrate the earth's fertility. This was also the midpoint of the Roman festival honoring Flora, the Goddess of flowers. In England, women bathe in the first dew of Mayday to meet their true loves, and others use its healing powers. Beltaine is celebrated by many Catholic churches as "The May Crowning" when, as in the pagan traditions, statues of Mary are crowned with wreathes of flowers. She is referred to as the Queen of the Angels, or the Queen of the May. Prior to its appropriation by the Catholic Church, the latter title referred to the Goddess, her priestess, or a young woman chosen from the community to embody the Goddess.

LITHA–June 21, Summer Solstice is the longest day of the year though from this day forth the sun's presence will wane. The fertile conjunction of sun and earth are celebrated as the divine union of Goddess and God. People rejoice in the richness of their lives, giving thanks for the fruitful blessings of the Great Mother Earth, without whom there would be no life. Appropriated by the Christian calendar as Midsummer's Day, Feast of St. John the Baptist.

LUGHNASSAD–August 1, Lughnassad is a first harvest celebration in which thanks are given for the fruits of the earth. It is also a wake for the Celtic God of the Sun, Lugh, who is said to enter the Underworld on this day (as the light of the sun wanes). It was celebrated with games and races, dancing, and ritual fires. The Saxons called this harvest festival *hlafmaesse* or Lammas, Feast of Bread. The Romans celebrated the birth of the Goddess Diana, and the Greeks honored Artemis, both of whom were Goddesses of the Animals, Forest, and the Moon. Also called Lammas by the Church of England, which appropriated the sabbat as St. Peter's Day, when the church hands out loaves of blessed bread. Also, August 13 was celebrated by the ancient Romans and pagan Italians as the birthday of the Goddess Diana, appropriated by the Christian calendar as the day of Mary's Assumption into Heaven.

MABON–September 21, Autumn Equinox, is when light and dark are again in perfect balance, though now the movement is toward darkness. On this holy day, the mystery of eternal life is contemplated as the sun goes into the seed that will sustain life through the dark months of winter ahead. The Goddess is thanked for her generosity with the completion of the harvest; the God is thanked for his gift of energy as it is embodied in the waning sun; and we reflect upon those goals we have brought to fruition and upon the aspects of our life we must release in order to grow. This holiday was appropriated by the Christian calendar as Michaelmas, for St. Michael, the Archangel of Fire, celebrated a week after Mabon, on September 29.

Resources

There are now hundreds of Wiccan and Goddess organizations, bookstores, catalogs, and special events. Unfortunately, space limitations prohibit listing them all. I have provided a selection of some of the oldest and best known in each category and have included catalogs and sources that will provide excellent and extensive lists as resources and guides to the Goddess and Wiccan community here and abroad.

Wiccan and Goddess Guides

Circle Guide to Pagan Groups and Resources, Circle Sanctuary, P.O. Box 219, Mt. Horeb, WI 53572

Nutshell Guide to Pagan Resources, Church of the Iron Oak, P.O. Box 060672, Palm Bay, FL 32906, (407) 722-0291

Periodicals, Newsletters, and Magazines
(some of these may no longer be in print)

The Beltane Papers (women's mysteries), 1333 Lincoln St., #240, Bellingham, WA 98226

Calendar of Events, c/o Larry Comett, 9355 Sibelius Dr., Vienna, VA 22182

Circle Network News, P.O. Box 219, Mt. Horeb, WI 53572

Crone Chronicles, P.O. Box 81, Kelly, WY 83011

Enchante, 30 Charlton St., Box 6F, New York, NY 10014

Gnosis, P.O. Box 14217, San Francisco, CA 94114

Green Egg, P.O. Box 1542, Ukiah, CA 95482, e-mail 5878037@mcimail.com

The Green Man (for men), P.O. Box 641, Pt. Arena, CA 95468

Goddess Regenerated, P.O. Box 73, Sliema, Malta, or P.O. Box 269, Valrico, FL 33595, e-mail goddssng@maltanet.net

Goddess Rising, 4006 First St., NE, Seattle, WA 98105

Magickal Blend, P.O. Box 11303, San Francisco, CA 94101-7303

Our Pagan Times (for New Yorkers) P.O. Box 1471, Mad. Sq. Station, New York, NY 10159-1449

Of Like Mind, P.O. Box 6677, Madison, WI 53716, (608) 257-5858

Sage Woman, P.O. Box 641, Pt. Arena, CA 95468, (707) 882-2052

The Shaman's Drum, Box 2636, Berkeley, CA 94702

The Web, 401 Cumberland Dr., No. Augusta, SC 29841

The Wise Woman, 2441 Cordova St., Oakland, CA 94602

The Witches' Almanac, P.O. Box 318, Milton, MA 02168

Woman of Power, P.O. Box 2785, Orleans, MA 02653

Woman Spirit, 2000 King Mountain Trail, Sunny Valley, Wolf Creek, OR 97497-9799 (Back issues)

Wood and Water (eco-pagan), 4 High Tor Close, Babbacombe Rd., Bromley, Kent, UK, BR1 3LQ

*Spiritual Organizations, Educational Institutions,
Centers, and Programs*

Aquarian Tabernacle Church, P.O. Box 409, Index, WA 98256, workshops and festivals

Ariadne Institute for the Study of Myth and Ritual, Ltd., 1306 Crestview Dr., Blacksburg, VA 24060, (540) 951-3070

Athena, 1741 Ninth St., Chicago, IL 60643, (773) 881-3124, programs on the Goddess

Bridges, Branches, and Braids, 472 Kentucky Ave., Berkeley, CA 94707, (510) 559-9342 workshops, trips, etc.

Brooke Medicine Eagle Resources, 1 Second Ave., E., C401, Polson, MT 59860, (406) 881-4488, workshops; women's mysteries, moontime

California Institute of Integral Studies, 9 Peter Yorke Way, San Francisco, CA 94109, (415) 674-5500, master's and doctoral degrees in women's spirituality

Center for Women and Religion, Graduate Theological Union, 2400 Ridge Rd., Berkeley, CA 94709

Center for Women, the Earth, and the Divine, 1114 Rising Ridge Rd., Ridgefield, CT 06877, founded by Dr. Eleanor Rae; workshops and lectures focusing on eco-feminism

Church of All Worlds, P.O. Box 1542, Ukiah, CA 95482

Church of the Iron Oak, P.O. Box 060672, Palm Bay, FL 32906, (407) 722-0291, classes, rituals, public sabbats

Circle of Ara, c/o H.Ps. Phyllis Curott, training coven

Circle Sanctuary, P.O. Box 219, Mt. Horeb, WI 53572, founded by Selene Fox; one of the oldest Wiccan organizations sponsors gatherings and publishes the very useful Circle Guide to Pagan Groups and Resources and Circle Network News

Covenant of the Goddess, P.O. Box 1226, Berkeley, CA 94704, e-mail pio@cog.org, organization of Wiccan covens

Covenant of Unitarian Universalist Pagans (CUUPS), P.O. Box 640, Cambridge, MA 02140

Crone's Cradle Conserve, P.O. Box 535, Orange Springs, FL 32182, (352) 595-3377, founded by Deborah Anne Light; Goddess workshops, lectures, events, newsletter

Drumsong Institute, P.O. Box 452, Catskill, NY 12414, (518) 678-0166, workshops and concerts

The Earthspirit Community, P.O. Box 340, Williamsburg, MA 01096, sponsors of Rites of Spring, one of the oldest festivals; also workshops, lectures, newsletter

Foundation for a Compassionate Society, P.O. Box 868, Kyle, TX, (512) 262-2300, projects for social change emphasizing women's values

Heart of the Goddess, 10 Leopard Rd., Berwyn, PA 19312, (610) 695-9494, workshops and gallery

MAMAROOTS: Ajama-Jebi, P.O. Box 16151, Oakland, CA 94610, (510) 238-9260, Afracentric Goddess spirituality, newsletter

The Mystery School, Box 3300, Pomona, NY 10970, founded by Jean Houston

Reclaiming Collective, P.O. Box 14404, San Francisco, CA 94114, founded by Starhawk and others; Wiccan workshops and rituals, newsletter

Reformed Congregation of the Goddess, (608) 257-5858

Rising Moon Healing Center, P.O. Box 553, Wenham, MA 01984, (508) 468-2021, holistic healing center, workshops, etc.

Temple of the Sacred Earth, c/o H.Ps. Curott, public rituals, classes, lectures

Temple of Isis, 20889 Geyserville Avel, Geyserville, CA 95441

Fellowship of Isis, Clonegal Castle, Enniscorthy, Ireland, founded by Lady Olivia Robertson; training of clergy

Unicorn Books, 1210 Massachusetts Ave., Arlington, MA 02174, (617) 646-3680, lectures and classes on women's spirituality

Unitarian Universalist Women's Federation, 25 Beacon St., Boston, MA 02108, (617) 742-2100, e-mail uuwf@uua.org, programs, conventions, classes, awards

The University of Creation Spirituality, 2141 Broadway, Oakland, CA 94612, (510) 835-4827, Matthew Fox, president

Women's Lodge, Watertown, MA, (617) 924-8022, open women's spirituality circle

Women's Spirituality Forum, P.O. Box 11363, Piedmont, CA 94611, (510) 893-3097, sponsors biannual Goddess festival and events with Z. Budapest

Merchant Catalogs

Church of the Iron Oak Legal Defense Fund Catalog, P.O. Box 060672, Palm Bay, FL 32906, (407) 722-0291

Earth Care, environmental household goods, 555 Leslie St., Ukian, CA 95482, (800) 347-0070

Enchantments, Attn: Mary, 341 E. 9th St., New York City, NY 10003, (212) 228-4394

Ladyslipper Inc., Recordings by Women, P.O. Box 3124, Durham, NC 27715

Special Events

Biannual International Goddess Festival, sponsored by Women's Spirituality Forum, P.O. Box 11363, Piedmont, CA 94611, (510) 893-3097 sponsors biannual Goddess festival and events with Z. Budapest

Michigan Womyn's Music Festival, (616) 757-4766, the oldest and largest women's music festival in the United States.

National Women's Music and Spirit Conference, (June), Women in the Arts, P.O. Box 1427, Indianapolis, IN 46206

Rites of Spring Festival, Earthspirit, P.O. Box 502, Medford, MA 02155

Goddess Pilgrimage Tours

Ariadne Institute, 1306 Crestview Dr., Blacksburg, VA 24060, (540) 951-3070, Crete

Avalon Travel Associates, 38 Federal St., Newburyport, MA 01950, (508) 462-3778, England, Wales, and Scotland

Sacred Site Tours with Luisah Teish, 2550 Sattuck Ave., #28, Berkeley, CA 94704, Caribbean, Africa, and South America

Additional Organizations and Resources

ACLU, 125 Broad St., New York, NY 10275

Amnesty International, 322 Eighth Ave., New York, NY 10001

Association for Union Democracy, 500 State St., Brooklyn, NY 11207

Greenpeace, P.O. Box 5013, Hagerstown, MD 21741

National Domestic Violence Hotline (800) 799-SAFE (7233)

Planned Parenthood, P.O. Box 96735, Washington, DC 20077

Rape Abuse Incest National Network Hotline, 1 (800) 656-4673

United Farm Workers of America, P.O. Box 62, Keene, CA 93531

BOOKS OF INTEREST

Many of the authors listed below have written more than one book. Due to space limitations, I've listed just one title to get you started.

Adler, Margot. *Drawing Down the Moon.* New York: Viking Press, 1982.

Allen, Paula Gunn. *The Sacred Hoop: Recovering the Feminine in American Indian Traditions.* Boston: Beacon Press, 1987.

Arroyo, S. *Astrology, Psychology and the Four Elements.* Sebastopol, CA: CRCS Publications, 1975.

Ashcroft-Nowicki, Dolores. *First Steps in Ritual.* Great Britain, 1982.

Berry, Thomas. *The Dream of the Earth.* San Francisco: Sierra Club, 1990.

Blum, Ralph. *The Book of Runes.* New York: St. Martin's Press, 1994.

Bolen, Jean Shinoda. *Goddesses in Every Woman.* 1983. Out of Print.

Briffault, Robert. *The Mothers: A Study of the Origins of Sentiments and Institutions.* London: Allen, 1927.

Buckland, Raymond. *Witchcraft from the Inside.* St. Paul: Lllewellyn, 1971.

Budapest, Z. *The Feminist Book of Lights and Shadows.* Venice, California: Luna Publications, 1976.

Bullfinch, Thomas. *Bullfinch's Mythology.* New York: Dell, 1967.

Campbell, Joseph. *Hero With a Thousand Faces.* Princeton: Princeton University Press, 1990.

Capra, Fritjof. *The Tao of Physics.* Boulder, Colorado: Shambhala, 1975.

Castaneda, Carlos. *The Teachings of Don Juan: A Yaqui Way of Knowledge.* New York: Ballantine Books, 1968.

Chadwick, Nora K. *Celtic Britain.* New York: Praeger, 1963.

Chopra, Deepak. *Ageless Body, Timeless Mind.* New York: Harmony Books, 1993.

Christ, Carol P., and Plasko, Judith, eds. *Womanspirit Rising.* San Francisco: Harper & Row, 1979.

Crowley, Vivianne. *Wicca: The Old Religion in the New Age.* London: Aquarian Press, 1989.

Cunningham, Scott. *Guide for the Solitary Practitioner.* St. Paul, Minnesota: Llewellyn Publications, 1989.

Daly, Mary. *Beyond God the Father: Toward a Philosophy of Women's Liberation.* Boston: Beacon Press, 1973.

De Beauvoir, Simone. *The Second Sex.* New York: Vintage Books, 1989.

Dunwich, Gerina. *The Wicca Garden.* New York: Citadel Press, 1996.

Ehrenreich, Barbara, and Deirdre English. *Witches, Midwives, and Nurses: A History of Women Healers.* Old Westbury, New York: The Feminist Press, 1973.

Eisler, Riane. *The Chalice and the Blade.* New York: Harper & Row, 1987.

Eller, Cynthia. *Living in the Lap of the Goddess: The Feminist Spirituality Movement in America.* New York: Crossroad, 1993.

Ellis, Normandi. *Awakening Osiris, The Egyptian Book of the Dead.* Trans. Ellis. Michigan: Phanes Press, 1988.

Estes, Clarissa Pinkola. *Women Who Run with the Wolves.* New York: Ballantine Books, 1992.

Farrar, Janet and Stewart. *Eight Sabbats for Witches.* London: Robert Hale, 1981.

Fortune, Dion. *Aspects of Occultism*. Aquarian Press, 1962.

Frazier, Sir James. *The New Golden Bough*. Ed. Thodor H. Gaster. New York: Criterion Books, 1959.

Gardner, Gerald B. *Witchcraft Today*. Cavendish, Suffolk, Great Britain: Ryder, 1954.

Gimbutas, Marija. *The Language of the Goddess*. San Francisco: Harper & Row, 1989.

Ginzburg, Carlo. *Ecstasies: Deciphering the Witches' Sabbath*. New York: Random House, 1991.

Gladstar, Rosemary. *Herbal Healing for Women*. New York: Fireside–Simon & Schuster, 1993.

Goldenberg, Naomi. *The Changing of the Gods*. Boston: Beacon Press, 1979.

Goodrich, Norma Lorre. *Priestesses*. New York: Franklin Watts, 1989.

Graves, Robert. *The White Goddess*. New York: Farrar, Straus & Giroux, 1966.

Griffin, Susan. *Woman and Nature: The Roaring Inside Her*. New York: Harper Colophon, 1978.

Harding, M. Esther. *Woman's Mysteries, Ancient and Modern*. New York: Harper & Row, 1971.

Harner, Michael. *The Way of the Shaman: A Guide to Power and Healing*. New York: Bantam Books, 1982.

Harrison, Jane Ellen. *Prolegomena to the Study of Greek Religion*. New York: Meridian, 1955.

Hawkes, Jaquetta. *The First Great Civilizations*. New York: Knopf, 1973; Random House, 1968.

Holzer, Hans. *The New Pagans*. New York: Doubleday, 1972.

Houston, Jean. *The Passion of Isis and Osiris*. 1995. Out of Print.

I Ching, Book of Changes. Trans. Richard Wilhelm. Bollingen Series. Princeton: Princeton University Press, 1950.

Jayakar, Pupul. *The Earth Mother: Legends, Goddesses, and Ritual Arts of India*. San Francisco: Harper & Row, 1990.

Johnson, Buffie. *Lady of the Beasts: Ancient Images of the Goddess and Her Sacred Animals*. San Francisco: Harper & Row, 1988.

Jong, Erica. *Witches*. New York: Harry N. Abrams, 1997.

Jung, C. G., and K. Kerenyi. *Essays on a Science of Mythology*. Bollingen Series. Princeton: Princeton University Press, 1949.

Kennealy Morrison, Patricia. *The Silver Branch*. New York: Penguin, 1988.

Lao Tzu. *Tao Te Ching*. Trans. Brian Walker. New York: St. Martins, 1996.

Leek, Sybil. *Diary of a Witch*. New York: Signet, 1968.

Leland, Charles. *Aradia: Gospel of the Witches*. New York: Weiser, 1974.

The Mabinogian. Ed. Lady Charlotte Guest. Wellingborough, Great Britain: Ballantyne Press, 1910.

Matthews, Caitlin. *Ladies of the Lake*. Wellingborough, Great Britain: Aquarian Press, 1992.

Matthews, John. *At the Table of the Grail.* Ed. John Matthews. Great Britain: Arkana, 1984.

Merchant, Carolyn. *The Death of Nature: Women, Ecology, and the Scientific Revolution.* San Francisco: Harper & Row, 1980.

Mernissi, Fatima. *Beyond the Veil: Male-Female Dynamics in a Modern Muslim Society.* Cambridge, Massachusetts: Schenkman Publishing, 1975.

Monaghan, Patricia. *The Book of Goddesses and Heroines.* New York: E. P. Dutton, 1981.

Morgan, Robin, ed. *Sisterhood Is Powerful: An Anthology of Writings from the Women's Liberation Movement.* New York: Vintage Books, 1970.

Murray, Margaret A. *The Witch-Cult in Western Europe.* New York: Oxford University Press, 1971.

Neimark, Philip John. *The Way of the Orisa.* New York: HarperCollins, 1993.

Neumann, Erich. *The Great Mother.* Trans. R. Manheim. Princeton: Princeton University Press, 1963.

Nilsson, Martin P. *Greek Folk Religion.* New York: Harper, 1940, 1961.

Noble, Vicki. *Motherpeace: A Way to the Goddess Through Myth, Art, and Tarot.* San Francisco: Harper & Row, 1983.

Paul, Diana Y. *Women in Buddhism: Images of the Feminine in Mahayana Tradition.* Berkeley: University of California Press, 1985.

Plant, Judith, ed. *Healing the Wounds: The Promise of Ecofeminism.* Philadelphia: New Society Publishers, 1989.

Rae, Eleanor. *Women, the Earth, the Divine.* Maryknoll, N.Y.: Orbis Books, 1994.

Reuther, Rosemary R. *New Woman/New Earth.* New York: Seabury Press, 1975.

Rig Veda, Bhagavad Gita, and *the Upanishads*

Robbins, Tom. *Skinny Legs and All.* New York: Bantam Doubleday Dell, 1995.

Sjoo, Monica, and Barbara Mor. *The Great Cosmic Mother: Rediscovering the Religions of the Earth.* San Francisco: Harper & Row, 1987.

Spretnak, Charlene. *Lost Goddesses of Early Greece.* Boston: Beacon Press, 1978, 1984.

Starhawk. *The Spiral Dance.* New York: Harper & Row, 1979.

Stein, Diane. *The Women's Spirituality Book.* St. Paul, Minn.: Llewellyn Publications, 1987.

Steinbeck, John. *The Acts of King Arthur and His Noble Knights.* New York: Farrar, Straus & Giroux, 1976.

Stewart, R. J. *The Underworld Initiation.* Wellingborough, Great Britain: Aquarian Press, 1985.

Stone, Merlin. *When God Was a Woman.* New York: Dial Press, 1976; New York: Harcourt Brace Jovanovich, 1976.

Teish, Luisah. *Jambalaya.* San Francisco: HarperCollins, 1985.

Valiente, Doreen. *An ABC of Witchcraft.* New York: St. Martin's Press, 1973.

Walker, Barbara. *The Woman's Dictionary of Symbols and Sacred Objects*. San Francisco: Harper & Row, 1985.

Weed, Susan. *Wise Woman Ways—Menopausal Years*. Woodstock, New York: Ash Tree Publishing, 1992.

White, T. H. *The Once and Future King*. Collins, 1952.

Wilson, Robert Anton. *The Cosmic Trigger*. New York: Simon & Schuster, 1977.

Wolkstein, Diane, and Samuel Noah Cramer. *Inanna, Queen of Heaven and Earth: Her Stories and Hymns from Sumer*. New York: Harper & Row, 1983.

Yeats, W. B. *The Collected Poems of W. B. Yeats*. R. Finneran, ed. New York: Macmillan Publishing Co., 1983.

Zimmer Bradley, Marian. *The Mists of Avalon*. Sphere, 1984.

For information on seminars, lectures, and other programs by H. Ps. Phyllis Curott, or to subscribe to a future newsletter, please contact her at:

P.O. Box 311
Prince Street Station
New York City, New York 10012